5000258318

THE ART OF
COMPUTER PROGRAMMING

VOLUME 1, FASCICLE 1

MMIX

A RISC Computer for the
New Millennium

DONALD E. KNUTH *Stanford University*

ADDISON–**WESLEY**

Upper Saddle River, NJ · Boston · India
New York · Toronto · Montréal · Londc
Capetown · Sydney · Tokyo · Singapore · Mexico City

D1333678

The author and publisher have taken care in the preparation of this book, but make no expressed or implied warranty of any kind and assume no responsibility for errors or omissions. No liability is assumed for incidental or consequential damages in connection with or arising out of the use of the information or programs contained herein.

TeX is a trademark of the American Mathematical Society

For sales outside the U.S., please contact:

>International Sales
>`international@pearsoned.com`

Visit us on the Web: `www.awprofessional.com`

Internet page `http://www-cs-faculty.stanford.edu/~knuth/taocp.html` contains current information about this book and related books.

See also `http://www-cs-faculty.stanford.edu/~knuth/mmix.html` for downloadable software, and `http://mmixmasters.sourceforge.net` for general news about MMIX.

Copyright © 2005 by Pearson Education, Inc.

All rights reserved. Printed in the United States of America. This publication is protected by copyright, and permission must be obtained from the publisher prior to any prohibited reproduction, storage in a retrieval system, or transmission in any form or by any means, electronic, mechanical, photocopying, recording, or likewise. For information regarding permissions, write to:

>Pearson Education, Inc.
>Rights and Contracts Department
>One Lake Street
>Upper Saddle River, NJ 07458

ISBN 0-201-85392-2

Text printed in the United States on recycled paper at the Courier Corporation plant in Stoughton, Massachusetts

First printing, February 2005

PREFACE

fas·ci·cle \'fasəkəl\ n ... 1: a small bundle ... an inflorescence consisting of
a compacted cyme less capitate than a glomerule
... 2: one of the divisions of a book published in parts
— P. B. GOVE, Webster's Third New International Dictionary (1961)

THIS IS THE FIRST of a series of updates that I plan to make available at regular intervals as I continue working toward the ultimate editions of *The Art of Computer Programming*.

I was inspired to prepare fascicles like this by the example of Charles Dickens, who issued his novels in serial form; he published a dozen installments of *Oliver Twist* before having any idea what would become of Bill Sikes! I was thinking also of James Murray, who began to publish 350-page portions of the Oxford English Dictionary in 1884, finishing the letter B in 1888 and the letter C in 1895. (Murray died in 1915 while working on the letter T; my task is, fortunately, much simpler than his.)

Unlike Dickens and Murray, I have computers to help me edit the material, so that I can easily make changes before putting everything together in its final form. Although I'm trying my best to write comprehensive accounts that need no further revision, I know that every page brings me hundreds of opportunities to make mistakes and to miss important ideas. My files are bursting with notes about beautiful algorithms that have been discovered, but computer science has grown to the point where I cannot hope to be an authority on all the material I wish to cover. Therefore I need extensive feedback from readers before I can finalize the official volumes.

In other words, I think these fascicles will contain a lot of Good Stuff, and I'm excited about the opportunity to present everything I write to whoever wants to read it, but I also expect that beta-testers like you can help me make it Way Better. As usual, I will gratefully pay a reward of $2.56 to the first person who reports anything that is technically, historically, typographically, or politically incorrect.

Charles Dickens usually published his work once a month, sometimes once a week; James Murray tended to finish a 350-page installment about once every 18 months. My goal, God willing, is to produce two 128-page fascicles per year. Most of the fascicles will represent new material destined for Volumes 4 and higher; but sometimes I will be presenting amendments to one or more of the earlier volumes. For example, Volume 4 will need to refer to topics that belong in Volume 3, but weren't invented when Volume 3 first came out. With luck, the entire work will make sense eventually.

Fascicle Number One is about MMIX, the long-promised replacement for MIX. Thirty-seven years have passed since the MIX computer was designed, and computer architecture has been converging during those years towards a rather different style of machine. Therefore I decided in 1990 to replace MIX with a new computer that would contain even less saturated fat than its predecessor.

Exercise 1.3.1–25 in the first three editions of Volume 1 spoke of an extended MIX called MixMaster, which was upward compatible with the old version. But MixMaster itself has long been hopelessly obsolete. It allowed for several gigabytes of memory, but one couldn't even use it with ASCII code to print lowercase letters. And ouch, its standard conventions for calling subroutines were irrevocably based on self-modifying instructions! Decimal arithmetic and self-modifying code were popular in 1962, but they sure have disappeared quickly as machines have gotten bigger and faster. Fortunately the modern RISC architecture has a very appealing structure, so I've had a chance to design a new computer that is not only up to date but also fun.

Many readers are no doubt thinking, "Why does Knuth replace MIX by another machine instead of just sticking to a high-level programming language? Hardly anybody uses assemblers these days." Such people are entitled to their opinions, and they need not bother reading the machine-language parts of my books. But the reasons for machine language that I gave in the preface to Volume 1, written in the early 1960s, remain valid today:

- One of the principal goals of my books is to show how high-level constructions are actually implemented in machines, not simply to show how they are applied. I explain coroutine linkage, tree structures, random number generation, high-precision arithmetic, radix conversion, packing of data, combinatorial searching, recursion, etc., from the ground up.

- The programs needed in my books are generally so short that their main points can be grasped easily.

- People who are more than casually interested in computers should have at least some idea of what the underlying hardware is like. Otherwise the programs they write will be pretty weird.

- Machine language is necessary in any case, as output of some of the software that I describe.

- Expressing basic methods like algorithms for sorting and searching in machine language makes it possible to carry out meaningful studies of the effects of cache and RAM size and other hardware characteristics (memory speed, pipelining, multiple issue, lookaside buffers, the size of cache blocks, etc.) when comparing different schemes.

Moreover, if I did use a high-level language, what language should it be? In the 1960s I would probably have chosen Algol W; in the 1970s, I would then have had to rewrite my books using Pascal; in the 1980s, I would surely have changed everything to C; in the 1990s, I would have had to switch to C++ and then probably to Java. In the 2000s, yet another language will no doubt be *de rigueur.* I cannot afford the time to rewrite my books as languages go in and out of fashion; languages aren't the point of my books, the point is rather what you can do in your favorite language. My books focus on timeless truths.

Therefore I will continue to use English as the high-level language in *The Art of Computer Programming*, and I shall continue to use a low-level language to indicate how machines actually compute. Readers who only want to see algorithms that are already packaged in a plug-in way, using a trendy language, should buy other people's books.

The good news is that programming for MMIX is pleasant and simple. This fascicle presents

1) a programmer's introduction to the machine (replacing Section 1.3.1 of the third edition of Volume 1);
2) the MMIX assembly language (replacing Section 1.3.2);
3) new material on subroutines, coroutines, and interpretive routines (replacing Sections 1.4.1, 1.4.2, and 1.4.3).

Of course, MIX appears in many places throughout the existing editions of Volumes 1–3, and dozens of programs need to be rewritten for MMIX before the next editions of those volumes are ready. Readers who would like to help with this conversion process are encouraged to join the MMIXmasters, a happy group of volunteers based at mmixmasters.sourceforge.net.

The fourth edition of Volume 1 will not be ready until after Volumes 4 and 5 have been completed; therefore two quite different versions of Sections 1.3.1, 1.3.2, 1.4.1, 1.4.2, and 1.4.3 will coexist for several years. In order to avoid potential confusion, I've temporarily assigned "prime numbers" 1.3.1′, 1.3.2′, 1.4.1′, 1.4.2′, and 1.4.3′ to the new material.

I am extremely grateful to all the people who helped me with the design of MMIX. In particular, John Hennessy and Richard L. Sites deserve special thanks for their active participation and substantial contributions. Thanks also to Vladimir Ivanović for volunteering to be the MMIX grandmaster/webmaster.

Stanford, California   D. E. K.
May 1999

> *You can, if you want, rewrite forever.*
> — NEIL SIMON, *Rewrites: A Memoir* (1996)

CONTENTS

1.3′. MMIX

IN MANY PLACES throughout this book we will have occasion to refer to a computer's internal machine language. The machine we use is a mythical computer called "MMIX." MMIX — pronounced *EM-micks* — is very much like nearly every general-purpose computer designed since 1985, except that it is, perhaps, nicer. The language of MMIX is powerful enough to allow brief programs to be written for most algorithms, yet simple enough so that its operations are easily learned.

The reader is urged to study this section carefully, since MMIX language appears in so many parts of this book. There should be no hesitation about learning a machine language; indeed, the author once found it not uncommon to be writing programs in a half dozen different machine languages during the same week! Everyone with more than a casual interest in computers will probably get to know at least one machine language sooner or later. Machine language helps programmers understand what really goes on inside their computers. And once one machine language has been learned, the characteristics of another are easy to assimilate. Computer science is largely concerned with an understanding of how low-level details make it possible to achieve high-level goals.

Software for running MMIX programs on almost any real computer can be downloaded from the website for this book (see page ii). The complete source code for the author's MMIX routines appears in the book *MMIXware* [*Lecture Notes in Computer Science* **1750** (1999)]; that book will be called "the *MMIXware* document" in the following pages.

1.3.1′. Description of MMIX

MMIX is a polyunsaturated, 100% natural computer. Like most machines, it has an identifying number — the 2009. This number was found by taking 14 actual computers very similar to MMIX and on which MMIX could easily be simulated, then averaging their numbers with equal weight:

$$
\begin{aligned}
\big(\text{Cray I} + \text{IBM 801} + \text{RISC II} &+ \text{Clipper C300} + \text{AMD 29K} + \text{Motorola 88K} \\
&+ \text{IBM 601} + \text{Intel i960} + \text{Alpha 21164} + \text{POWER 2} + \text{MIPS R4000} \\
&+ \text{Hitachi SuperH4} + \text{StrongARM 110} + \text{Sparc 64}\big)/14 \\
&= 28126/14 = 2009.
\end{aligned}
\tag{1}
$$

The same number may also be obtained in a simpler way by taking Roman numerals.

Bits and bytes. MMIX works with patterns of 0s and 1s, commonly called binary digits or *bits*, and it usually deals with 64 bits at a time. For example, the 64-bit quantity

$$1001111000110111011110011011100101111111010010100111110000010110 \tag{2}$$

is a typical pattern that the machine might encounter. Long patterns like this can be expressed more conveniently if we group the bits four at a time and use *hexadecimal digits* to represent each group. The sixteen hexadecimal digits are

$$
\begin{array}{llll}
0 = 0000, & 4 = 0100, & 8 = 1000, & \texttt{c} = 1100, \\
1 = 0001, & 5 = 0101, & 9 = 1001, & \texttt{d} = 1101, \\
2 = 0010, & 6 = 0110, & \texttt{a} = 1010, & \texttt{e} = 1110, \\
3 = 0011, & 7 = 0111, & \texttt{b} = 1011, & \texttt{f} = 1111.
\end{array}
\tag{3}
$$

We shall always use a distinctive typeface for hexadecimal digits, as shown here, so that they won't be confused with the decimal digits 0–9; and we will usually also put the symbol # just before a hexadecimal number, to make the distinction even clearer. For example, (2) becomes

$$
{}^{\#}\texttt{9e3779b97f4a7c16}
\tag{4}
$$

in hexadecimalese. Uppercase digits `ABCDEF` are often used instead of `abcdef`, because `#9E3779B97F4A7C16` looks better than `#9e3779b97f4a7c16` in some contexts; there is no difference in meaning.

A sequence of eight bits, or two hexadecimal digits, is commonly called a *byte*. Most computers now consider bytes to be their basic, individually addressable units of data; we will see that an MMIX program can refer to as many as 2^{64} bytes, each of which has its own address from `#0000000000000000` to `#ffffffffffffffff`. Letters, digits, and punctuation marks of languages like English are often represented with one byte per character, using the American Standard Code for Information Interchange (ASCII). For example, the ASCII equivalent of MMIX is `#4d4d4958`. ASCII is actually a 7-bit code with control characters `#00`–`#1f`, printing characters `#20`–`#7e`, and a "delete" character `#7f` [see *CACM* **8** (1965), 207–214; **11** (1968), 849–852; **12** (1969), 166–178]. It was extended during the 1980s to an international standard 8-bit code known as Latin-1 or ISO 8859-1, thereby encoding accented letters: *pâté* is `#70e274e9`.

> *"Of the 256th squadron?"*
> *"Of the fighting 256th Squadron," Yossarian replied.*
> *... "That's two to the fighting eighth power."*
>
> — JOSEPH HELLER, *Catch-22* (1961)

A 16-bit code that supports nearly *every* modern language became an international standard during the 1990s. This code, known as Unicode UTF-16 or ISO/IEC 10646 UCS-2, includes not only Greek letters like Σ and σ (`#03a3` and `#03c3`), Cyrillic letters like Щ and щ (`#0429` and `#0449`), Armenian letters like Ͻ and ? (`#0547` and `#0577`), Hebrew letters like ש (`#05e9`), Arabic letters like ش (`#0634`), and Indian letters like श (`#0936`) or শ (`#09b6`) or ଶ (`#0b36`) or ஷ (`#0bb7`), etc., but also tens of thousands of East Asian ideographs such as the Chinese character for mathematics and computing, 算 (`#7b97`). It even has special codes for Roman numerals: MMIX = `#216f 216f 2160 2169`. Ordinary ASCII or Latin-1 characters are represented by simply giving them a leading byte of zero: *pâté* is `#0070 00e2 0074 00e9`, *à l'Unicode*.

We will use the convenient term *wyde* to describe a 16-bit quantity like the wide characters of Unicode, because two-byte quantities are quite important in practice. We also need convenient names for four-byte and eight-byte quantities, which we shall call *tetrabytes* (or "tetras") and *octabytes* (or "octas"). Thus

$$2 \text{ bytes} = 1 \text{ wyde};$$
$$2 \text{ wydes} = 1 \text{ tetra};$$
$$2 \text{ tetras} = 1 \text{ octa}.$$

One octabyte equals four wydes equals eight bytes equals sixty-four bits.

Bytes and multibyte quantities can, of course, represent numbers as well as alphabetic characters. Using the binary number system,

an unsigned byte can express the numbers 0 .. 255;
an unsigned wyde can express the numbers 0 .. 65,535;
an unsigned tetra can express the numbers 0 .. 4,294,967,295;
an unsigned octa can express the numbers 0 .. 18,446,744,073,709,551,615.

Integers are also commonly represented by using *two's complement notation,* in which the leftmost bit indicates the sign: If the leading bit is 1, we subtract 2^n to get the integer corresponding to an n-bit number in this notation. For example, -1 is the signed byte $^\#\texttt{ff}$; it is also the signed wyde $^\#\texttt{ffff}$, the signed tetrabyte $^\#\texttt{ffffffff}$, and the signed octabyte $^\#\texttt{ffffffffffffffff}$. In this way

a signed byte can express the numbers -128 .. 127;
a signed wyde can express the numbers $-32,768$ .. 32,767;
a signed tetra can express the numbers $-2,147,483,648$ .. 2,147,483,647;
a signed octa can express the numbers $-9,223,372,036,854,775,808$ .. 9,223,372,036,854,775,807.

Memory and registers. From a programmer's standpoint, an MMIX computer has 2^{64} cells of *memory* and 2^8 general-purpose *registers,* together with 2^5 special registers (see Fig. 13). Data is transferred from the memory to the registers, transformed in the registers, and transferred from the registers to the memory. The cells of memory are called M[0], M[1], ..., M[$2^{64} - 1$]; thus if x is any octabyte, M[x] is a byte of memory. The general-purpose registers are called \$0, \$1, ..., \$255; thus if x is any byte, \$$x$ is an octabyte.

The 2^{64} bytes of memory are grouped into 2^{63} wydes, $M_2[0] = M_2[1] = $ M[0]M[1], $M_2[2] = M_2[3] = $ M[2]M[3], ...; each wyde consists of two consecutive bytes M[$2k$]M[$2k+1$] = M[$2k$] $\times 2^8 + $ M[$2k+1$], and is denoted either by $M_2[2k]$ or by $M_2[2k+1]$. Similarly there are 2^{62} tetrabytes

$$M_4[4k] = M_4[4k+1] = \cdots = M_4[4k+3] = M[4k]M[4k+1]\ldots M[4k+3],$$

and 2^{61} octabytes

$$M_8[8k] = M_8[8k+1] = \cdots = M_8[8k+7] = M[8k]M[8k+1]\ldots M[8k+7].$$

In general if x is any octabyte, the notations $M_2[x]$, $M_4[x]$, and $M_8[x]$ denote the wyde, the tetra, and the octa that contain byte M[x]; we ignore the least

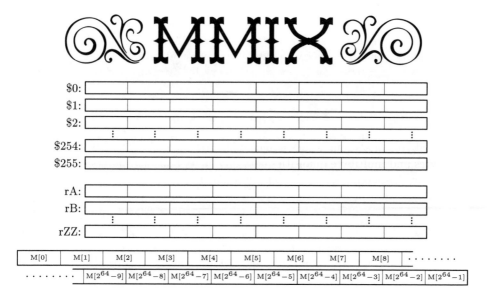

Fig. 13. The MMIX computer, as seen by a programmer, has 256 general-purpose registers and 32 special-purpose registers, together with 2^{64} bytes of virtual memory. Each register holds 64 bits of data.

significant $\lg t$ bits of x when referring to $M_t[x]$. For completeness, we also write $M_1[x] = M[x]$, and we define $M[x] = M[x \bmod 2^{64}]$ when $x < 0$ or $x \geq 2^{64}$.

The 32 special registers of MMIX are called rA, rB, ..., rZ, rBB, rTT, rWW, rXX, rYY, and rZZ. Like their general-purpose cousins, they each hold an octabyte. Their uses will be explained later; for example, we will see that rA controls arithmetic interrupts while rR holds the remainder after division.

Instructions. MMIX's memory contains instructions as well as data. An *instruction* or "command" is a tetrabyte whose four bytes are conventionally called OP, X, Y, and Z. OP is the *operation code* (or "opcode," for short); X, Y, and Z specify the *operands*. For example, #20010203 is an instruction with OP = #20, X = #01, Y = #02, and Z = #03, and it means "Set \$1 to the sum of \$2 and \$3." The operand bytes are always regarded as unsigned integers.

Each of the 256 possible opcodes has a symbolic form that is easy to remember. For example, opcode #20 is ADD. We will deal almost exclusively with symbolic opcodes; the numeric equivalents can be found, if needed, in Table 1 below, and also in the endpapers of this book.

The X, Y, and Z bytes also have symbolic representations, consistent with the assembly language that we will discuss in Section 1.3.2′. For example, the instruction #20010203 is conventionally written 'ADD \$1,\$2,\$3', and the addition instruction in general is written 'ADD \$X,\$Y,\$Z'. Most instructions have three operands, but some of them have only two, and a few have only one. When there are two operands, the first is X and the second is the two-byte quantity YZ; the symbolic notation then has only one comma. For example, the instruction

'INCL $X,YZ' increases register $X by the amount YZ. When there is only one operand, it is the unsigned three-byte number XYZ, and the symbolic notation has no comma at all. For example, we will see that 'JMP @+4*XYZ' tells MMIX to find its next instruction by skipping ahead XYZ tetrabytes; the instruction 'JMP @+1000000' has the hexadecimal form $^\#$f003d090, because JMP = $^\#$f0 and 250000 = $^\#$03d090.

We will describe each MMIX instruction both informally and formally. For example, the informal meaning of 'ADD $X,$Y,$Z' is "Set $X to the sum of $Y and $Z"; the formal definition is 's($X) ← s($Y) + s($Z)'. Here s($x$) denotes the *signed integer* corresponding to the bit pattern x, according to the conventions of two's complement notation. An assignment like s(x) ← N means that x is to be set to the bit pattern for which s(x) = N. (Such an assignment causes *integer overflow* if N is too large or too small to fit in x. For example, an ADD will overflow if s($Y) + s($Z) is less than -2^{63} or greater than $2^{63} - 1$. When we're discussing an instruction informally, we will often gloss over the possibility of overflow; the formal definition, however, will make everything precise. In general the assignment s(x) ← N sets x to the binary representation of $N \bmod 2^n$, where n is the number of bits in x, and it signals overflow if $N < -2^{n-1}$ or $N \geq 2^{n-1}$; see exercise 5.)

Loading and storing. Although MMIX has 256 different opcodes, we will see that they fall into a few easily learned categories. Let's start with the instructions that transfer information between the registers and the memory.

Each of the following instructions has a *memory address* A obtained by adding $Y to $Z. Formally,

$$A = \bigl(u(\$Y) + u(\$Z)\bigr) \bmod 2^{64} \tag{5}$$

is the sum of the *unsigned integers* represented by $Y and $Z, reduced to a 64-bit number by ignoring any carry that occurs at the left when those two integers are added. In this formula the notation u(x) is analogous to s(x), but it considers x to be an unsigned binary number.

- LDB $X,$Y,$Z (load byte): s($X) ← s$\bigl(M_1[A]\bigr)$.
- LDW $X,$Y,$Z (load wyde): s($X) ← s$\bigl(M_2[A]\bigr)$.
- LDT $X,$Y,$Z (load tetra): s($X) ← s$\bigl(M_4[A]\bigr)$.
- LDO $X,$Y,$Z (load octa): s($X) ← s$\bigl(M_8[A]\bigr)$.

These instructions bring data from memory into register $X, changing the data if necessary from a signed byte, wyde, or tetrabyte to a signed octabyte of the same value. For example, suppose the octabyte $M_8[1002] = M_8[1000]$ is

$$M[1000]M[1001] \ldots M[1007] = {}^\#01\,23\,45\,67\,89\,ab\,cd\,ef. \tag{6}$$

Then if $2 = 1000 and $3 = 2, we have A = 1002, and

        LDB $1,$2,$3 sets $1 ← $^\#$0000000000000045;
        LDW $1,$2,$3 sets $1 ← $^\#$0000000000004567;
        LDT $1,$2,$3 sets $1 ← $^\#$0000000001234567;
        LDO $1,$2,$3 sets $1 ← $^\#$0123456789abcdef.

But if $3 = 5$, so that $A = 1005$,

LDB $1,$2,$3 sets $1 ← #ffff ffff ffff ffab;
LDW $1,$2,$3 sets $1 ← #ffff ffff ffff 89ab;
LDT $1,$2,$3 sets $1 ← #ffff ffff 89ab cdef;
LDO $1,$2,$3 sets $1 ← #0123 4567 89ab cdef.

When a signed byte or wyde or tetra is converted to a signed octa, its sign bit is "extended" into all positions to the left.

- LDBU $X,$Y,$Z (load byte unsigned): $u(\$X) \leftarrow u\big(M_1[A]\big)$.
- LDWU $X,$Y,$Z (load wyde unsigned): $u(\$X) \leftarrow u\big(M_2[A]\big)$.
- LDTU $X,$Y,$Z (load tetra unsigned): $u(\$X) \leftarrow u\big(M_4[A]\big)$.
- LDOU $X,$Y,$Z (load octa unsigned): $u(\$X) \leftarrow u\big(M_8[A]\big)$.

These instructions are analogous to LDB, LDW, LDT, and LDO, but they treat the memory data as *unsigned*; bit positions at the left of the register are set to zero when a short quantity is being lengthened. Thus, in the example above, LDBU $1,$2,$3 with $2 + $3 = 1005 would set $1 ← #0000 0000 0000 00ab.

The instructions LDO and LDOU actually have exactly the same behavior, because no sign extension or padding with zeros is necessary when an octabyte is loaded into a register. But a good programmer will use LDO when the sign is relevant and LDOU when it is not; then readers of the program can better understand the significance of what is being loaded.

- LDHT $X,$Y,$Z (load high tetra): $u(\$X) \leftarrow u\big(M_4[A]\big) \times 2^{32}$.

Here the tetrabyte $M_4[A]$ is loaded into the *left* half of $X, and the right half is set to zero. For example, LDHT $1,$2,$3 sets $1 ← #89ab cdef 0000 0000, assuming (6) with $2 + $3 = 1005.

- LDA $X,$Y,$Z (load address): $u(\$X) \leftarrow A$.

This instruction, which puts a memory address into a register, is essentially the same as the ADDU instruction described below. Sometimes the words "load address" describe its purpose better than the words "add unsigned."

- STB $X,$Y,$Z (store byte): $s\big(M_1[A]\big) \leftarrow s(\$X)$.
- STW $X,$Y,$Z (store wyde): $s\big(M_2[A]\big) \leftarrow s(\$X)$.
- STT $X,$Y,$Z (store tetra): $s\big(M_4[A]\big) \leftarrow s(\$X)$.
- STO $X,$Y,$Z (store octa): $s\big(M_8[A]\big) \leftarrow s(\$X)$.

These instructions go the other way, placing register data into the memory. Overflow is possible if the (signed) number in the register lies outside the range of the memory field. For example, suppose register $1 contains the number $-65536 = {}^\#$ffff ffff ffff 0000. Then if $2 = 1000, $3 = 2, and (6) holds,

STB $1,$2,$3 sets $M_8[1000] ← #0123 0067 89ab cdef$ (with overflow);
STW $1,$2,$3 sets $M_8[1000] ← #0123 0000 89ab cdef$ (with overflow);
STT $1,$2,$3 sets $M_8[1000] ← #ffff 0000 89ab cdef$;
STO $1,$2,$3 sets $M_8[1000] ← #ffff ffff ffff 0000$.

- STBU $X,$Y,$Z (store byte unsigned):
  $u\big(M_1[A]\big) \leftarrow u(\$X) \bmod 2^8$.
- STWU $X,$Y,$Z (store wyde unsigned):
  $u\big(M_2[A]\big) \leftarrow u(\$X) \bmod 2^{16}$.
- STTU $X,$Y,$Z (store tetra unsigned):
  $u\big(M_4[A]\big) \leftarrow u(\$X) \bmod 2^{32}$.
- STOU $X,$Y,$Z (store octa unsigned): $u\big(M_8[A]\big) \leftarrow u(\$X)$.

These instructions have exactly the same effect on memory as their signed counterparts STB, STW, STT, and STO, but overflow never occurs.

- STHT $X,$Y,$Z (store high tetra): $u\big(M_4[A]\big) \leftarrow \lfloor u(\$X)/2^{32} \rfloor$.

The left half of register $X is stored in memory tetrabyte $M_4[A]$.

- STCO X,$Y,$Z (store constant octabyte): $u\big(M_8[A]\big) \leftarrow X$.

A constant between 0 and 255 is stored in memory octabyte $M_8[A]$.

Arithmetic operators. Most of MMIX's operations take place strictly between registers. We might as well begin our study of the register-to-register operations by considering addition, subtraction, multiplication, and division, because computers are supposed to be able to compute.

- ADD $X,$Y,$Z (add): $s(\$X) \leftarrow s(\$Y) + s(\$Z)$.
- SUB $X,$Y,$Z (subtract): $s(\$X) \leftarrow s(\$Y) - s(\$Z)$.
- MUL $X,$Y,$Z (multiply): $s(\$X) \leftarrow s(\$Y) \times s(\$Z)$.
- DIV $X,$Y,$Z (divide): $s(\$X) \leftarrow \lfloor s(\$Y)/s(\$Z) \rfloor \ [\$Z \neq 0]$, and
  $s(rR) \leftarrow s(\$Y) \bmod s(\$Z)$.

Sums, differences, and products need no further discussion. The DIV command forms the quotient and remainder as defined in Section 1.2.4; the remainder goes into the special *remainder register* rR, where it can be examined by using the instruction GET $X,rR described below. If the divisor $Z is zero, DIV sets $X ← 0 and rR ← $Y (see Eq. 1.2.4–(1)); an "integer divide check" also occurs.

- ADDU $X,$Y,$Z (add unsigned): $u(\$X) \leftarrow \big(u(\$Y) + u(\$Z)\big) \bmod 2^{64}$.
- SUBU $X,$Y,$Z (subtract unsigned): $u(\$X) \leftarrow \big(u(\$Y) - u(\$Z)\big) \bmod 2^{64}$.
- MULU $X,$Y,$Z (multiply unsigned): $u(rH \, \$X) \leftarrow u(\$Y) \times u(\$Z)$.
- DIVU $X,$Y,$Z (divide unsigned): $u(\$X) \leftarrow \lfloor u(rD \, \$Y)/u(\$Z) \rfloor$, $u(rR) \leftarrow u(rD \, \$Y) \bmod u(\$Z)$, if $u(\$Z) > u(rD)$; otherwise $X ← rD, rR ← $Y.

Arithmetic on unsigned numbers never causes overflow. A full 16-byte product is formed by the MULU command, and the upper half goes into the special *himult register* rH. For example, when the unsigned number #9e3779b97f4a7c16 in (2) and (4) above is multiplied by itself we get

$$rH \leftarrow {}^{\#}61c8\,8646\,80b5\,83ea, \quad \$X \leftarrow {}^{\#}1bb3\,2095\,ccdd\,51e4. \tag{7}$$

In this case the value of rH has turned out to be exactly 2^{64} minus the original number #9e3779b97f4a7c16; this is not a coincidence! The reason is that (2) actually gives the first 64 bits of the binary representation of the golden ratio $\phi^{-1} = \phi - 1$, if we place a binary radix point at the *left*. (See Table 2 in Appendix A.) Squaring gives us an approximation to the binary representation of $\phi^{-2} = 1 - \phi^{-1}$, with the radix point now at the left of rH.

Division with DIVU yields the 8-byte quotient and remainder of a 16-byte dividend with respect to an 8-byte divisor. The upper half of the dividend appears in the special *dividend register* rD, which is zero at the beginning of a program; this register can be set to any desired value with the command PUT rD,$Z described below. If rD is greater than or equal to the divisor, DIVU $X,$Y,$Z simply sets $X ← rD and rR ← $Y. (This case always arises when $Z is zero.) But DIVU never causes an integer divide check.

The ADDU instruction computes a memory address A, according to definition (5); therefore, as discussed earlier, we sometimes give ADDU the alternative name LDA. The following related commands also help with address calculation.

- 2ADDU $X,$Y,$Z (times 2 and add unsigned):
  $u(\$X) \leftarrow \big(u(\$Y) \times 2 + u(\$Z)\big) \bmod 2^{64}$.
- 4ADDU $X,$Y,$Z (times 4 and add unsigned):
  $u(\$X) \leftarrow \big(u(\$Y) \times 4 + u(\$Z)\big) \bmod 2^{64}$.
- 8ADDU $X,$Y,$Z (times 8 and add unsigned):
  $u(\$X) \leftarrow \big(u(\$Y) \times 8 + u(\$Z)\big) \bmod 2^{64}$.
- 16ADDU $X,$Y,$Z (times 16 and add unsigned):
  $u(\$X) \leftarrow \big(u(\$Y) \times 16 + u(\$Z)\big) \bmod 2^{64}$.

It is faster to execute the command 2ADDU $X,$Y,$Y than to multiply by 3, if overflow is not an issue.

- NEG $X,Y,$Z (negate): $s(\$X) \leftarrow Y - s(\$Z)$.
- NEGU $X,Y,$Z (negate unsigned): $u(\$X) \leftarrow \big(Y - u(\$Z)\big) \bmod 2^{64}$.

In these commands Y is simply an unsigned constant, not a register number (just as X was an unsigned constant in the STCO instruction). Usually Y is zero, in which case we can write simply NEG $X,$Z or NEGU $X,$Z.

- SL $X,$Y,$Z (shift left): $s(\$X) \leftarrow s(\$Y) \times 2^{u(\$Z)}$.
- SLU $X,$Y,$Z (shift left unsigned): $u(\$X) \leftarrow \big(u(\$Y) \times 2^{u(\$Z)}\big) \bmod 2^{64}$.
- SR $X,$Y,$Z (shift right): $s(\$X) \leftarrow \lfloor s(\$Y)/2^{u(\$Z)} \rfloor$.
- SRU $X,$Y,$Z (shift right unsigned): $u(\$X) \leftarrow \lfloor u(\$Y)/2^{u(\$Z)} \rfloor$.

SL and SLU both produce the same result in $X, but SL might overflow while SLU never does. SR extends the sign when shifting right, but SRU shifts zeros in from the left. Therefore SR and SRU produce the same result in $X if and only if $Y is nonnegative or $Z is zero. The SL and SR instructions are much faster than MUL and DIV by powers of 2. An SLU instruction is much faster than MULU by a power of 2, although it does not affect rH as MULU does. An SRU instruction is much faster than DIVU by a power of 2, although it is not affected by rD. The notation $y \ll z$ is often used to denote the result of shifting a binary value y to the left by z bits; similarly, $y \gg z$ denotes shifting to the right.

- CMP $X,$Y,$Z (compare):
  $s(\$X) \leftarrow \big[s(\$Y) > s(\$Z)\big] - \big[s(\$Y) < s(\$Z)\big]$.
- CMPU $X,$Y,$Z (compare unsigned):
  $s(\$X) \leftarrow \big[u(\$Y) > u(\$Z)\big] - \big[u(\$Y) < u(\$Z)\big]$.

These instructions each set $X to either −1, 0, or 1, depending on whether register $Y is less than, equal to, or greater than register $Z.

Conditional instructions. Several instructions base their actions on whether a register is positive, or negative, or zero, etc.

- CSN $X,$Y,$Z (conditional set if negative): if s($Y) < 0, set $X ← $Z.
- CSZ $X,$Y,$Z (conditional set if zero): if $Y = 0, set $X ← $Z.
- CSP $X,$Y,$Z (conditional set if positive): if s($Y) > 0, set $X ← $Z.
- CSOD $X,$Y,$Z (conditional set if odd): if s($Y) mod 2 = 1, set $X ← $Z.
- CSNN $X,$Y,$Z (conditional set if nonnegative): if s($Y) ≥ 0, set $X ← $Z.
- CSNZ $X,$Y,$Z (conditional set if nonzero): if $Y ≠ 0, set $X ← $Z.
- CSNP $X,$Y,$Z (conditional set if nonpositive): if s($Y) ≤ 0, set $X ← $Z.
- CSEV $X,$Y,$Z (conditional set if even): if s($Y) mod 2 = 0, set $X ← $Z.

If register $Y satisfies the stated condition, register $Z is copied to register $X; otherwise nothing happens. A register is negative if and only if its leading (leftmost) bit is 1. A register is odd if and only if its trailing (rightmost) bit is 1.

- ZSN $X,$Y,$Z (zero or set if negative): $X ← $Z [s($Y) < 0].
- ZSZ $X,$Y,$Z (zero or set if zero): $X ← $Z [$Y = 0].
- ZSP $X,$Y,$Z (zero or set if positive): $X ← $Z [s($Y) > 0].
- ZSOD $X,$Y,$Z (zero or set if odd): $X ← $Z [s($Y) mod 2 = 1].
- ZSNN $X,$Y,$Z (zero or set if nonnegative): $X ← $Z [s($Y) ≥ 0].
- ZSNZ $X,$Y,$Z (zero or set if nonzero): $X ← $Z [$Y ≠ 0].
- ZSNP $X,$Y,$Z (zero or set if nonpositive): $X ← $Z [s($Y) ≤ 0].
- ZSEV $X,$Y,$Z (zero or set if even): $X ← $Z [s($Y) mod 2 = 0].

If register $Y satisfies the stated condition, register $Z is copied to register $X; otherwise register $X is set to zero.

Bitwise operations. We often find it useful to think of an octabyte x as a *vector* v(x) of 64 individual bits, and to perform operations simultaneously on each component of two such vectors.

- AND $X,$Y,$Z (bitwise and): v($X) ← v($Y) ∧ v($Z).
- OR $X,$Y,$Z (bitwise or): v($X) ← v($Y) ∨ v($Z).
- XOR $X,$Y,$Z (bitwise exclusive-or): v($X) ← v($Y) ⊕ v($Z).
- ANDN $X,$Y,$Z (bitwise and-not): v($X) ← v($Y) ∧ v̄($Z).
- ORN $X,$Y,$Z (bitwise or-not): v($X) ← v($Y) ∨ v̄($Z).
- NAND $X,$Y,$Z (bitwise not-and): v̄($X) ← v($Y) ∧ v($Z).
- NOR $X,$Y,$Z (bitwise not-or): v̄($X) ← v($Y) ∨ v($Z).
- NXOR $X,$Y,$Z (bitwise not-exclusive-or): v̄($X) ← v($Y) ⊕ v($Z).

Here v̄ denotes the *complement* of vector v, obtained by changing 0 to 1 and 1 to 0. The binary operations ∧, ∨, and ⊕, defined by the rules

$$
\begin{array}{llll}
0 \wedge 0 = 0, & 0 \vee 0 = 0, & 0 \oplus 0 = 0, & \\
0 \wedge 1 = 0, & 0 \vee 1 = 1, & 0 \oplus 1 = 1, & \\
1 \wedge 0 = 0, & 1 \vee 0 = 1, & 1 \oplus 0 = 1, & (8)\\
1 \wedge 1 = 1, & 1 \vee 1 = 1, & 1 \oplus 1 = 0, &
\end{array}
$$

are applied independently to each bit. Anding is the same as multiplying or taking the minimum; oring is the same as taking the maximum. Exclusive-oring is the same as adding mod 2.

• MUX $X,$Y,$Z (bitwise multiplex): $v(\$X) \leftarrow \big(v(\$Y) \wedge v(rM)\big) \vee \big(v(\$Z) \wedge \bar{v}(rM)\big)$.
The MUX operation combines two bit vectors by looking at the special *multiplex mask register* rM, choosing bits of $Y where rM is 1 and bits of $Z where rM is 0.

• SADD $X,$Y,$Z (sideways add): $s(\$X) \leftarrow s\big(\sum(v(\$Y) \wedge \bar{v}(\$Z))\big)$.
The SADD operation counts the number of bit positions in which register $Y has a 1 while register $Z has a 0.

Bytewise operations. Similarly, we can regard an octabyte x as a vector $b(x)$ of eight individual bytes, each of which is an integer between 0 and 255; or we can think of it as a vector $w(x)$ of four individual wydes, or a vector $t(x)$ of two unsigned tetras. The following operations deal with all components at once.

• BDIF $X,$Y,$Z (byte difference): $b(\$X) \leftarrow b(\$Y) \mathbin{\dot-} b(\$Z)$.
• WDIF $X,$Y,$Z (wyde difference): $w(\$X) \leftarrow w(\$Y) \mathbin{\dot-} w(\$Z)$.
• TDIF $X,$Y,$Z (tetra difference): $t(\$X) \leftarrow t(\$Y) \mathbin{\dot-} t(\$Z)$.
• ODIF $X,$Y,$Z (octa difference): $u(\$X) \leftarrow u(\$Y) \mathbin{\dot-} u(\$Z)$.

Here $\dot-$ denotes the operation of *saturating subtraction*,

$$y \mathbin{\dot-} z = \max(0, y - z). \tag{9}$$

These operations have important applications to text processing, as well as to computer graphics (when the bytes or wydes represent pixel values). Exercises 27–30 discuss some of their basic properties.

We can also regard an octabyte as an 8×8 *Boolean matrix*, that is, as an 8×8 array of 0s and 1s. Let $m(x)$ be the matrix whose rows from top to bottom are the bytes of x from left to right; and let $m^T(x)$ be the transposed matrix, whose *columns* are the bytes of x. For example, if $x = {}^{\#}9e\,37\,79\,b9\,7f\,4a\,7c\,16$ is the octabyte (2), we have

$$m(x) = \begin{pmatrix} 1&0&0&1&1&1&1&0 \\ 0&0&1&1&0&1&1&1 \\ 0&1&1&1&1&0&0&1 \\ 1&0&1&1&1&0&0&1 \\ 0&1&1&1&1&1&1&1 \\ 0&1&0&0&1&0&1&0 \\ 0&1&1&1&1&1&0&0 \\ 0&0&0&1&0&1&1&0 \end{pmatrix}, \quad m^T(x) = \begin{pmatrix} 1&0&0&1&0&0&0&0 \\ 0&0&1&0&1&1&1&0 \\ 0&1&1&1&1&0&1&0 \\ 1&1&1&1&1&0&1&1 \\ 1&0&1&1&1&1&1&0 \\ 1&1&0&0&1&0&1&1 \\ 1&1&0&0&1&1&0&1 \\ 0&1&1&1&1&0&0&0 \end{pmatrix}. \tag{10}$$

This interpretation of octabytes suggests two operations that are quite familiar to mathematicians, but we will pause a moment to define them from scratch.

If A is an $m \times n$ matrix and B is an $n \times s$ matrix, and if $\circ$ and $\bullet$ are binary operations, the *generalized matrix product* $A \mathbin{\overset{\circ}{\underset{\bullet}{}}} B$ is the $m \times s$ matrix C defined by

$$C_{ij} = (A_{i1} \bullet B_{1j}) \circ (A_{i2} \bullet B_{2j}) \circ \cdots \circ (A_{in} \bullet B_{nj}) \tag{11}$$

for $1 \le i \le m$ and $1 \le j \le s$. [See K. E. Iverson, *A Programming Language* (Wiley, 1962), 23–24; we assume that $\circ$ is associative.] An ordinary matrix product is obtained when $\circ$ is $+$ and $\bullet$ is $\times$, but we obtain important operations on Boolean matrices if we let $\circ$ be $\vee$ or $\oplus$:

$$(A \overset{\vee}{\times} B)_{ij} = A_{i1}B_{1j} \vee A_{i2}B_{2j} \vee \cdots \vee A_{in}B_{nj}; \tag{12}$$

$$(A \overset{\oplus}{\times} B)_{ij} = A_{i1}B_{1j} \oplus A_{i2}B_{2j} \oplus \cdots \oplus A_{in}B_{nj}. \tag{13}$$

Notice that if the rows of A each contain at most one 1, at most one term in (12) or (13) is nonzero. The same is true if the columns of B each contain at most one 1. Therefore $A \overset{\vee}{\times} B$ and $A \overset{\oplus}{\times} B$ both turn out to be the same as the ordinary matrix product $A \overset{+}{\times} B = AB$ in such cases.

- MOR $X,$Y,$Z (multiple or): $m^T(\$X) \leftarrow m^T(\$Y) \overset{\vee}{\times} m^T(\$Z)$;
  equivalently, $m(\$X) \leftarrow m(\$Z) \overset{\vee}{\times} m(\$Y)$. (See exercise 32.)
- MXOR $X,$Y,$Z (multiple exclusive-or): $m^T(\$X) \leftarrow m^T(\$Y) \overset{\oplus}{\times} m^T(\$Z)$;
  equivalently, $m(\$X) \leftarrow m(\$Z) \overset{\oplus}{\times} m(\$Y)$.

These operations essentially set each byte of $X by looking at the corresponding byte of $Z and using its bits to select bytes of $Y; the selected bytes are then ored or xored together. If, for example, we have

$$\$Z = {}^{\#}0102040810204080, \tag{14}$$

then both MOR and MXOR will set register $X to the *byte reversal* of register $Y: The kth byte from the left of $X will be set to the kth byte from the right of $Y, for $1 \le k \le 8$. On the other hand if $Z = {}^{\#}00000000000000ff$, MOR and MXOR will set all bytes of $X to zero except for the rightmost byte, which will become either the OR or the XOR of all eight bytes of $Y. Exercises 33–37 illustrate some of the many practical applications of these versatile commands.

Floating point operators. MMIX includes a full implementation of the famous IEEE/ANSI Standard 754 for floating point arithmetic. Complete details of the floating point operations appear in Section 4.2 and in the *MMIXware* document; a rough summary will suffice for our purposes here.

Every octabyte x represents a floating binary number $f(x)$ determined as follows: The leftmost bit of x is the sign (0 = '+', 1 = '−'); the next 11 bits are the *exponent* E; the remaining 52 bits are the *fraction* F. The value represented is then

$$\pm 0.0, \text{ if E} = \text{F} = 0 \text{ (zero)};$$
$$\pm 2^{-1074}\text{F}, \text{ if E} = 0 \text{ and F} \ne 0 \text{ (denormal)};$$
$$\pm 2^{\text{E}-1023}(1 + \text{F}/2^{52}), \text{ if } 0 < \text{E} < 2047 \text{ (normal)};$$
$$\pm\infty, \text{ if E} = 2047 \text{ and F} = 0 \text{ (infinite)};$$
$$\pm\text{NaN}(\text{F}/2^{52}), \text{ if E} = 2047 \text{ and F} \ne 0 \text{ (Not-a-Number)}.$$

The "short" floating point number $f(t)$ represented by a tetrabyte t is similar, but its exponent part has only 8 bits and its fraction has only 23; the normal case $0 < \text{E} < 255$ of a short float represents $\pm 2^{\text{E}-127}(1 + \text{F}/2^{23})$.

- FADD $X,$Y,$Z (floating add): $f(\$X) \leftarrow f(\$Y) + f(\$Z)$.
- FSUB $X,$Y,$Z (floating subtract): $f(\$X) \leftarrow f(\$Y) - f(\$Z)$.
- FMUL $X,$Y,$Z (floating multiply): $f(\$X) \leftarrow f(\$Y) \times f(\$Z)$.
- FDIV $X,$Y,$Z (floating divide): $f(\$X) \leftarrow f(\$Y)/f(\$Z)$.

- FREM $X,$Y,$Z (floating remainder): f($X) ← f($Y) rem f($Z).
- FSQRT $X,$Z or FSQRT $X,Y,$Z (floating square root): f($X) ← f($Z)$^{1/2}$.
- FINT $X,$Z or FINT $X,Y,$Z (floating integer): f($X) ← int f($Z).
- FCMP $X,$Y,$Z (floating compare): s($X) ← [f($Y) > f($Z)] − [f($Y) < f($Z)].
- FEQL $X,$Y,$Z (floating equal to): s($X) ← [f($Y) = f($Z)].
- FUN $X,$Y,$Z (floating unordered): s($X) ← [f($Y) ∥ f($Z)].
- FCMPE $X,$Y,$Z (floating compare with respect to epsilon):
  s($X) ← [f($Y) ≻ f($Z) (f(rE))] − [f($Y) ≺ f($Z) (f(rE))], see 4.2.2–(21).
- FEQLE $X,$Y,$Z (floating equivalent with respect to epsilon):
  s($X) ← [f($Y) ≈ f($Z) (f(rE))], see 4.2.2–(24).
- FUNE $X,$Y,$Z (floating unordered with respect to epsilon):
  s($X) ← [f($Y) ∥ f($Z) (f(rE))].
- FIX $X,$Z or FIX $X,Y,$Z (convert floating to fixed): s($X) ← int f($Z).
- FIXU $X,$Z or FIXU $X,Y,$Z (convert floating to fixed unsigned):
  u($X) ← (int f($Z)) mod 2^{64}.
- FLOT $X,$Z or FLOT $X,Y,$Z (convert fixed to floating): f($X) ← s($Z).
- FLOTU $X,$Z or FLOTU $X,Y,$Z (convert fixed to floating unsigned):
  f($X) ← u($Z).
- SFLOT $X,$Z or SFLOT $X,Y,$Z (convert fixed to short float):
  f($X) ← f(T) ← s($Z).
- SFLOTU $X,$Z or SFLOTU $X,Y,$Z (convert fixed to short float unsigned):
  f($X) ← f(T) ← u($Z).
- LDSF $X,$Y,$Z or LDSF $X,A (load short float): f($X) ← f($M_4$[A]).
- STSF $X,$Y,$Z or STSF $X,A (store short float): f(M_4[A]) ← f($X).

Assignment to a floating point quantity uses the current rounding mode to determine the appropriate value when an exact value cannot be assigned. Four rounding modes are supported: 1 (ROUND_OFF), 2 (ROUND_UP), 3 (ROUND_DOWN), and 4 (ROUND_NEAR). The Y field of FSQRT, FINT, FIX, FIXU, FLOT, FLOTU, SFLOT, and SFLOTU can be used to specify a rounding mode other than the current one, if desired. For example, FIX $X,ROUND_UP,$Z sets s($X) ← ⌈f($Z)⌉. Operations SFLOT and SFLOTU first round as if storing into an anonymous tetrabyte T, then they convert that number to octabyte form.

The 'int' operation rounds to an integer. The operation y rem z is defined to be $y − nz$, where n is the nearest integer to y/z, or the nearest *even* integer in case of a tie. Special rules apply when the operands are infinite or NaN, and special conventions govern the sign of a zero result. The values +0.0 and −0.0 have different floating point representations, but FEQL calls them equal. All such technicalities are explained in the *MMIXware* document, and Section 4.2 explains why the technicalities are important.

Immediate constants. Programs often need to deal with small constant numbers. For example, we might want to add or subtract 1 from a register, or we might want to shift by 32, etc. In such cases it's a nuisance to load the small constant from memory into another register. So MMIX provides a general mechanism by which such constants can be obtained "immediately" from an instruction itself: *Every instruction we have discussed so far has a variant in which $\$Z$ is replaced by the number Z*, unless the instruction treats $\$Z$ as a floating point number.

For example, 'ADD $\$X,\$Y,\$Z$' has a counterpart 'ADD $\$X,\$Y,Z$', meaning $s(\$X) \leftarrow s(\$Y) + Z$; 'SRU $\$X,\$Y,\$Z$' has a counterpart 'SRU $\$X,\$Y,Z$', meaning $u(\$X) \leftarrow \lfloor u(\$Y)/2^Z \rfloor$; 'FLOT $\$X,\$Z$' has a counterpart 'FLOT $\$X,Z$', meaning $f(\$X) \leftarrow Z$. But 'FADD $\$X,\$Y,\$Z$' has no immediate counterpart.

The opcode for 'ADD $\$X,\$Y,\$Z$' is $^\#20$ and the opcode for 'ADD $\$X,\$Y,Z$' is $^\#21$; we use the same symbol ADD in both cases for simplicity. In general the opcode for the immediate variant of an operation is one greater than the opcode for the register variant.

Several instructions also feature *wyde immediate* constants, which range from $^\#0000 = 0$ to $^\#ffff = 65535$. These constants, which appear in the YZ bytes, can be shifted into the high, medium high, medium low, or low wyde positions of an octabyte.

- SETH $\$X,YZ$ (set high wyde): $u(\$X) \leftarrow YZ \times 2^{48}$.
- SETMH $\$X,YZ$ (set medium high wyde): $u(\$X) \leftarrow YZ \times 2^{32}$.
- SETML $\$X,YZ$ (set medium low wyde): $u(\$X) \leftarrow YZ \times 2^{16}$.
- SETL $\$X,YZ$ (set low wyde): $u(\$X) \leftarrow YZ$.
- INCH $\$X,YZ$ (increase by high wyde): $u(\$X) \leftarrow \big(u(\$X) + YZ \times 2^{48}\big) \bmod 2^{64}$.
- INCMH $\$X,YZ$ (increase by medium high wyde):
  $u(\$X) \leftarrow \big(u(\$X) + YZ \times 2^{32}\big) \bmod 2^{64}$.
- INCML $\$X,YZ$ (increase by medium low wyde):
  $u(\$X) \leftarrow \big(u(\$X) + YZ \times 2^{16}\big) \bmod 2^{64}$.
- INCL $\$X,YZ$ (increase by low wyde): $u(\$X) \leftarrow \big(u(\$X) + YZ\big) \bmod 2^{64}$.
- ORH $\$X,YZ$ (bitwise or with high wyde): $v(\$X) \leftarrow v(\$X) \lor v(YZ \ll 48)$.
- ORMH $\$X,YZ$ (bitwise or with medium high wyde):
  $v(\$X) \leftarrow v(\$X) \lor v(YZ \ll 32)$.
- ORML $\$X,YZ$ (bitwise or with medium low wyde):
  $v(\$X) \leftarrow v(\$X) \lor v(YZ \ll 16)$.
- ORL $\$X,YZ$ (bitwise or with low wyde): $v(\$X) \leftarrow v(\$X) \lor v(YZ)$.
- ANDNH $\$X,YZ$ (bitwise and-not high wyde): $v(\$X) \leftarrow v(\$X) \land \bar{v}(YZ \ll 48)$.
- ANDNMH $\$X,YZ$ (bitwise and-not medium high wyde):
  $v(\$X) \leftarrow v(\$X) \land \bar{v}(YZ \ll 32)$.
- ANDNML $\$X,YZ$ (bitwise and-not medium low wyde):
  $v(\$X) \leftarrow v(\$X) \land \bar{v}(YZ \ll 16)$.
- ANDNL $\$X,YZ$ (bitwise and-not low wyde): $v(\$X) \leftarrow v(\$X) \land \bar{v}(YZ)$.

Using at most four of these instructions, we can get any desired octabyte into a register without loading anything from the memory. For example, the commands

```
SETH $0,#0123;  INCMH $0,#4567;  INCML $0,#89ab;  INCL $0,#cdef
```

put $^\#0123\,4567\,89ab\,cdef$ into register $\$0$.

The MMIX assembly language allows us to write SET as an abbreviation for SETL, and SET $\$X,\$Y$ as an abbreviation for the common operation OR $\$X,\$Y,0$.

Jumps and branches. Instructions are normally executed in their natural sequence. In other words, the command that is performed after MMIX has obeyed the tetrabyte in memory location @ is normally the tetrabyte found in memory location @ + 4. (The symbol @ denotes the place where we're "at.") But jump and branch instructions allow this sequence to be interrupted.

- JMP RA (jump): @ ← RA.

Here RA denotes a three-byte *relative address*, which could be written more explicitly as @+4*XYZ, namely XYZ tetrabytes following the current location @. For example, 'JMP @+4*2' is a symbolic form for the tetrabyte #f0000002; if this instruction appears in location #1000, the next instruction to be executed will be the one in location #1008. We might in fact write 'JMP #1008'; but then the value of XYZ would depend on the location jumped from.

Relative offsets can also be negative, in which case the opcode increases by 1 and XYZ is the offset plus 2^{24}. For example, 'JMP @-4*2' is the tetrabyte #f1fffffe. Opcode #f0 tells the computer to "jump forward" and opcode #f1 tells it to "jump backward," but we write both as JMP. In fact, we usually write simply 'JMP Addr' when we want to jump to location Addr, and the MMIX assembly program figures out the appropriate opcode and the appropriate value of XYZ. Such a jump will be possible unless we try to stray more than about 67 million bytes from our present location.

- GO $X,$Y,$Z (go): u($X) ← @ + 4, then @ ← A.

The GO instruction allows us to jump to an *absolute address*, anywhere in memory; this address A is calculated by formula (5), exactly as in the load and store commands. Before going to the specified address, the location of the instruction that would ordinarily have come next is placed into register $X. Therefore we could return to that location later by saying, for example, 'GO $X,$X,0', with Z = 0 as an immediate constant.

- BN $X,RA (branch if negative): if s($X) < 0, set @ ← RA.
- BZ $X,RA (branch if zero): if $X = 0, set @ ← RA.
- BP $X,RA (branch if positive): if s($X) > 0, set @ ← RA.
- BOD $X,RA (branch if odd): if s($X) mod 2 = 1, set @ ← RA.
- BNN $X,RA (branch if nonnegative): if s($X) ≥ 0, set @ ← RA.
- BNZ $X,RA (branch if nonzero): if $X ≠ 0, set @ ← RA.
- BNP $X,RA (branch if nonpositive): if s($X) ≤ 0, set @ ← RA.
- BEV $X,RA (branch if even): if s($X) mod 2 = 0, set @ ← RA.

A *branch* instruction is a conditional jump that depends on the contents of register $X. The range of destination addresses RA is more limited than it was with JMP, because only two bytes are available to express the relative offset; but still we can branch to any tetrabyte between @ − 2^{18} and @ + 2^{18} − 4.

- PBN $X,RA (probable branch if negative): if s($X) < 0, set @ ← RA.
- PBZ $X,RA (probable branch if zero): if $X = 0, set @ ← RA.
- PBP $X,RA (probable branch if positive): if s($X) > 0, set @ ← RA.
- PBOD $X,RA (probable branch if odd): if s($X) mod 2 = 1, set @ ← RA.
- PBNN $X,RA (probable branch if nonnegative): if s($X) ≥ 0, set @ ← RA.

- **PBNZ $X,RA** (probable branch if nonzero): if $X \neq 0$, set @ ← RA.
- **PBNP $X,RA** (probable branch if nonpositive): if s($X) ≤ 0, set @ ← RA.
- **PBEV $X,RA** (probable branch if even): if s($X) mod 2 = 0, set @ ← RA.

High-speed computers usually work fastest if they can anticipate when a branch will be taken, because foreknowledge helps them look ahead and get ready for future instructions. Therefore MMIX encourages programmers to give hints about whether branching is likely or not. Whenever a branch is expected to be taken more than half of the time, a wise programmer will say PB instead of B.

*Subroutine calls.   MMIX also has several instructions that facilitate efficient communication between subprograms, via a *register stack*. The details are somewhat technical and we will defer them until Section 1.4′; an informal description will suffice here. Short programs do not need to use these features.

- **PUSHJ $X,RA** (push registers and jump): push(X) and set rJ ← @ + 4, then set @ ← RA.
- **PUSHGO $X,$Y,$Z** (push registers and go): push(X) and set rJ ← @ + 4, then set @ ← A.

The special *return-jump register* rJ is set to the address of the tetrabyte following the PUSH command. The action "push(X)" means, roughly speaking, that local registers $0 through $X are saved and made temporarily inaccessible. What used to be $(X+1) is now $0, what used to be $(X+2) is now $1, etc. But all registers $k for $k \geq$ rG remain unchanged; rG is the special *global threshold register*, whose value always lies between 32 and 255, inclusive.

Register $k is called *global* if $k \geq$ rG. It is called *local* if $k <$ rL; here rL is the special *local threshold register*, which tells how many local registers are currently active. Otherwise, namely if rL ≤ $k <$ rG, register $k is called *marginal*, and $k is equal to zero whenever it is used as a source operand in a command. If a marginal register $k is used as a destination operand in a command, rL is automatically increased to $k + 1$ before the command is performed, thereby making $k local.

- **POP X,YZ** (pop registers and return): pop(X), then @ ← rJ + 4 * YZ.

Here "pop(X)" means, roughly speaking, that all but X of the current local registers become marginal, and then the local registers hidden by the most recent "push" that has not yet been "popped" are restored to their former values. Full details appear in Section 1.4′, together with numerous examples.

- **SAVE $X,0** (save process state): u($X) ← context.
- **UNSAVE $Z** (restore process state): context ← u($Z).

The SAVE instruction stores all current registers in memory at the top of the register stack, and puts the address of the topmost stored octabyte into u($X). Register $X must be global; that is, X must be ≥ rG. All of the currently local and global registers are saved, together with special registers like rA, rD, rE, rG, rH, rJ, rM, rR, and several others that we have not yet discussed. The UNSAVE instruction takes the address of such a topmost octabyte and restores the associated context, essentially undoing a previous SAVE. The value of rL is set to zero by SAVE, but restored by UNSAVE. MMIX has special registers called the *register stack offset* (rO) and *register stack pointer* (rS), which control the PUSH, POP, SAVE, and UNSAVE operations. (Again, full details can be found in Section 1.4´.)

*System considerations. Several opcodes, intended primarily for ultrafast and/or parallel versions of the MMIX architecture, are of interest only to advanced users, but we should at least mention them here. Some of the associated operations are similar to the "probable branch" commands, in the sense that they give hints to the machine about how to plan ahead for maximum efficiency. Most programmers do not need to use these instructions, except perhaps SYNCID.

• LDUNC $X,$Y,$Z (load octa uncached): $s(\$X) \leftarrow s(M_8[A])$.

• STUNC $X,$Y,$Z (store octa uncached): $s(M_8[A]) \leftarrow s(\$X)$.

These commands perform the same operations as LDO and STO, but they also inform the machine that the loaded or stored octabyte and its near neighbors will probably not be read or written in the near future.

• PRELD X,$Y,$Z (preload data).

Says that many of the bytes $M[A]$ through $M[A + X]$ will probably be loaded or stored in the near future.

• PREST X,$Y,$Z (prestore data).

Says that all of the bytes $M[A]$ through $M[A + X]$ will definitely be written (stored) before they are next read (loaded).

• PREGO X,$Y,$Z (prefetch to go).

Says that many of the bytes $M[A]$ through $M[A + X]$ will probably be used as instructions in the near future.

• SYNCID X,$Y,$Z (synchronize instructions and data).

Says that all of the bytes $M[A]$ through $M[A + X]$ must be fetched again before being interpreted as instructions. *MMIX is allowed to assume that a program's instructions do not change after the program has begun*, unless the instructions have been prepared by SYNCID. (See exercise 57.)

• SYNCD X,$Y,$Z (synchronize data).

Says that all of bytes $M[A]$ through $M[A + X]$ must be brought up to date in the physical memory, so that other computers and input/output devices can read them.

• SYNC XYZ (synchronize).

Restricts parallel activities so that different processors can cooperate reliably; see *MMIXware* for details. XYZ must be 0, 1, 2, or 3.

• CSWAP $X,$Y,$Z (compare and swap octabytes).

If $u(M_8[A]) = u(rP)$, where rP is the special *prediction register*, set $u(M_8[A]) \leftarrow u(\$X)$ and $u(\$X) \leftarrow 1$. Otherwise set $u(rP) \leftarrow u(M_8[A])$ and $u(\$X) \leftarrow 0$. This is an atomic (indivisible) operation, useful when independent computers share a common memory.

• LDVTS $X,$Y,$Z (load virtual translation status).

This instruction, described in *MMIXware*, is for the operating system only.

*Interrupts. The normal flow of instructions from one tetrabyte to the next can be changed not only by jumps and branches but also by less predictable events like overflow or external signals. Real-world machines must also cope with such things as security violations and hardware failures. MMIX distinguishes two kinds of program interruptions: "trips" and "traps." A trip sends control to a *trip handler*, which is part of the user's program; a trap sends control to a *trap handler*, which is part of the operating system.

Eight kinds of exceptional conditions can arise when MMIX is doing arithmetic, namely integer divide check (D), integer overflow (V), float-to-fix overflow (W), invalid floating operation (I), floating overflow (O), floating underflow (U), floating division by zero (Z), and floating inexact (X). The special *arithmetic status register* rA holds current information about all these exceptions. The eight bits of its rightmost byte are called its *event bits*, and they are named D_BIT (#80), V_BIT (#40), ..., X_BIT (#01), in order DVWIOUZX.

The eight bits just to the left of the event bits in rA are called the *enable bits*; they appear in the same order DVWIOUZX. When an exceptional condition occurs during some arithmetic operation, MMIX looks at the corresponding enable bit before proceeding to the next instruction. If the enable bit is 0, the corresponding event bit is set to 1; otherwise the machine invokes a trip handler by "tripping" to location #10 for exception D, #20 for exception V, ..., #80 for exception X. Thus the event bits of rA record the exceptions that have not caused trips. (If more than one enabled exception occurs, the leftmost one takes precedence. For example, simultaneous O and X is handled by O.)

The two bits of rA just to the left of the enable bits hold the current rounding mode, mod 4. The other 46 bits of rA should be zero. A program can change the setting of rA at any time, using the PUT command discussed below.

- TRIP X,Y,Z or TRIP X,YZ or TRIP XYZ (trip).
This command forces a trip to the handler at location #00.

Whenever a trip occurs, MMIX uses five special registers to record the current state: the *bootstrap register* rB, the *where-interrupted register* rW, the *execution register* rX, the *Y operand register* rY, and the *Z operand register* rZ. First rB is set to $255, then $255 is set to rJ, and rW is set to @ + 4. The left half of rX is set to #8000 0000, and the right half is set to the instruction that tripped. If the interrupted instruction was not a store command, rY is set to $Y and rZ is set to $Z (or to Z in case of an immediate constant); otherwise rY is set to A (the memory address of the store command) and rZ is set to $X (the quantity to be stored). Finally control passes to the handler by setting @ to the handler address (#00 or #10 or ⋯ or #80).

- TRAP X,Y,Z or TRAP X,YZ or TRAP XYZ (trap).
This command is analogous to TRIP, but it forces a trap to the operating system. Special registers rBB, rWW, rXX, rYY, and rZZ take the place of rB, rW, rX, rY, and rZ; the special *trap address register* rT supplies the address of the trap handler, which is placed in @. Section 1.3.2′ describes several TRAP commands that provide simple input/output operations. The normal way to conclude a

program is to say 'TRAP 0'; this instruction is the tetrabyte $^\#$00000000, so you might run into it by mistake.

The *MMIXware* document gives further details about external interrupts, which are governed by the special *interrupt mask register* rK and *interrupt request register* rQ. Dynamic traps, which arise when rK $\land$ rQ $\ne$ 0, are handled at address rTT instead of rT.

- RESUME 0 (resume after interrupt).

If s(rX) is negative, MMIX simply sets @ $\leftarrow$ rW and takes its next instruction from there. Otherwise, if the leading byte of rX is zero, MMIX sets @ $\leftarrow$ rW $-$ 4 and executes the instruction in the lower half of rX as if it had appeared in that location. (This feature can be used even if no interrupt has occurred. The inserted instruction must not itself be RESUME.) Otherwise MMIX performs special actions described in the *MMIXware* document and of interest primarily to the operating system; see exercise 1.4.3′–14.

The complete instruction set. Table 1 shows the symbolic names of all 256 opcodes, arranged by their numeric values in hexadecimal notation. For example, ADD appears in the upper half of the row labeled $^\#$2x and in the column labeled $^\#$0 at the top, so ADD is opcode $^\#$20; ORL appears in the lower half of the row labeled $^\#$Ex and in the column labeled $^\#$B at the bottom, so ORL is opcode $^\#$EB.

Table 1 actually says 'ADD[I]', not 'ADD', because the symbol ADD really stands for two opcodes. Opcode $^\#$20 arises from ADD \$X,\$Y,\$Z using register \$Z, while opcode $^\#$21 arises from ADD \$X,\$Y,Z using the immediate constant Z. When a distinction is necessary, we say that opcode $^\#$20 is ADD and opcode $^\#$21 is ADDI ("add immediate"); similarly, $^\#$F0 is JMP and $^\#$F1 is JMPB ("jump backward"). This gives every opcode a unique name. However, the extra I and B are generally dropped for convenience when we write MMIX programs.

We have discussed nearly all of MMIX's opcodes. Two of the stragglers are

- GET \$X,Z (get from special register): u(\$X) $\leftarrow$ u(g[Z]), where $0 \le Z < 32$.
- PUT X,\$Z (put into special register): u(g[X]) $\leftarrow$ u(\$Z), where $0 \le X < 32$.

Each special register has a code number between 0 and 31. We speak of registers rA, rB, ..., as aids to human understanding; but register rA is really g[21] from the machine's point of view, and register rB is really g[0], etc. The code numbers appear in Table 2 on page 21.

GET commands are unrestricted, but certain things cannot be PUT: No value can be put into rG that is greater than 255, less than 32, or less than the current setting of rL. No value can be put into rA that is greater than $^\#$3ffff. If a program tries to increase rL with the PUT command, rL will stay unchanged. Moreover, a program cannot PUT anything into rC, rN, rO, rS, rI, rT, rTT, rK, rQ, rU, or rV; these "extraspecial" registers have code numbers in the range 8–18.

Most of the special registers have already been mentioned in connection with specific instructions, but MMIX also has a "clock register" or *cycle counter*, rC, which keeps advancing; an *interval counter*, rI, which keeps decreasing, and which requests an interrupt when it reaches zero; a *serial number register*, rN, which gives each MMIX machine a unique number; a *usage counter*, rU, which

Table 1

THE OPCODES OF MMIX

	#0	#1	#2	#3	#4	#5	#6	#7	
#0x	TRAP 5υ	FCMP υ	FUN υ	FEQL υ	FADD 4υ	FIX 4υ	FSUB 4υ	FIXU 4υ	#0x
	FLOT[I] 4υ		FLOTU[I] 4υ		SFLOT[I] 4υ		SFLOTU[I] 4υ		
#1x	FMUL 4υ	FCMPE 4υ	FUNE υ	FEQLE 4υ	FDIV 40υ	FSQRT 40υ	FREM 4υ	FINT 4υ	#1x
	MUL[I] 10υ		MULU[I] 10υ		DIV[I] 60υ		DIVU[I] 60υ		
#2x	ADD[I] υ		ADDU[I] υ		SUB[I] υ		SUBU[I] υ		#2x
	2ADDU[I] υ		4ADDU[I] υ		8ADDU[I] υ		16ADDU[I] υ		
#3x	CMP[I] υ		CMPU[I] υ		NEG[I] υ		NEGU[I] υ		#3x
	SL[I] υ		SLU[I] υ		SR[I] υ		SRU[I] υ		
#4x	BN[B] υ+π		BZ[B] υ+π		BP[B] υ+π		BOD[B] υ+π		#4x
	BNN[B] υ+π		BNZ[B] υ+π		BNP[B] υ+π		BEV[B] υ+π		
#5x	PBN[B] 3υ−π		PBZ[B] 3υ−π		PBP[B] 3υ−π		PBOD[B] 3υ−π		#5x
	PBNN[B] 3υ−π		PBNZ[B] 3υ−π		PBNP[B] 3υ−π		PBEV[B] 3υ−π		
#6x	CSN[I] υ		CSZ[I] υ		CSP[I] υ		CSOD[I] υ		#6x
	CSNN[I] υ		CSNZ[I] υ		CSNP[I] υ		CSEV[I] υ		
#7x	ZSN[I] υ		ZSZ[I] υ		ZSP[I] υ		ZSOD[I] υ		#7x
	ZSNN[I] υ		ZSNZ[I] υ		ZSNP[I] υ		ZSEV[I] υ		
#8x	LDB[I] μ+υ		LDBU[I] μ+υ		LDW[I] μ+υ		LDWU[I] μ+υ		#8x
	LDT[I] μ+υ		LDTU[I] μ+υ		LDO[I] μ+υ		LDOU[I] μ+υ		
#9x	LDSF[I] μ+υ		LDHT[I] μ+υ		CSWAP[I] 2μ+2υ		LDUNC[I] μ+υ		#9x
	LDVTS[I] υ		PRELD[I] υ		PREGO[I] υ		GO[I] 3υ		
#Ax	STB[I] μ+υ		STBU[I] μ+υ		STW[I] μ+υ		STWU[I] μ+υ		#Ax
	STT[I] μ+υ		STTU[I] μ+υ		STO[I] μ+υ		STOU[I] μ+υ		
#Bx	STSF[I] μ+υ		STHT[I] μ+υ		STCO[I] μ+υ		STUNC[I] μ+υ		#Bx
	SYNCD[I] υ		PREST[I] υ		SYNCID[I] υ		PUSHGO[I] 3υ		
#Cx	OR[I] υ		ORN[I] υ		NOR[I] υ		XOR[I] υ		#Cx
	AND[I] υ		ANDN[I] υ		NAND[I] υ		NXOR[I] υ		
#Dx	BDIF[I] υ		WDIF[I] υ		TDIF[I] υ		ODIF[I] υ		#Dx
	MUX[I] υ		SADD[I] υ		MOR[I] υ		MXOR[I] υ		
#Ex	SETH υ	SETMH υ	SETML υ	SETL υ	INCH υ	INCMH υ	INCML υ	INCL υ	#Ex
	ORH υ	ORMH υ	ORML υ	ORL υ	ANDNH υ	ANDNMH υ	ANDNML υ	ANDNL υ	
#Fx	JMP[B] υ		PUSHJ[B] υ		GETA[B] υ		PUT[I] υ		#Fx
	POP 3υ	RESUME 5υ	[UN]SAVE 20μ+υ		SYNC υ	SWYM υ	GET υ	TRIP 5υ	
	#8	#9	#A	#B	#C	#D	#E	#F	

$\pi = 2\upsilon$ if the branch is taken, $\pi = 0$ if the branch is not taken

increases by 1 whenever specified opcodes are executed; and a *virtual translation register*, rV, which defines a mapping from the "virtual" 64-bit addresses used in programs to the "actual" physical locations of installed memory. These special registers help make MMIX a complete, viable machine that could actually be built and run successfully; but they are not of importance to us in this book. The *MMIXware* document explains them fully.

- **GETA $X,RA** (get address): u($X) ← RA.

This instruction loads a relative address into register $X, using the same conventions as the relative addresses in branch commands. For example, GETA $0,@ will set $0 to the address of the instruction itself.

Table 2
SPECIAL REGISTERS OF MMIX

		code	saved?	put?
rA	arithmetic status register	21	✓	✓
rB	bootstrap register (trip)	0	✓	✓
rC	cycle counter	8		
rD	dividend register	1	✓	✓
rE	epsilon register	2	✓	✓
rF	failure location register	22		✓
rG	global threshold register	19	✓	✓
rH	himult register	3	✓	✓
rI	interval counter	12		
rJ	return-jump register	4	✓	✓
rK	interrupt mask register	15		
rL	local threshold register	20	✓	✓
rM	multiplex mask register	5	✓	✓
rN	serial number	9		
rO	register stack offset	10		
rP	prediction register	23	✓	✓
rQ	interrupt request register	16		
rR	remainder register	6	✓	✓
rS	register stack pointer	11		
rT	trap address register	13		
rU	usage counter	17		
rV	virtual translation register	18		
rW	where-interrupted register (trip)	24	✓	✓
rX	execution register (trip)	25	✓	✓
rY	Y operand (trip)	26	✓	✓
rZ	Z operand (trip)	27	✓	✓
rBB	bootstrap register (trap)	7		✓
rTT	dynamic trap address register	14		
rWW	where-interrupted register (trap)	28		✓
rXX	execution register (trap)	29		✓
rYY	Y operand (trap)	30		✓
rZZ	Z operand (trap)	31		✓

- SWYM X,Y,Z or SWYM X,YZ or SWYM XYZ (sympathize with your machinery). The last of MMIX's 256 opcodes is, fortunately, the simplest of all. In fact, it is often called a no-op, because it performs no operation. It does, however, keep the machine running smoothly, just as real-world swimming helps to keep programmers healthy. Bytes X, Y, and Z are ignored.

Timing. In later parts of this book we will often want to compare different MMIX programs to see which is faster. Such comparisons aren't easy to make, in general, because the MMIX architecture can be implemented in many different ways. Although MMIX is a mythical machine, its mythical hardware exists in cheap, slow versions as well as in costly high-performance models. The running time of a program depends not only on the clock rate but also on the number of functional units that can be active simultaneously and the degree to which they are pipelined; it depends on the techniques used to prefetch instructions before they are executed; it depends on the size of the random-access memory that is used to give the illusion of 2^{64} virtual bytes; and it depends on the sizes and allocation strategies of caches and other buffers, etc., etc.

For practical purposes, the running time of an MMIX program can often be estimated satisfactorily by assigning a fixed cost to each operation, based on the approximate running time that would be obtained on a high-performance machine with lots of main memory; so that's what we will do. Each operation will be assumed to take an integer number of v, where v (pronounced "oops")* is a unit that represents the clock cycle time in a pipelined implementation. Although the value of v decreases as technology improves, we always keep up with the latest advances because we measure time in units of v, not in nanoseconds. The running time in our estimates will also be assumed to depend on the number of memory references or *mems* that a program uses; this is the number of load and store instructions. For example, we will assume that each LDO (load octa) instruction costs $\mu + v$, where μ is the average cost of a memory reference. The total running time of a program might be reported as, say, $35\mu + 1000v$, meaning "35 mems plus 1000 oops." The ratio μ/v has been increasing steadily for many years; nobody knows for sure whether this trend will continue, but experience has shown that μ and v deserve to be considered independently.

Table 1, which is repeated also in the endpapers of this book, displays the assumed running time together with each opcode. Notice that most instructions take just $1v$, while loads and stores take $\mu + v$. A branch or probable branch takes $1v$ if predicted correctly, $3v$ if predicted incorrectly. Floating point operations usually take $4v$ each, although FDIV and FSQRT cost $40v$. Integer multiplication takes $10v$; integer division weighs in at $60v$.

Even though we will often use the assumptions of Table 1 for seat-of-the-pants estimates of running time, we must remember that the actual running time might be quite sensitive to the ordering of instructions. For example, integer division might cost only one cycle if we can find 60 other things to do between the time we issue the command and the time we need the result. Several LDB (load byte) instructions might need to reference memory only once, if they refer to the same octabyte. Yet the result of a load command is usually not ready for use in the immediately following instruction. Experience has shown that some algorithms work well with cache memory, and others do not; therefore μ is not really constant. Even the location of instructions in memory can have a significant effect on performance, because some instructions can be fetched together with others. Therefore the *MMIXware* package includes not only a simple simulator, which calculates running times by the rules of Table 1, but also a comprehensive *meta-simulator*, which runs MMIX programs under a wide range of different technological assumptions. Users of the meta-simulator can specify the

---

  * The Greek letter upsilon (v) is wider than an italic letter vee (v), but the author admits that this distinction is rather subtle. Readers who prefer to say vee instead of oops are free to do as they wish. The symbol is, however, an upsilon.

characteristics of the memory bus and the parameters of such things as caches for instructions and data, virtual address translation, pipelining and simultaneous instruction issue, branch prediction, etc. Given a configuration file and a program file, the meta-simulator determines precisely how long the specified hardware would need to run the program. Only the meta-simulator can be trusted to give reliable information about a program's actual behavior in practice; but such results can be difficult to interpret, because infinitely many configurations are possible. That's why we often resort to the much simpler estimates of Table 1.

> *No benchmark result should ever be taken at face value.*
> — BRIAN KERNIGHAN and CHRISTOPHER VAN WYK (1998)

MMIX versus reality. A person who understands the rudiments of MMIX programming has a pretty good idea of what today's general-purpose computers can do easily; MMIX is very much like all of them. But MMIX has been idealized in several ways, partly because the author has tried to design a machine that is somewhat "ahead of its time" so that it won't become obsolete too quickly. Therefore a brief comparison between MMIX and the computers actually being built at the turn of the millennium is appropriate. The main differences between MMIX and those machines are:

- Commercial machines do not ignore the low-order bits of memory addresses, as MMIX does when accessing $M_8[A]$; they usually insist that A be a multiple of 8. (We will find many uses for those precious low-order bits.)

- Commercial machines are usually deficient in their support of integer arithmetic. For example, they almost never produce the true quotient $\lfloor x/y \rfloor$ and true remainder $x \bmod y$ when x is negative or y is negative; they often throw away the upper half of a product. They don't treat left and right shifts as strict equivalents of multiplication and division by powers of 2. Sometimes they do not implement division in hardware at all; and when they do handle division, they usually assume that the upper half of the 128-bit dividend is zero. Such restrictions make high-precision calculations more difficult.

- Commercial machines do not perform FINT and FREM efficiently.

- Commercial machines do not (yet?) have the powerful MOR and MXOR operations. They usually have a half dozen or so ad hoc instructions that handle only the most common special cases of MOR.

- Commercial machines rarely have more than 64 general-purpose registers. The 256 registers of MMIX significantly decrease program length, because many variables and constants of a program can live entirely in those registers instead of in memory. Furthermore, MMIX's register stack is more flexible than the comparable mechanisms in existing computers.

All of these pluses for MMIX have associated minuses, because computer design always involves tradeoffs. The primary design goal for MMIX was to keep the machine as simple and clean and consistent and forward-looking as possible, without sacrificing speed and realism too greatly.

And now I see with eye serene
The very pulse of the machine.
— WILLIAM WORDSWORTH, *She Was a Phantom of Delight* (1804)

Summary. MMIX is a programmer-friendly computer that operates on 64-bit quantities called octabytes. It has the general characteristics of a so-called RISC ("reduced instruction set computer"); that is, its instructions have only a few different formats (OP X, Y, Z or OP X, YZ or OP XYZ), and each instruction either transfers data between memory and a register or involves only registers. Table 1 summarizes the 256 opcodes and their default running times; Table 2 summarizes the special registers that are sometimes important.

The following exercises give a quick review of the material in this section. Most of them are quite simple, and the reader should try to do nearly all of them.

EXERCISES

1. [*00*] The binary form of 2009 is $(11111011001)_2$; what is 2009 in hexadecimal?

2. [*05*] Which of the letters {A, B, C, D, E, F, a, b, c, d, e, f} are *odd* when considered as (a) hexadecimal digits? (b) ASCII characters?

3. [*10*] Four-bit quantities — half-bytes, or hexadecimal digits — are often called *nybbles*. Suggest a good name for *two-bit* quantities, so that we have a complete binary nomenclature ranging from bits to octabytes.

4. [*15*] A kilobyte (kB or KB) is 1000 bytes, and a megabyte (MB) is 1000 kB. What are the official names and abbreviations for larger numbers of bytes?

5. [*M13*] If α is any string of 0s and 1s, let $s(\alpha)$ and $u(\alpha)$ be the integers that it represents when regarded as a signed or unsigned binary number. Prove that, if x is any integer, we have

$$x = s(\alpha) \quad \text{if and only if} \quad x \equiv u(\alpha) \ (\text{modulo } 2^n) \text{ and } -2^{n-1} \le x < 2^{n-1},$$

where n is the length of α.

▶ **6.** [*M20*] Prove or disprove the following rule for negating an n-bit number in two's complement notation: "Complement all the bits, then add 1." (For example, $^\#0\ldots01$ becomes $^\#f\ldots fe$, then $^\#f\ldots ff$; also $^\#f\ldots ff$ becomes $^\#0\ldots00$, then $^\#0\ldots01$.)

7. [*M15*] Could the formal definitions of LDHT and STHT have been stated as

$$s(\$X) \leftarrow s(M_4[A]) \times 2^{32} \quad \text{and} \quad s(M_4[A]) \leftarrow \lfloor s(\$X)/2^{32} \rfloor,$$

thus treating the numbers as signed rather than unsigned?

8. [*10*] If registers $Y and $Z represent numbers between 0 and 1 in which the binary radix point is assumed to be at the left of each register, (7) illustrates the fact that MULU forms a product in which the assumed radix point appears at the left of register rH. Suppose, on the other hand, that $Z is an integer, with the radix point assumed at its right, while $Y is a fraction between 0 and 1 as before. Where does the radix point lie after MULU in such a case?

9. [*M10*] Does the equation $s(\$Y) = s(\$X) \cdot s(\$Z) + s(rR)$ always hold after the instruction DIV $X,$Y,$Z has been performed?

10. [*M16*] Give an example of DIV in which overflow occurs.

11. [*M16*] True or false: (a) Both MUL $X,$Y,$Z and MULU $X,$Y,$Z produce the same result in $X. (b) If register rD is zero, both DIV $X,$Y,$Z and DIVU $X,$Y,$Z produce the same result in $X.

▶ **12.** [*M20*] Although ADDU $X,$Y,$Z never signals overflow, we might want to know if a carry occurs at the left when adding $Y to $Z. Show that the carry can be computed with two further instructions.

13. [*M21*] Suppose MMIX had no ADD command, only its unsigned counterpart ADDU. How could a programmer tell whether overflow occurred when computing s($Y)+s($Z)?

14. [*M21*] Suppose MMIX had no SUB command, only its unsigned counterpart SUBU. How could a programmer tell whether overflow occurred when computing s($Y)−s($Z)?

15. [*M25*] The product of two signed octabytes always lies between -2^{126} and 2^{126}, so it can always be expressed as a signed 16-byte quantity. Explain how to calculate the upper half of such a signed product.

16. [*M23*] Suppose MMIX had no MUL command, only its unsigned counterpart MULU. How could a programmer tell whether overflow occurred when computing s($Y)×s($Z)?

▶ **17.** [*M22*] Prove that unsigned integer division by 3 can always be done by multiplication: If register $Y contains any unsigned integer y, and if register $1 contains the constant $^\#$aaaa aaaa aaaa aaab, then the sequence

$$\text{MULU } \$0,\$Y,\$1; \quad \text{GET } \$0,\text{rH}; \quad \text{SRU } \$X,\$0,1$$

puts $\lfloor y/3 \rfloor$ into register $X.

18. [*M23*] Continuing the previous exercise, prove or disprove that the instructions

$$\text{MULU } \$0,\$Y,\$1; \quad \text{GET } \$0,\text{rH}; \quad \text{SRU } \$X,\$0,2$$

put $\lfloor y/5 \rfloor$ in $X if $1 is an appropriate constant.

▶ **19.** [*M26*] Continuing exercises 17 and 18, prove or disprove the following statement: Unsigned integer division by a constant can always be done using "high multiplication" followed by a right shift. More precisely, if $2^e < z < 2^{e+1}$ we can compute $\lfloor y/z \rfloor$ by computing $\lfloor ay/2^{64+e} \rfloor$, where $a = \lceil 2^{64+e}/z \rceil$, for $0 \le y < 2^{64}$.

20. [*16*] Show that two cleverly chosen MMIX instructions will multiply by 25 faster than the single instruction MUL $X,$Y,25, if we assume that overflow will not occur.

21. [*15*] Describe the effects of SL, SLU, SR, and SRU when the unsigned value in register $Z is 64 or more.

▶ **22.** [*15*] Mr. B. C. Dull wrote a program in which he wanted to branch to location Case1 if the signed number in register $1 was less than the signed number in register $2. His solution was to write 'SUB $0,$1,$2; BN $0,Case1'.
What terrible mistake did he make? What should he have written instead?

▶ **23.** [*10*] Continuing the previous exercise, what should Dull have written if his problem had been to branch if s($1) was *less than or equal to* s($2)?

24. [*M10*] If we represent a subset S of $\{0, 1, \ldots, 63\}$ by the bit vector

$$([0 \in S], [1 \in S], \ldots, [63 \in S]),$$

the bitwise operations $\wedge$ and $\vee$ correspond respectively to set intersection $(S \cap T)$ and set union $(S \cup T)$. Which bitwise operation corresponds to set difference $(S \setminus T)$?

25. [10] The *Hamming distance* between two bit vectors is the number of positions in which they differ. Show that two MMIX instructions suffice to set register $X equal to the Hamming distance between v($Y) and v($Z).

26. [10] What's a good way to compute 64 bit differences, v($X) ← v($Y) $\dot-$ v($Z)?

▶ **27.** [20] Show how to use BDIF to compute the *maximum* and *minimum* of eight bytes at a time: b($X) ← max(b($Y), b($Z)), b($W) ← min(b($Y), b($Z)).

28. [16] How would you calculate eight *absolute pixel differences* |b($Y) − b($Z)| simultaneously?

29. [21] The operation of *saturating addition* on n-bit pixels is defined by the formula

$$y \dot+ z \;=\; \min(2^n - 1, y + z).$$

Show that a sequence of three MMIX instructions will set b($X) ← b($Y) $\dot+$ b($Z).

▶ **30.** [25] Suppose register $0 contains eight ASCII characters. Find a sequence of three MMIX instructions that counts the number of *blank spaces* among those characters. (You may assume that auxiliary constants have been preloaded into other registers. A blank space is ASCII code #20.)

31. [22] Continuing the previous exercise, show how to count the number of characters in $0 that have *odd parity* (an odd number of 1 bits).

32. [M20] True or false: If $C = A \mathbin{\overset{\circ}{\bullet}} B$ then $C^T = B^T \mathbin{\overset{\circ}{\bullet}} A^T$. (See (11).)

33. [20] What is the shortest sequence of MMIX instructions that will *cyclically shift* a register eight bits to the right? For example, #9e3779b97f4a7c16 would become #169e3779b97f4a7c.

▶ **34.** [21] Given eight bytes of ASCII characters in $Z, explain how to convert them to the corresponding eight wyde characters of Unicode, using only two MMIX instructions to place the results in $X and $Y. How would you go the other way (back to ASCII)?

▶ **35.** [22] Show that two cleverly chosen MOR instructions will reverse the left-to-right order of all 64 bits in a given register $Y.

▶ **36.** [20] Using only two instructions, create a mask that has #ff in all byte positions where $Y differs from $Z, #00 in all byte positions where $Y equals $Z.

▶ **37.** [HM30] (*Finite fields.*) Explain how to use MXOR for arithmetic in a field of 256 elements; each element of the field should be represented by a suitable octabyte.

38. [20] What does the following little program do?

```
SETL $1,0; SR $2,$0,56; ADD $1,$1,$2; SLU $0,$0,8; PBNZ $0,@-4*3.
```

▶ **39.** [20] Which of the following equivalent sequences of code is faster, based on the timing information of Table 1?

    a) BN $0,@+4*2; ADDU $1,$2,$3 versus ADDU $4,$2,$3; CSNN $1,$0,$4.

    b) BN $0,@+4*3; SET $1,$2; JMP @+4*2; SET $1,$3 versus
       CSNN $1,$0,$2; CSN $1,$0,$3.

    c) BN $0,@+4*3; ADDU $1,$2,$3; JMP @+4*2; ADDU $1,$4,$5 versus
       ADDU $1,$2,$3; ADDU $6,$4,$5; CSN $1,$0,$6.

    d, e, f) Same as (a), (b), and (c), but with PBN in place of BN.

40. [10] What happens if you GO to an address that is not a multiple of 4?

41. [*20*] True or false:

a) The instructions CSOD $X,$Y,0 and ZSEV $X,$Y,$X have exactly the same effect.

b) The instructions CMPU $X,$Y,0 and ZSNZ $X,$Y,1 have exactly the same effect.

c) The instructions MOR $X,$Y,1 and AND $X,$Y,#ff have exactly the same effect.

d) The instructions MXOR $X,$Y,#80 and SR $X,$Y,56 have exactly the same effect.

42. [*20*] What is the best way to set register $1 to the *absolute value* of the number in register $0, if $0 holds (a) a signed integer? (b) a floating point number?

▶ **43.** [*28*] Given a nonzero octabyte in $Z, what is the fastest way to count how many leading and trailing zero bits it has? (For example, #13fd8124f32434a2 has three leading zeros and one trailing zero.)

▶ **44.** [*M25*] Suppose you want to emulate 32-bit arithmetic with MMIX. Show that it is easy to add, subtract, multiply, and divide signed tetrabytes, with overflow occurring whenever the result does not lie in the interval $[-2^{31} .. 2^{31})$.

45. [*10*] Think of a way to remember the sequence DVWIOUZX.

46. [*05*] The all-zeros tetrabyte #00000000 halts a program when it occurs as an MMIX instruction. What does the all-ones tetrabyte #ffffffff do?

47. [*05*] What are the symbolic names of opcodes #DF and #55?

48. [*11*] The text points out that opcodes LDO and LDOU perform exactly the same operation, with the same efficiency, regardless of the operand bytes X, Y, and Z. What other pairs of opcodes are equivalent in this sense?

▶ **49.** [*22*] After the following "number one" program has been executed, what changes to registers and memory have taken place? (For example, what is the final setting of $1? of rA? of rB?)

```
NEG     $1,1
STCO    1,$1,1
CMPU    $1,$1,1
STB     $1,$1,$1
LDOU    $1,$1,$1
INCH    $1,1
16ADDU  $1,$1,$1
MULU    $1,$1,$1
PUT     rA,1
STW     $1,$1,1
SADD    $1,$1,1
FLOT    $1,$1
PUT     rB,$1
XOR     $1,$1,1
PBOD    $1,@-4*1
NOR     $1,$1,$1
SR      $1,$1,1
SRU     $1,$1,1  ∎
```

▶ **50.** [*14*] What is the execution time of the program in the preceding exercise?

51. [*14*] Convert the "number one" program of exercise 49 to a sequence of tetrabytes in hexadecimal notation.

52. [*22*] For each MMIX opcode, consider whether there is a way to set the X, Y, and Z bytes so that the result of the instruction is precisely equivalent to SWYM (except that the execution time may be longer). Assume that nothing is known about the contents of any registers or any memory locations. Whenever it is possible to produce a no-op, state how it can be done. *Examples:* INCL is a no-op if X = 255 and Y = Z = 0. BZ is a no-op if Y = 0 and Z = 1. MULU can never be a no-op, since it affects rH.

53. [*15*] List all MMIX opcodes that can possibly change the value of rH.

54. [*20*] List all MMIX opcodes that can possibly change the value of rA.

55. [*21*] List all MMIX opcodes that can possibly change the value of rL.

▶ **56.** [*28*] Location $^\#2000\,0000\,0000\,0000$ contains a signed integer number, x. Write two programs that compute x^{13} in register \$0. One program should use the minimum number of MMIX memory locations; the other should use the minimum possible execution time. Assume that x^{13} fits into a single octabyte, and that all necessary constants have been preloaded into global registers.

▶ **57.** [*20*] When a program changes one or more of its own instructions in memory, it is said to have *self-modifying code*. MMIX insists that a SYNCID command be issued before such modified commands are executed. Explain why self-modifying code is usually undesirable in a modern computer.

58. [*50*] Write a book about operating systems, which includes the complete design of an NNIX kernel for the MMIX architecture.

Them fellers is a-mommixin' *everything.*

— V. RANDOLPH and G. P. WILSON, *Down in the Holler* (1953)

1.3.2'. The MMIX Assembly Language

A symbolic language is used to make MMIX programs considerably easier to read and to write, and to save the programmer from worrying about tedious clerical details that often lead to unnecessary errors. This language, MMIXAL ("MMIX Assembly Language"), is an extension of the notation used for instructions in the previous section. Its main features are the optional use of alphabetic names to stand for numbers, and a label field to associate names with memory locations and register numbers.

MMIXAL can readily be comprehended if we consider first a simple example. The following code is part of a larger program; it is a subroutine to find the maximum of n elements $X[1]$, ..., $X[n]$, according to Algorithm 1.2.10M.

Program M (*Find the maximum*). Initially n is in register \$0, and the address of $X[0]$ is in register x0, a global register defined elsewhere.

Assembled code	Line no.	LABEL	OP	EXPR	Times	Remarks
	01	j	IS	\$0		j
	02	m	IS	\$1		m
	03	kk	IS	\$2		$8k$
	04	xk	IS	\$3		$X[k]$
	05	t	IS	\$255		Temp storage
	06		LOC	#100		
$^\#100$: $^\#39\,02\,00\,03$	*07*	Maximum	SL	kk,\$0,3	1	<u>M1. Initialize.</u> $k \leftarrow n,\ j \leftarrow n$.
$^\#104$: $^\#8c\,01\,fe\,02$	*08*		LDO	m,x0,kk	1	$m \leftarrow X[n]$.
$^\#108$: $^\#f0\,00\,00\,06$	*09*		JMP	DecrK	1	To M2 with $k \leftarrow n-1$.

#10c: #8c 03 fe 02	*10*	Loop	LDO	xk,x0,kk	$n-1$	*M3. Compare.*
#110: #30 ff 03 01	*11*		CMP	t,xk,m	$n-1$	$t \leftarrow [X[k] > m] - [X[k] < m]$.
#114: #5c ff 00 03	*12*		PBNP	t,DecrK	$n-1$	To M5 if $X[k] \leq m$.
#118: #c1 01 03 00	*13*	ChangeM	SET	m,xk	A	*M4. Change m.* $m \leftarrow X[k]$.
#11c: #3d 00 02 03	*14*		SR	j,kk,3	A	$j \leftarrow k$.
#120: #25 02 02 08	*15*	DecrK	SUB	kk,kk,8	n	*M5. Decrease k.* $k \leftarrow k - 1$.
#124: #55 00 ff fa	*16*		PBP	kk,Loop	n	*M2. All tested?* To M3 if $k > 0$.
#128: #f8 02 00 00	*17*		POP	2,0	1	Return to main program. ▮

This program is an example of several things simultaneously:

a) The columns headed "LABEL", "OP", and "EXPR" are of principal interest; they contain a program in the MMIXAL symbolic machine language, and we shall explain the details of this program below.

b) The column headed "Assembled code" shows the actual numeric machine language that corresponds to the MMIXAL program. MMIXAL has been designed so that any MMIXAL program can easily be translated into numeric machine language; the translation is usually carried out by another computer program called an *assembly program* or *assembler*. Thus, programmers can do all of their machine language programming in MMIXAL, never bothering to determine the equivalent numeric codes by hand. Virtually all MMIX programs in this book are written in MMIXAL.

c) The column headed "Line no." is not an essential part of the MMIXAL program; it is merely included with MMIXAL examples in this book so that we can readily refer to parts of the program.

d) The column headed "Remarks" gives explanatory information about the program, and it is cross-referenced to the steps of Algorithm 1.2.10M. The reader should compare that algorithm (page 96) with the program above. Notice that a little "programmer's license" was used during the transcription into MMIX code; for example, step M2 has been put last.

e) The column headed "Times" will be instructive in many of the MMIX programs we will be studying in this book; it represents the *profile*, the number of times the instruction on that line will be executed during the course of the program. Thus, line 10 will be performed $n-1$ times, etc. From this information we can determine the length of time required to perform the subroutine; it is $n\mu + (5n + 4A + 5)\upsilon$, where A is the quantity that was analyzed carefully in Section 1.2.10. (The PBNP instruction costs $(n - 1 + 2A)\upsilon$.)

Now let's discuss the MMIXAL part of Program M. Line 01, 'j IS $0', says that symbol j stands for register $0; lines 02–05 are similar. The effect of lines 01 and 03 can be seen on line 14, where the numeric equivalent of the instruction 'SR j,kk,3' appears as #3d 00 02 03, that is, 'SR $0,$2,3'.

Line 06 says that the locations for succeeding lines should be chosen sequentially, beginning with #100. Therefore the symbol Maximum that appears in the label field of line 07 becomes equivalent to the number #100; the symbol Loop in line 10 is three tetrabytes further along, so it is equivalent to #10c.

On lines 07 through 17 the OP field contains the symbolic names of MMIX instructions: SL, LDO, etc. But the symbolic names IS and LOC, found in the OP column of lines 01–06, are somewhat different; IS and LOC are called *pseudo-operations*, because they are operators of MMIXAL but not operators of MMIX. Pseudo-operations provide special information about a symbolic program, without being instructions of the program itself. Thus the line 'j IS $0' only talks *about* Program M; it does not signify that any variable is to be set equal to the contents of register $0 when the program is run. Notice that no instructions are assembled for lines 01–06.

Line 07 is a "shift left" instruction that sets $k \leftarrow n$ by setting $\text{kk} \leftarrow 8n$. This program works with the value of $8k$, not k, because $8k$ is needed for octabyte addresses in lines 08 and 10.

Line 09 jumps the control to line 15. The assembler, knowing that this JMP instruction is in location $\#108$ and that DecrK is equivalent to $\#120$, computes the relative offset $(\#120 - \#108)/4 = 6$. Similar relative addresses are computed for the branch commands in lines 12 and 16.

The rest of the symbolic code is self-explanatory. As mentioned earlier, Program M is intended to be part of a larger program; elsewhere the sequence

```
SET    $2,100
PUSHJ  $1,Maximum
STO    $1,Max
```

would, for example, jump to Program M with n set to 100. Program M would then find the largest of the elements $X[1], \ldots, X[100]$ and would return to the instruction 'STO $1,Max' with the maximum value in $1 and with its position, j, in $2. (See exercise 3.)

Let's look now at a program that is *complete*, not merely a subroutine. If the following program is named Hello, it will print out the famous message 'Hello, world' and stop.

Program H (*Hail the world*).

Assembled code	Line	LABEL	OP	EXPR	Remarks
	01	argv	IS	$1	The argument vector
	02		LOC	#100	
#100: #8f ff 01 00	03	Main	LDOU	$255,argv,0	$255 ← address of program name.
#104: #00 00 07 01	04		TRAP	0,Fputs,StdOut	Print that name.
#108: #f4 ff 00 03	05		GETA	$255,String	$255 ← address of ", world".
#10c: #00 00 07 01	06		TRAP	0,Fputs,StdOut	Print that string.
#110: #00 00 00 00	07		TRAP	0,Halt,0	Stop.
#114: #2c 20 77 6f	08	String	BYTE	", world",#a,0	String of characters
#118: #72 6c 64 0a	09				with newline
#11c: #00	10				and terminator ∎

Readers who have access to an MMIX assembler and simulator should take a moment to prepare a short computer file containing the LABEL OP EXPR portions of Program H before reading further. Name the file 'Hello.mms' and assemble it by saying, for example, 'mmixal Hello.mms'. (The assembler will produce a file called 'Hello.mmo'; the suffix .mms means "MMIX symbolic" and .mmo means "MMIX object.") Now invoke the simulator by saying 'mmix Hello'.

The MMIX simulator implements some of the simplest features of a hypothetical operating system called NNIX. If an object file called, say, foo.mmo is present, NNIX will launch it when a command line such as

$$\text{foo bar xyzzy} \tag{1}$$

is given. You can obtain the corresponding behavior by invoking the simulator with the command line 'mmix ⟨options⟩ foo bar xyzzy', where ⟨options⟩ is a sequence of zero or more special requests. For example, option -P will print a profile of the program after it has halted.

An MMIX program always begins at symbolic location Main. At that time register $0 contains the number of *command line arguments*, namely the number of words on the command line. Register $1 contains the memory address of the first such argument, which is always the name of the program. The operating system has placed all of the arguments into consecutive octabytes, starting at the address in $1 and ending with an octabyte of all zeros. Each argument is represented as a *string*, meaning that it is the address in memory of a sequence of zero or more nonzero bytes followed by a byte that is zero; the nonzero bytes are the *characters* of the string.

For example, the command line (1) would cause $0 to be initially 3, and we might have

	$1 = #4000000000000008	Pointer to the first string
M_8[#4000000000000008]	= #4000000000000028	First argument, the string "foo"
M_8[#4000000000000010]	= #4000000000000030	Second argument, the string "bar"
M_8[#4000000000000018]	= #4000000000000038	Third argument, the string "xyzzy"
M_8[#4000000000000020]	= #0000000000000000	Null pointer after the last argument
M_8[#4000000000000028]	= #666f6f0000000000	'f','o','o',0,0,0,0,0
M_8[#4000000000000030]	= #6261720000000000	'b','a','r',0,0,0,0,0
M_8[#4000000000000038]	= #78797a7a79000000	'x','y','z','z','y',0,0,0

NNIX sets up each argument string so that its characters begin at an octabyte boundary; strings in general can, however, start anywhere within an octabyte.

The first instruction of Program H, in line 03, puts the string pointer M_8[$1] into register $255; this string is the program name 'Hello'. Line 04 is a special TRAP instruction, which asks the operating system to put string $255 into the *standard output* file. Similarly, lines 05 and 06 ask NNIX to contribute ', world' and a newline character to the standard output. The symbol Fputs is predefined to equal 7, and the symbol StdOut is predefined to equal 1. Line 07, 'TRAP 0,Halt,0', is the normal way to terminate a program. We will discuss all such special TRAP commands at the end of this section.

The characters of the string output by lines 05 and 06 are generated by the BYTE command in line 08. BYTE is a pseudo-operation of MMIXAL, not an operation of MMIX; but BYTE is different from pseudo-ops like IS and LOC, because it does assemble data into memory. In general, BYTE assembles a sequence of expressions into one-byte constants. The construction ", world" in line 08 is MMIXAL's shorthand for the list

$$',',' ','w','o','r','l','d'$$

of seven one-character constants. The constant #a on line 08 is the ASCII *newline* character, which causes a new line to begin when it appears in a file being printed. The final ',0' on line 08 terminates the string. Thus line 08 is a list of nine expressions, and it leads to the nine bytes shown at the left of lines 08–10.

Our third example introduces a few more features of the assembly language. The object is to compute and print a table of the first 500 prime numbers, with 10 columns of 50 numbers each. The table should appear as follows, when the standard output of our program is listed as a text file:

```
First Five Hundred Primes
  0002 0233 0547 0877 1229 1597 1993 2371 2749 3187
  0003 0239 0557 0881 1231 1601 1997 2377 2753 3191
  0005 0241 0563 0883 1237 1607 1999 2381 2767 3203
    ⋮                                           ⋮
  0229 0541 0863 1223 1583 1987 2357 2741 3181 3571
```

We will use the following method.

Algorithm P (*Print table of 500 primes*). This algorithm has two distinct parts: Steps P1–P8 prepare an internal table of 500 primes, and steps P9–P11 print the answer in the form shown above.

P1. [Start table.] Set PRIME[1] ← 2, $n ← 3$, $j ← 1$. (In this program, n runs through the odd numbers that are candidates for primes; j keeps track of how many primes have been found so far.)

P2. [n is prime.] Set $j ← j + 1$, PRIME[j] ← n.

P3. [500 found?] If $j = 500$, go to step P9.

P4. [Advance n.] Set $n ← n + 2$.

P5. [$k ← 2$.] Set $k ← 2$. (PRIME[k] will run through n's possible prime divisors.)

P6. [PRIME[k]\n?] Divide n by PRIME[k]; let q be the quotient and r the remainder. If $r = 0$ (hence n is not prime), go to P4.

P7. [PRIME[k] large?] If $q ≤$ PRIME[k], go to P2. (In such a case, n must be prime; the proof of this fact is interesting and a little unusual — see exercise 11.)

P8. [Advance k.] Increase k by 1, and go to P6.

P9. [Print title.] Now we are ready to print the table. Output the title line and set $m ← 1$.

P10. [Print line.] Output a line that contains PRIME[m], PRIME[$50 + m$], ..., PRIME[$450 + m$] in the proper format.

P11. [500 printed?] Increase m by 1. If $m ≤ 50$, return to P10; otherwise the algorithm terminates. ▮

Program P (*Print table of 500 primes*). This program has deliberately been written in a slightly clumsy fashion in order to illustrate most of the features of MMIXAL in a single program.

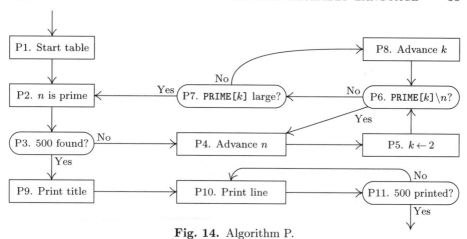

Fig. 14. Algorithm P.

```
01  % Example program ...  Table of primes
02  L        IS     500              The number of primes to find
03  t        IS     $255             Temporary storage
04  n        GREG   0                Prime candidate
05  q        GREG   0                Quotient
06  r        GREG   0                Remainder
07  jj       GREG   0                Index for PRIME[j]
08  kk       GREG   0                Index for PRIME[k]
09  pk       GREG   0                Value of PRIME[k]
10  mm       IS     kk               Index for output lines
11           LOC    Data_Segment
12  PRIME1   WYDE   2                PRIME[1] = 2
13           LOC    PRIME1+2*L
14  ptop     GREG   @                Address of PRIME[501]
15  j0       GREG   PRIME1+2-@       Initial value of jj
16  BUF      OCTA   0                Place to form decimal string
17
18           LOC    #100
19  Main     SET    n,3              P1. Start table. n ← 3.
20           SET    jj,j0            j ← 1.
21  2H       STWU   n,ptop,jj        P2. n is prime. PRIME[j+1] ← n.
22           INCL   jj,2             j ← j + 1.
23  3H       BZ     jj,2F            P3. 500 found?
24  4H       INCL   n,2              P4. Advance n.
25  5H       SET    kk,j0            P5. k ← 2.
26  6H       LDWU   pk,ptop,kk       P6. PRIME[k]\n?
27           DIV    q,n,pk           q ← ⌊n/PRIME[k]⌋.
28           GET    r,rR             r ← n mod PRIME[k].
29           BZ     r,4B             To P4 if r = 0.
30  7H       CMP    t,q,pk           P7. PRIME[k] large?
31           BNP    t,2B             To P2 if q ≤ PRIME[k].
32  8H       INCL   kk,2             P8. Advance k. k ← k + 1.
33           JMP    6B               To P6.
```

```
34              GREG    @                           Base address
35   Title      BYTE    "First Five Hundred Primes"
36   NewLn      BYTE    #a,0                        Newline and string terminator
37   Blanks     BYTE    "   ",0                     String of three blanks
38   2H         LDA     t,Title                     P9. Print title.
39              TRAP    0,Fputs,StdOut
40              NEG     mm,2                        Initialize m.
41   3H         ADD     mm,mm,j0                    P10. Print line.
42              LDA     t,Blanks                    Output "   ".
43              TRAP    0,Fputs,StdOut
44   2H         LDWU    pk,ptop,mm                  pk ← prime to be printed.
45   0H         GREG    #2030303030000000           " 0000",0,0,0
46              STOU    0B,BUF                      Prepare buffer for decimal conversion.
47              LDA     t,BUF+4                     t ← position of units digit.
48   1H         DIV     pk,pk,10                    pk ← ⌊pk/10⌋.
49              GET     r,rR                        r ← next digit.
50              INCL    r,'0'                       r ← ASCII digit r.
51              STBU    r,t,0                       Store r in the buffer.
52              SUB     t,t,1                       Move one byte to the left.
53              PBNZ    pk,1B                       Repeat on remaining digits.
54              LDA     t,BUF                       Output " " and four digits.
55              TRAP    0,Fputs,StdOut
56              INCL    mm,2*L/10                   Advance by 50 wydes.
57              PBN     mm,2B
58              LDA     t,NewLn                     Output a newline.
59              TRAP    0,Fputs,StdOut
60              CMP     t,mm,2*(L/10-1)             P11. 500 printed?
61              PBNZ    t,3B                        To P10 if not done.
62              TRAP    0,Halt,0                    ▮
```

The following points of interest should be noted about this program:

1. Line 01 begins with a percent sign and line 17 is blank. Such "comment" lines are merely explanatory; they have no effect on the assembled program.

Each non-comment line has three fields called LABEL, OP, and EXPR, separated by spaces. The EXPR field contains one or more symbolic expressions separated by commas. Comments may follow the EXPR field.

2. As in Program M, the pseudo-operation IS sets the equivalent of a symbol. For example, in line 02 the equivalent of L is set to 500, which is the number of primes to be computed. Notice that in line 03, the equivalent of t is set to $255, a *register number*, while L's equivalent was 500, a *pure number*. Some symbols have register number equivalents, ranging from $0 to $255; others have pure equivalents, which are octabytes. We will generally use symbolic names that begin with a lowercase letter to denote registers, and names that begin with an uppercase letter to denote pure values, although MMIXAL does not enforce this convention.

3. The pseudo-op GREG on line 04 allocates a *global register*. Register $255 is always global; the first GREG causes $254 to be global, and the next GREG does

the same for $253, etc. Lines 04–09 therefore allocate six global registers, and they cause the symbols n, q, r, jj, kk, pk to be respectively equivalent to $254, $253, $252, $251, $250, $249. Line 10 makes mm equivalent to $250.

If the EXPR field of a GREG definition is zero, as it is on lines 04–09, the global register is assumed to have a dynamically varying value when the program is run. But if a nonzero expression is given, as on lines 14, 15, 34, and 45, the global register is assumed to be constant throughout a program's execution. MMIXAL uses such global registers as *base addresses* when subsequent instructions refer to memory. For example, consider the instruction 'LDA t,BUF+4' in line 47. MMIXAL is able to discover that global register ptop holds the address of BUF; therefore 'LDA t,BUF+4' can be assembled as 'LDA t,ptop,4'. Similarly, the LDA instructions on lines 38, 42, and 58 make use of the nameless base address introduced by the instruction 'GREG @' on line 34. (Recall from Section 1.3.1′ that @ denotes the current location.)

4. A good assembly language should mimic the way a programmer *thinks* about machine programs. One example of this philosophy is the automatic allocation of global registers and base addresses. Another example is the idea of *local symbols* such as the symbol 2H, which appears in the label field of lines 21, 38, and 44.

Local symbols are special symbols whose equivalents can be *redefined* as many times as desired. A global symbol like PRIME1 has but one significance throughout a program, and if it were to appear in the label field of more than one line an error would be indicated by the assembler. But local symbols have a different nature; we write, for example, 2H ("2 here") in the LABEL field, and 2F ("2 forward") or 2B ("2 backward") in the EXPR field of an MMIXAL line:

> 2B means the closest *previous* label 2H;
> 2F means the closest *following* label 2H.

Thus the 2F in line 23 refers to line 38; the 2B in line 31 refers back to line 21; and the 2B in line 57 refers to line 44. The symbols 2F and 2B never refer to their *own* line. For example, the MMIXAL instructions

```
2H    IS    $10
2H    BZ    2B,2F
2H    IS    2B-4
```

are virtually equivalent to the single instruction

BZ $10,@-4 .

The symbols 2F and 2B should never be used in the LABEL field; the symbol 2H should never be used in the EXPR field. If 2B occurs before any appearance of 2H, it denotes zero. There are ten local symbols, which can be obtained by replacing '2' in these examples by any digit from 0 to 9.

The idea of local symbols was introduced by M. E. Conway in 1958, in connection with an assembly program for the UNIVAC I. Local symbols free us from the obligation to choose a symbolic name when we merely want to refer to an instruction a few lines away. There often is no appropriate name for nearby locations, so programmers have tended to introduce meaningless symbols like X1, X2, X3, etc., with the potential danger of duplication.

5. The reference to Data_Segment on line 11 introduces another new idea. In most embodiments of MMIX, the 2^{64}-byte virtual address space is broken into two parts, called *user space* (addresses $^\#$0000000000000000 .. $^\#$7fffffffffffffff) and *kernel space* (addresses $^\#$8000000000000000 .. $^\#$ffffffffffffffff). The "negative" addresses of kernel space are reserved for the operating system.

User space is further subdivided into four segments of 2^{61} bytes each. First comes the *text segment*; the user's program generally resides here. Then comes the *data segment*, beginning at virtual address $^\#$2000000000000000; this is for variables whose memory locations are allocated once and for all by the assembler, and for other variables allocated by the user without the help of the system library. Next is the *pool segment*, beginning at $^\#$4000000000000000; command line arguments and other dynamically allocated data go here. Finally the *stack segment*, which starts at $^\#$6000000000000000, is used by the MMIX hardware to maintain the register stack governed by PUSH, POP, SAVE, and UNSAVE. Three symbols,

$$\text{Data\_Segment} = {}^\#2000000000000000,$$
$$\text{Pool\_Segment} = {}^\#4000000000000000,$$
$$\text{Stack\_Segment} = {}^\#6000000000000000,$$

are predefined for convenience in MMIXAL. Nothing should be assembled into the pool segment or the stack segment, although a program may refer to data found there. References to addresses near the beginning of a segment might be more efficient than references to addresses that come near the end; for example, MMIX might not be able to access the last byte of the text segment, M[$^\#$1fffffffffffffff], as fast as it can read the first byte of the data segment.

Our programs for MMIX will always consider the text segment to be *read-only*: Everything in memory locations less than $^\#$2000000000000000 will remain constant once a program has been assembled and loaded. Therefore Program P puts the prime table and the output buffer into the data segment.

6. The text and data segments are entirely zero at the beginning of a program, except for instructions and data that have been loaded in accordance with the MMIXAL specification of the program. If two or more bytes of data are destined for the same cell of memory, the loader will fill that cell with their bitwise exclusive-or.

7. The symbolic expression 'PRIME1+2*L' on line 13 indicates that MMIXAL has the ability to do arithmetic on octabytes. See also the more elaborate example '2*(L/10-1)' on line 60.

8. As a final note about Program P, we can observe that its instructions have been organized so that registers are counted towards zero, and tested against zero, whenever possible. For example, register jj holds a quantity that is related to the positive variable *j* of Algorithm P, but jj is normally negative; this change

makes it easy for the machine to decide when j has reached 500 (line 23). Lines 40–61 are particularly noteworthy in this regard, although perhaps a bit tricky. The binary-to-decimal conversion routine in lines 45–55, based on division by 10, is simple but not the fastest possible. More efficient methods are discussed in Section 4.4.

It may be of interest to note a few of the statistics observed when Program P was actually run. The division instruction in line 27 was executed 9538 times. The total time to perform steps P1–P8 (lines 19–33) was $10036\mu+641543v$; steps P9–P11 cost an additional $2804\mu + 124559v$, not counting the time taken by the operating system to handle TRAP requests.

Language summary. Now that we have seen three examples of what can be done in MMIXAL, it is time to discuss the rules more carefully, observing in particular the things that *cannot* be done. The following comparatively few rules define the language.

1. A *symbol* is a string of letters and/or digits, beginning with a letter. The underscore character '_' is regarded as a letter, for purposes of this definition, and so are all Unicode characters whose code value exceeds 126. *Examples:* PRIME1, Data_Segment, Main, __, pâté.

The special constructions dH, dF, and dB, where d is a single digit, are effectively replaced by unique symbols according to the "local symbol" convention explained above.

2. A *constant* is either

a) a *decimal constant*, consisting of one or more decimal digits $\{0, 1, 2, 3, 4, 5, 6, 7, 8, 9\}$, representing an unsigned octabyte in radix 10 notation; or

b) a *hexadecimal constant*, consisting of a hash mark # followed by one or more hexadecimal digits $\{0, 1, 2, 3, 4, 5, 6, 7, 8, 9, a, b, c, d, e, f, A, B, C, D, E, F\}$, representing an unsigned octabyte in radix 16 notation; or

c) a *character constant*, consisting of a quote character ' followed by any character other than newline, followed by another quote '; this represents the ASCII or Unicode value of the quoted character.

Examples: 65, #41, 'A', 39, #27, ''', 31639, #7B97, '算'.

A *string constant* is a double-quote character " followed by one or more characters other than newline or double-quote, followed by another double-quote ". This construction is equivalent to a sequence of character constants for the individual characters, separated by commas.

3. Each appearance of a symbol in an MMIXAL program is said to be either a "defined symbol" or a "future reference." A *defined symbol* is a symbol that has appeared in the LABEL field of a preceding line of this MMIXAL program. A *future reference* is a symbol that has not yet been defined in this way.

A few symbols, like rR and ROUND_NEAR and V_BIT and W_Handler and Fputs, are predefined because they refer to constants associated with the MMIX hardware or with its rudimentary operating system. Such symbols can be re-defined, because MMIXAL does not assume that every programmer knows all their names. But no symbol should appear as a label more than once.

Every defined symbol has an equivalent value, which is either *pure* (an unsigned octabyte) or a *register number* ($0 or $1 or ... or $255).

4. A *primary* is either

a) a symbol; or

b) a constant; or

c) the character @, denoting the current location; or

d) an expression enclosed in parentheses; or

e) a unary operator followed by a primary.

The unary operators are + (affirmation, which does nothing), - (negation, which subtracts from zero), ~ (complementation, which changes all 64 bits), and $ (registerization, which converts a pure value to a register number).

5. A *term* is a sequence of one or more primaries separated by strong binary operators; an *expression* is a sequence of one or more terms separated by weak binary operators. The *strong binary operators* are * (multiplication), / (division), // (fractional division), % (remainder), << (left shift), >> (right shift), and & (bitwise and). The *weak binary operators* are + (addition), - (subtraction), | (bitwise or), and ^ (bitwise exclusive-or). These operations act on unsigned octabytes; $x//y$ denotes $\lfloor 2^{64}x/y \rfloor$ if $x < y$, and it is undefined if $x \geq y$. Binary operators of the same strength are performed from left to right; thus a/b/c is (a/b)/c and a-b+c is (a-b)+c.

Example: #ab<<32+k&~(k-1) is an expression, the sum of terms #ab<<32 and k&~(k-1). The latter term is the bitwise and of primaries k and ~(k-1). The latter primary is the complement of (k-1), a parenthesized expression that is the difference of two terms k and 1. The term 1 is also a primary, and also a constant, in fact it is a decimal constant. If symbol k is equivalent to #cdef00, say, the entire expression #ab<<32+k&~(k-1) is equivalent to #ab00000100.

Binary operations are allowed only on pure numbers, except in cases like $1+2 = $3 and $3-$1 = 2. Future references cannot be combined with anything else; an expression like 2F+1 is always illegal, because 2F never corresponds to a defined symbol.

6. An *instruction* consists of three fields:

a) the LABEL field, which is either blank or a symbol;

b) the OP field, which is either an MMIX opcode or an MMIXAL pseudo-op;

c) the EXPR field, which is a list of one or more expressions separated by commas. The EXPR field can also be blank, in which case it is equivalent to the single expression 0.

7. Assembly of an instruction takes place in three steps:

a) The current location @ is aligned, if necessary, by increasing it to the next multiple of

       8,   if OP is OCTA;

       4,   if OP is TETRA or an MMIX opcode;

       2,   if OP is WYDE.

b) The symbol in LABEL, if present, is defined to be @, unless OP = IS or OP = GREG.

c) If OP is a pseudo-operation, see rule 8. Otherwise OP is an MMIX instruction; the OP and EXPR fields define a tetrabyte as explained in Section 1.3.1′, and @ advances by 4. Some MMIX opcodes have three operands in the EXPR field, others have two, and others have only one.

If OP is ADD, say, MMIXAL will expect three operands, and will check that the first and second operands are register numbers. If the third operand is pure, MMIXAL will change the opcode from #20 ("add") to #21 ("add immediate"), and will check that the immediate value is less than 256.

If OP is SETH, say, MMIXAL will expect two operands. The first operand should be a register number; the second should be a pure value less than 65536.

An OP like BNZ takes two operands: a register and a pure number. The pure number should be expressible as a relative address; in other words, its value should be expressible as $@ + 4k$ where $-65536 \leq k < 65536$.

Any OP that refers to memory, like LDB or GO, has a two-operand form $X,A as well as the three-operand forms $X,$Y,$Z or $X,$Y,Z. The two-operand option can be used when the memory address A is expressible as the sum $Y + Z of a base address and a one-byte value; see rule 8(b).

8. MMIXAL includes the following pseudo-operations.

a) OP = IS: The EXPR should be a single expression; the symbol in LABEL, if present, is made equivalent to the value of this expression.

b) OP = GREG: The EXPR should be a single expression with a pure equivalent, x. The symbol in LABEL, if present, is made equivalent to the largest previously unallocated global register number, and this global register will contain x when the program begins. If $x \neq 0$, the value of x is considered to be a *base address*, and the program should not change that global register.

c) OP = LOC: The EXPR should be a single expression with a pure equivalent, x. The value of @ is set to x. For example, the instruction 'T LOC @+1000' defines symbol T to be the address of the first of a sequence of 1000 bytes, and advances @ to the byte following that sequence.

d) OP = BYTE, WYDE, TETRA, or OCTA: The EXPR field should be a list of pure expressions that each fit in 1, 2, 4, or 8 bytes, respectively.

9. MMIXAL restricts future references so that the assembly process can work quickly in one pass over the program. A future reference is permitted only

a) in a relative address: as the operand of JMP, or as the second operand of a branch, probable branch, PUSHJ, or GETA; or

b) in an expression assembled by OCTA.

```
% Example program ... Table of primes
L IS 500            The number of primes to find
t  IS  $255     Temporary storage
n GREG        ;; Prime candidate
q GREG  /* Quotient */
r GREG  // Remainder
jj GREG 0       Index for PRIME[j]
   .
   .
   .
  PBN   mm,2B
 LDA t,NewLn; TRAP 0,Fputs,StdOut
 CMP t,mm,2*(L/10-1) ; PBNZ t,3B;      TRAP 0,Halt,0
```

Fig. 15. Program P as a computer file: The assembler tolerates many formats.

MMIXAL also has a few additional features relevant to system programming that do not concern us here. Complete details of the full language appear in the *MMIXware* document, together with the complete logic of a working assembler.

A free format can be used when presenting an MMIXAL program to the assembler (see Fig. 15). The LABEL field starts at the beginning of a line and continues up to the first blank space. The next nonblank character begins the OP field, which continues to the next blank, etc. The whole line is a comment if the first nonblank character is not a letter or digit; otherwise comments start after the EXPR field. Notice that the GREG definitions for n, q, and r in Fig. 15 have a blank EXPR field (which is equivalent to the single expression '0'); therefore the comments on those lines need to be introduced by some sort of special delimiter. But no such delimiter is necessary on the GREG line for jj, because an explicit EXPR of 0 appears there.

The final lines of Fig. 15 illustrate the fact that two or more instructions can be placed on a single line of input to the assembler, if they are separated by semicolons. If an instruction following a semicolon has a nonblank label, the label must immediately follow the ';'.

A consistent format would obviously be better than the hodgepodge of different styles shown in Fig. 15, because computer files are easier to read when they aren't so chaotic. But the assembler itself is very forgiving; it doesn't mind occasional sloppiness.

Primitive input and output. Let us conclude this section by discussing the special TRAP operations supported by the MMIX simulator. These operations provide basic input and output functions on which facilities at a much higher level could be built. A two-instruction sequence of the form

$$\text{SET } \$255, \langle\text{arg}\rangle; \ \text{TRAP } 0, \langle\text{function}\rangle, \langle\text{handle}\rangle \tag{2}$$

is usually used to invoke such a function, where $\langle\text{arg}\rangle$ points to a parameter and $\langle\text{handle}\rangle$ identifies the relevant file. For example, Program H uses

$$\text{GETA } \$255, \text{String}; \ \text{TRAP } 0, \text{Fputs}, \text{StdOut}$$

to put a string into the standard output file, and Program P is similar.

After the TRAP has been serviced by the operating system, register $255 will contain a return value. In each case *this value will be negative if and only if an error occurred.* Programs H and P do not check for file errors, because they assume that the correctness or incorrectness of the standard output will speak for itself; but error detection and error recovery are usually important in well-written programs.

• Fopen(*handle, name, mode*). Each of the ten primitive input/output traps applies to a *handle*, which is a one-byte integer. Fopen associates *handle* with an external file whose name is the string *name*, and prepares to do input and/or output on that file. The third parameter, *mode*, must be one of the values TextRead, TextWrite, BinaryRead, BinaryWrite, or BinaryReadWrite, all of which are predefined in MMIXAL. In the three ...Write modes, any previous file contents are discarded. The value returned is 0 if the handle was successfully opened, otherwise −1.

The calling sequence for Fopen is

$$\text{LDA } \$255, \text{Arg}; \quad \text{TRAP } 0, \text{Fopen}, \langle\text{handle}\rangle \tag{3}$$

where Arg is a two-octabyte sequence

$$\text{Arg OCTA } \langle\text{name}\rangle, \langle\text{mode}\rangle \tag{4}$$

that has been placed elsewhere in memory. For example, to call the function Fopen(5, "foo", BinaryWrite) in an MMIXAL program, we could put

```
Arg  OCTA  1F,BinaryWrite
1H   BYTE  "foo",0
```

into, say, the data segment, and then give the instructions

LDA $255,Arg; TRAP 0,Fopen,5 .

This would open handle 5 for writing a new file of binary output,* to be named "foo".

Three handles are already open at the beginning of each program: The standard input file StdIn (handle 0) has mode TextRead; the standard output file StdOut (handle 1) has mode TextWrite; the standard error file StdErr (handle 2) also has mode TextWrite.

• Fclose(*handle*). If *handle* has been opened, Fclose causes it to be closed, hence no longer associated with any file. Again the result is 0 if successful, or −1 if the file was already closed or unclosable. The calling sequence is simply

$$\text{TRAP } 0, \text{Fclose}, \langle\text{handle}\rangle \tag{5}$$

because there is no need to put anything in $255.

---

* Different computer systems have different notions of what constitutes a text file and what constitutes a binary file. Each MMIX simulator adopts the conventions of the operating system on which it resides.

• Fread(*handle*, *buffer*, *size*). The file handle should have been opened with mode TextRead, BinaryRead, or BinaryReadWrite. The next *size* bytes are read from the file into MMIX's memory starting at address *buffer*. The value $n - size$ is returned, where n is the number of bytes successfully read and stored, or $-1 - size$ if an error occurred. The calling sequence is

$$\text{LDA \$255,Arg; TRAP 0,Fread,}\langle\text{handle}\rangle \qquad (6)$$

with two octabytes for the other arguments

$$\text{Arg OCTA } \langle\text{buffer}\rangle, \langle\text{size}\rangle \qquad (7)$$

as in (3) and (4).

• Fgets(*handle*, *buffer*, *size*). The file handle should have been opened with mode TextRead, BinaryRead, or BinaryReadWrite. One-byte characters are read into MMIX's memory starting at address *buffer*, until either $size-1$ characters have been read and stored or a newline character has been read and stored; the next byte in memory is then set to zero. If an error or end of file occurs before reading is complete, the memory contents are undefined and the value -1 is returned; otherwise the number of characters successfully read and stored is returned. The calling sequence is the same as (6) and (7), except of course that Fgets replaces Fread in (6).

• Fgetws(*handle*, *buffer*, *size*). This command is the same as Fgets, except that it applies to wyde characters instead of one-byte characters. Up to $size - 1$ wyde characters are read; a wyde newline is #000a.

• Fwrite(*handle*, *buffer*, *size*). The file handle should have been opened with one of the modes TextWrite, BinaryWrite, or BinaryReadWrite. The next *size* bytes are written from MMIX's memory starting at address *buffer*. The value $n - size$ is returned, where n is the number of bytes successfully written. The calling sequence is analogous to (6) and (7).

• Fputs(*handle*, *string*). The file handle should have been opened with mode TextWrite, BinaryWrite, or BinaryReadWrite. One-byte characters are written from MMIX's memory to the file, starting at address *string*, up to but not including the first byte equal to zero. The number of bytes written is returned, or -1 on error. The calling sequence is

$$\text{SET \$255,}\langle\text{string}\rangle; \text{ TRAP 0,Fputs,}\langle\text{handle}\rangle. \qquad (8)$$

• Fputws(*handle*, *string*). This command is the same as Fputs, except that it applies to wyde characters instead of one-byte characters.

• Fseek(*handle*, *offset*). The file handle should have been opened with mode BinaryRead, BinaryWrite, or BinaryReadWrite. This operation causes the next input or output operation to begin at *offset* bytes from the beginning of the file, if $offset \geq 0$, or at $-offset-1$ bytes before the end of the file, if $offset < 0$. (For example, $offset = 0$ "rewinds" the file to its very beginning; $offset = -1$

moves forward all the way to the end.) The result is 0 if successful, or −1 if the stated positioning could not be done. The calling sequence is

$$\text{SET \$255},\langle\text{offset}\rangle; \quad \text{TRAP 0,Fseek},\langle\text{handle}\rangle. \tag{9}$$

An Fseek command must be given when switching from input to output or from output to input in BinaryReadWrite mode.

• Ftell(*handle*). The given file handle should have been opened with mode BinaryRead, BinaryWrite, or BinaryReadWrite. This operation returns the current file position, measured in bytes from the beginning, or −1 if an error has occurred. The calling sequence is simply

$$\text{TRAP 0,Ftell},\langle\text{handle}\rangle. \tag{10}$$

Complete details about all ten of these input/output functions appear in the *MMIXware* document, together with a reference implementation. The symbols

$$
\begin{array}{llll}
\text{Fopen} = 1, & \text{Fwrite} = 6, & \text{TextRead} = 0, & \\
\text{Fclose} = 2, & \text{Fputs} = 7, & \text{TextWrite} = 1, & \\
\text{Fread} = 3, & \text{Fputws} = 8, & \text{BinaryRead} = 2, & (11) \\
\text{Fgets} = 4, & \text{Fseek} = 9, & \text{BinaryWrite} = 3, & \\
\text{Fgetws} = 5, & \text{Ftell} = 10, & \text{BinaryReadWrite} = 4 &
\end{array}
$$

are predefined in MMIXAL; also Halt = 0.

EXERCISES — First set

1. [*05*] (a) What is the meaning of '4B' in line 29 of Program P? (b) Would the program still work if the label of line 24 were changed to '2H' and the EXPR field of line 29 were changed to 'r,2B'?

2. [*10*] Explain what happens if an MMIXAL program contains several instances of the line

$$\text{9H} \quad \text{IS} \quad \text{9B+1}$$

and no other occurrences of 9H.

▶ **3.** [*23*] What is the effect of the following program?

```
          LOC     Data_Segment
    X0    IS      @
    N     IS      100
    x0    GREG    X0
    ⟨Insert Program M here⟩
    Main  GETA    t,9F; TRAP 0,Fread,StdIn
          SET     $0,N<<3
    1H    SR      $2,$0,3; PUSHJ $1,Maximum
          LDO     $3,x0,$0
          SL      $2,$2,3
          STO     $1,x0,$0; STO $3,x0,$2
          SUB     $0,$0,1<<3; PBNZ $0,1B
          GETA    t,9F; TRAP 0,Fwrite,StdOut
          TRAP    0,Halt,0
    9H    OCTA    X0+1<<3,N<<3    ▮
```

4. [*10*] What is the value of the constant #112233445566778899?

5. [*11*] What do you get from 'BYTE 3+"pills"+6'?

▶ **6.** [*15*] True or false: The single instruction TETRA ⟨expr1⟩,⟨expr2⟩ always has the same effect as the pair of instructions TETRA ⟨expr1⟩; TETRA ⟨expr2⟩.

7. [*05*] John H. Quick (a student) was shocked, shocked to find that the instruction GETA $0,@+1 gave the same result as GETA $0,@. Explain why he should not have been surprised.

▶ **8.** [*15*] What's a good way to align the current location @ so that it is a multiple of 16, increasing it by 0..15 as necessary?

9. [*10*] What changes to Program P will make it print a table of 600 primes?

▶ **10.** [*25*] Assemble Program P by hand. (It won't take as long as you think.) What are the actual numerical contents of memory, corresponding to that symbolic program?

11. [*HM20*] (a) Show that every nonprime $n > 1$ has a divisor d with $1 < d \le \sqrt{n}$. (b) Use this fact to show that n is prime if it passes the test in step P7 of Algorithm P.

12. [*15*] The GREG instruction on line 34 of Program P defines a base address that is used for the string constants Title, NewLn, and Blank on lines 38, 42, and 58. Suggest a way to avoid using this extra global register, without making the program run slower.

13. [*20*] Unicode characters make it possible to print the first 500 primes as

أول خمس ميات الأرقام الأولية

٣١٨٧	٢٧٤٩	٢٢٧١	١٩٩٣	١٥٩٧	١٢٢٩	٠٨٧٧	٠٥٤٧	٠٢٣٣	٠٠٠٢
٣١٩١	٢٧٥٣	٢٢٧٧	١٩٩٧	١٦٠١	١٢٣١	٠٨٨١	٠٥٥٧	٠٢٣٩	٠٠٠٣
٣٢٠٣	٢٧٦٧	٢٢٨١	١٩٩٩	١٦٠٧	١٢٣٧	٠٨٨٣	٠٥٦٣	٠٢٤١	٠٠٠٥

⋮ ⋮

| ٣٥٧١ | ٣١٨١ | ٢٧٤١ | ٢٣٥٧ | ١٩٨٧ | ١٥٨٣ | ١٢٢٣ | ٠٨٦٣ | ٠٥٤١ | ٠٢٢٩ |

with "authentic" Arabic numerals. One simply uses wyde characters instead of bytes, translating the English title and then substituting Arabic-Indic digits #0660–#0669 for the ASCII digits #30–#39. (Arabic script is written from right to left, but numbers still appear with their least significant digits at the right. The bidirectional presentation rules of Unicode automatically take care of the necessary reversals when the output is formatted.) What changes to Program P will accomplish this?

▶ **14.** [*21*] Change Program P so that it uses floating point arithmetic for the divisibility test in step P6. (The FREM instruction always gives an exact result.) Use $\sqrt{n}$ instead of q in step P7. Do these changes increase or decrease the running time?

▶ **15.** [*22*] What does the following program do? (Do not run it on a computer, figure it out by hand!)

```
      * Mystery Program
a       GREG    '*'
b       GREG    ' '
c       GREG    Data_Segment
        LOC     #100
Main    NEG     $1,1,75
        SET     $2,0
2H      ADD     $3,$1,75
3H      STB     b,c,$2
        ADD     $2,$2,1
```

```
          SUB    $3,$3,1
          PBP    $3,3B
          STB    a,c,$2
          INCL   $2,1
          INCL   $1,1
          PBN    $1,2B
          SET    $255,c;  TRAP 0,Fputs,StdOut
          TRAP   0,Halt,0  ▌
```

16. [*46*] MMIXAL was designed with simplicity and efficiency in mind, so that people can easily prepare machine language programs for MMIX when those programs are relatively short. Longer programs are usually written in a higher-level language like C or Java, ignoring details at the machine level. But sometimes there is a need to write large-scale programs specifically for a particular machine, and to have precise control over each instruction. In such cases we ought to have a machine-oriented language with a much richer structure than the line-for-line approach of a traditional assembler.

Design and implement a language called PL/MMIX, which is analogous to Niklaus Wirth's PL/360 language [*JACM* **15** (1968), 37–74]. Your language should also incorporate the ideas of literate programming [D. E. Knuth, *Literate Programming* (1992)].

EXERCISES — Second set

The next exercises are short programming problems, representing typical computer applications and covering a wide range of techniques. Every reader is encouraged to choose a few of these problems in order to get some experience using MMIX, as well as to practice basic programming skills. If desired, these exercises may be worked concurrently as the rest of Chapter 1 is being read. The following list indicates the types of programming techniques that are involved:

The use of switching tables for multiway decisions: exercise 17.
Computation with two-dimensional arrays: exercises 18, 28, and 35.
Text and string manipulation: exercises 24, 25, and 35.
Integer and scaled decimal arithmetic: exercises 21, 27, 30, and 32.
Elementary floating point arithmetic: exercises 27 and 32.
The use of subroutines: exercises 23, 24, 32, 33, 34, and 35.
List processing: exercise 29.
Real-time control: exercise 34.
Typographic display: exercise 35.
Loop and pipeline optimization: exercises 23 and 26.

Whenever an exercise in this book says "write an MMIX program" or "write an MMIX subroutine," you need only write symbolic MMIXAL code for what is asked. This code will not be complete in itself; it will merely be a fragment of a (hypothetical) complete program. No input or output need be done in a code fragment, if the data is to be supplied externally; one need write only LABEL, OP, and EXPR fields of MMIXAL instructions, together with appropriate remarks. The numeric machine language, line number, and "Times" columns (see Program M) are not required unless specifically requested, nor will there be a Main label.

On the other hand, if an exercise says "write a *complete* MMIX program," it implies that an executable program should be written in MMIXAL, including in particular the Main label. Such programs should preferably be tested with the help of an MMIX assembler and simulator.

▶ **17.** [*25*] Register $0 contains the address of a tetrabyte that purportedly is a valid, unprivileged `MMIX` instruction. (This means that $0 ≥ 0 and that the X, Y, and Z bytes of M₄[$0] obey all restrictions imposed by the OP byte, according to the rules of Section 1.3.1′. For example, a valid instruction with opcode `FIX` will have Y ≤ `ROUND_NEAR`; a valid instruction with opcode `PUT` will have Y = 0 and either X < 8 or 18 < X < 32. The opcode `LDVTS` is always privileged, for use by the operating system only. But most opcodes define instructions that are valid and unprivileged for all X, Y, and Z.) Write an `MMIX` subroutine that checks the given tetrabyte for validity in this sense; try to make your program as efficient as possible.

Note: Inexperienced programmers tend to tackle a problem like this by writing a long series of tests on the OP byte, such as "`SR op,tetra,24; CMP t,op,#18; BN t,1F; CMP t,op,#98; BN t,2F; ...`". This is *not* good practice! The best way to make multiway decisions is to prepare an auxiliary *table* containing information that encapsulates the desired logic. For example, a table of 256 octabytes, one for each opcode, could be accessed by saying "`SR t,tetra,21; LDO t,Table,t`", followed perhaps by a `GO` instruction if many different kinds of actions need to be done. A tabular approach often makes a program dramatically faster and more flexible.

▶ **18.** [*31*] Assume that a 9 × 8 matrix of signed one-byte elements

$$\begin{pmatrix} a_{11} & a_{12} & a_{13} & \cdots & a_{18} \\ a_{21} & a_{22} & a_{23} & \cdots & a_{28} \\ \vdots & & & & \vdots \\ a_{91} & a_{92} & a_{93} & \cdots & a_{98} \end{pmatrix}$$

has been stored so that a_{ij} is in location $A + 8i + j$ for some constant A. The matrix therefore appears as follows in `MMIX`'s memory:

$$\begin{pmatrix} M[A+9] & M[A+10] & M[A+11] & \cdots & M[A+16] \\ M[A+17] & M[A+18] & M[A+19] & \cdots & M[A+24] \\ \vdots & & & & \vdots \\ M[A+73] & M[A+74] & M[A+75] & \cdots & M[A+80] \end{pmatrix}.$$

An $m \times n$ matrix is said to have a "saddle point" if some position is the smallest value in its row and the largest value in its column. In symbols, a_{ij} is a saddle point if

$$a_{ij} = \min_{1 \le k \le n} a_{ik} = \max_{1 \le k \le m} a_{kj}.$$

Write an `MMIX` program that computes the location of a saddle point (if there is at least one) or zero (if there is no saddle point), and puts this value in register $0.

19. [*M29*] What is the *probability* that the matrix in the preceding exercise has a saddle point, assuming that the 72 elements are distinct and assuming that all 72! permutations are equally likely? What is the corresponding probability if we assume instead that the elements of the matrix are zeros and ones, and that all 2^{72} such matrices are equally likely?

20. [*HM42*] Two solutions are given for exercise 18 (see page 102), and a third is suggested; it is not clear which of them is better. Analyze the algorithms, using each of the assumptions of exercise 19, and decide which is the better method.

21. [*25*] The ascending sequence of all reduced fractions between 0 and 1 that have denominators $\leq n$ is called the "Farey series of order n." For example, the Farey series of order 7 is

$$\frac{0}{1}, \frac{1}{7}, \frac{1}{6}, \frac{1}{5}, \frac{1}{4}, \frac{2}{7}, \frac{1}{3}, \frac{2}{5}, \frac{3}{7}, \frac{1}{2}, \frac{4}{7}, \frac{3}{5}, \frac{2}{3}, \frac{5}{7}, \frac{3}{4}, \frac{4}{5}, \frac{5}{6}, \frac{6}{7}, \frac{1}{1}.$$

If we denote this series by x_0/y_0, x_1/y_1, x_2/y_2, ..., exercise 22 proves that

$$x_0 = 0, \quad y_0 = 1; \qquad x_1 = 1, \quad y_1 = n;$$
$$x_{k+2} = \lfloor (y_k + n)/y_{k+1} \rfloor x_{k+1} - x_k;$$
$$y_{k+2} = \lfloor (y_k + n)/y_{k+1} \rfloor y_{k+1} - y_k.$$

Write an MMIX subroutine that computes the Farey series of order n, by storing the values of x_k and y_k in tetrabytes X + 4k and Y + 4k, respectively. (The total number of terms in the series is approximately $3n^2/\pi^2$; thus we may assume that $n < 2^{32}$.)

22. [*M30*] (a) Show that the numbers x_k and y_k defined by the recurrence in the preceding exercise satisfy the relation $x_{k+1}y_k - x_k y_{k+1} = 1$. (b) Show that the fractions x_k/y_k are indeed the Farey series of order n, using the fact proved in (a).

23. [*25*] Write an MMIX subroutine that sets n consecutive bytes of memory to zero, given a starting address in \$0 and an integer $n \geq 0$ in \$1. Try to make your subroutine blazingly fast, when n is large; use an MMIX pipeline simulator to obtain realistic running-time statistics.

▶ **24.** [*30*] Write an MMIX subroutine that copies a string, starting at the address in \$0, to bytes of memory starting at the address in \$1. Strings are terminated by null characters (that is, bytes equal to zero). Assume that there will be no overlap in memory between the string and its copy. Your routine should minimize the number of memory references by loading and storing eight bytes at a time when possible, so that long strings are copied efficiently. Compare your program to the trivial byte-at-a-time code

```
SUBU $1,$1,$0;1H LDBU $2,$0,0; STBU $2,$0,$1; INCL $0,1; PBNZ $2,1B
```

which takes $(2n + 2)\mu + (4n + 7)v$ to copy a string of length n.

25. [*26*] A cryptanalyst wants to count how often each character occurs in a long string of ciphertext. Write an MMIX program that computes 255 frequency counts, one for each nonnull character; the first null byte ends the given string. Try for a solution that is efficient in terms of the "mems and oops" criteria of Table 1 in Section 1.3.1′.

▶ **26.** [*32*] Improve the solution to the previous exercise by optimizing its performance with respect to realistic configurations of the MMIX pipeline simulator.

27. [*26*] (*Fibonacci approximations.*) Equation 1.2.8–(15) states that the formula $F_n = \text{round}(\phi^n/\sqrt{5})$ holds for all $n \geq 0$, where 'round' denotes rounding to the nearest integer. (a) Write a complete MMIX program to test how well this formula behaves with respect to floating point arithmetic: Compute straightforward approximations to $\phi^n/\sqrt{5}$ for $n = 0, 1, 2, \ldots$, and find the smallest n for which the approximation does not round to F_n. (b) Exercise 1.2.8–28 proves that $F_n = \text{round}(\phi F_{n-1})$ for all $n \geq 3$. Find the smallest $n \geq 3$ for which this equation fails when we compute ϕF_{n-1} approximately by *fixed point* multiplication of unsigned octabytes. (See Eq. 1.3.1′–(7).)

28. [*26*] A *magic square of order* n is an arrangement of the numbers 1 through n^2 in a square array in such a way that the sum of each row and column is $n(n^2 + 1)/2$, and so is the sum of the two main diagonals. Figure 16 shows a magic square of order 7.

22	47	16	41	10	35	04
05	23	48	17	42	11	29
30	06	24	49	18	36	12
13	31	07	25	43	19	37
38	14	32	01	26	44	20
21	39	08	33	02	27	45
46	15	40	09	34	03	28

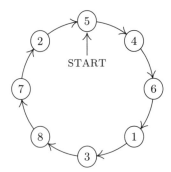

Fig. 16. A magic square.   **Fig. 17.** Josephus's problem, $n = 8$, $m = 4$.

The rule for generating it is easily seen: Start with 1 just below the middle square, then go down and to the right diagonally until reaching a filled square; if you run off the edge, "wrap around" by imagining an entire plane tiled with squares. When you reach a nonempty position, drop down two spaces from the most-recently-filled square and continue. This method works whenever n is odd.

Using memory allocated in a fashion like that of exercise 18, write a complete MMIX program to generate a 19×19 magic square by the method above, and to format the result in the standard output file. [This algorithm is due to Ibn al-Haytham, who was born in Basra about 965 and died in Cairo about 1040. Many other magic square constructions make good programming exercises; see W. W. Rouse Ball, *Mathematical Recreations and Essays*, revised by H. S. M. Coxeter (New York: Macmillan, 1939), Chapter 7.]

29. [*30*] (*The Josephus problem.*) There are n men arranged in a circle. Beginning at a particular position, we count around the circle and brutally execute every mth man; the circle closes as men die. For example, the execution order when $n = 8$ and $m = 4$ is 54613872, as shown in Fig. 17: The first man is fifth to go, the second man is fourth, etc. Write a complete MMIX program that prints out the order of execution when $n = 24$, $m = 11$. Try to design a clever algorithm that works at high speed when m and n are large (it may save your life). *Reference:* W. Ahrens, *Mathematische Unterhaltungen und Spiele* **2** (Leipzig: Teubner, 1918), Chapter 15.

30. [*31*] We showed in Section 1.2.7 that the sum $1 + \frac{1}{2} + \frac{1}{3} + \cdots$ becomes infinitely large. But if it is calculated with finite accuracy by a computer, the sum actually exists, in some sense, because the terms eventually get so small that they contribute nothing to the sum if added one by one. For example, suppose we calculate the sum by rounding to one decimal place; then we have $1 + 0.5 + 0.3 + 0.2 + 0.2 + 0.2 + 0.1 + 0.1 + 0.1 + 0.1 + 0.1 + 0.1 + 0.1 + 0.1 + 0.1 + 0.1 + 0.1 + 0.1 + 0.0 + \cdots = 3.7$.

More precisely, let $r_n(x)$ be the number x rounded to n decimal places, rounding to an even digit in case of ties. For the purposes of this problem we can use the formula $r_n(x) = \lceil 10^n x - \frac{1}{2} \rceil / 10^n$. Then we wish to find

$$S_n = r_n(1) + r_n\left(\tfrac{1}{2}\right) + r_n\left(\tfrac{1}{3}\right) + \cdots;$$

we know that $S_1 = 3.7$, and the problem is to write a complete MMIX program that calculates and prints S_n for $1 \le n \le 10$.

Note: There is a much faster way to do this than the simple procedure of adding $r_n(1/m)$, one number at a time, until $r_n(1/m)$ becomes zero. For example, we have $r_5(1/m) = 0.00001$ for all values of m from 66667 to 199999; it's wise to avoid calculating $1/m$ all 133333 times! An algorithm along the following lines is better.

H1. Start with $m_1 = 1$, $S \leftarrow 1$, $k \leftarrow 1$.

H2. Calculate $r \leftarrow r_n\big(1/(m_k + 1)\big)$, and stop if $r = 0$.

H3. Find m_{k+1}, the largest m for which $r_n(1/m) = r$.

H4. Set $S \leftarrow S + (m_{k+1} - m_k)r$, $k \leftarrow k + 1$, and return to H2.   ▮

31. [*HM30*] Using the notation of the preceding exercise, prove or disprove the formula

$$\lim_{n \to \infty}(S_{n+1} - S_n) = \ln 10.$$

▶ **32.** [*31*] The following algorithm, due to the Neapolitan astronomer Aloysius Lilius and the German Jesuit mathematician Christopher Clavius in the late 16th century, is used by most Western churches to determine the date of Easter Sunday for any year after 1582.

Algorithm E (*Date of Easter*). Let Y be the year for which Easter date is desired.

E1. [Golden number.] Set $G \leftarrow (Y \bmod 19) + 1$. ($G$ is the so-called "golden number" of the year in the 19-year Metonic cycle.)

E2. [Century.] Set $C \leftarrow \lfloor Y/100 \rfloor + 1$. (When Y is not a multiple of 100, C is the century number; for example, 1984 is in the twentieth century.)

E3. [Corrections.] Set $X \leftarrow \lfloor 3C/4 \rfloor - 12$, $Z \leftarrow \lfloor (8C + 5)/25 \rfloor - 5$. (Here X is the number of years, such as 1900, in which leap year was dropped in order to keep in step with the sun; Z is a special correction designed to synchronize Easter with the moon's orbit.)

E4. [Find Sunday.] Set $D \leftarrow \lfloor 5Y/4 \rfloor - X - 10$. (March $((-D) \bmod 7)$ will actually be a Sunday.)

E5. [Epact.] Set $E \leftarrow (11G + 20 + Z - X) \bmod 30$. If $E = 25$ and the golden number G is greater than 11, or if $E = 24$, increase E by 1. (This number E is the *epact*, which specifies when a full moon occurs.)

E6. [Find full moon.] Set $N \leftarrow 44 - E$. If $N < 21$ then set $N \leftarrow N + 30$. (Easter is supposedly the first Sunday following the first full moon that occurs on or after March 21. Actually perturbations in the moon's orbit do not make this strictly true, but we are concerned here with the "calendar moon" rather than the actual moon. The Nth of March is a calendar full moon.)

E7. [Advance to Sunday.] Set $N \leftarrow N + 7 - ((D + N) \bmod 7)$.

E8. [Get month.] If $N > 31$, the date is $(N - 31)$ APRIL; otherwise the date is N MARCH.   ▮

Write a subroutine to calculate and print Easter date given the year, assuming that the year is less than 100000. The output should have the form "*dd* MONTH, *yyyyy*" where *dd* is the day and *yyyyy* is the year. Write a complete MMIX program that uses this subroutine to prepare a table of the dates of Easter from 1950 through 2000.

33. [*M30*] Some computers — not MMIX! — give a negative remainder when a negative number is divided by a positive number. Therefore a program for calculating the date of Easter by the algorithm in the previous exercise might fail when the quantity $(11G + 20 + Z - X)$ in step E5 is negative. For example, in the year 14250 we obtain $G = 1$, $X = 95$, $Z = 40$; so if we had $E = -24$ instead of $E = +6$ we would get the ridiculous answer "42 APRIL". [See *CACM* **5** (1962), 556.] Write a complete MMIX program that finds the *earliest* year for which this error would actually cause the wrong date to be calculated for Easter.

▶ **34.** [*33*] Assume that an MMIX computer has been wired up to the traffic signals at the corner of Del Mar Boulevard and Berkeley Avenue, via special "files" named /dev/lights and /dev/sensor. The computer activates the lights by outputting one byte to /dev/lights, specifying the sum of four two-bit codes as follows:

Del Mar traffic light: #00 off, #40 green, #80 amber, #c0 red;
Berkeley traffic light: #00 off, #10 green, #20 amber, #30 red;
Del Mar pedestrian light: #00 off, #04 WALK, #0c DON'T WALK;
Berkeley pedestrian light: #00 off, #01 WALK, #03 DON'T WALK.

Cars or pedestrians wishing to travel on Berkeley across the boulevard must activate a sensor; if this condition never occurs, the light for Del Mar should remain green. When MMIX reads a byte from /dev/sensor, the input is nonzero if and only if the sensor has been activated since the previous input.

Cycle times are as follows:

Del Mar traffic light is green ≥ 30 sec, amber 8 sec;
Berkeley traffic light is green 20 sec, amber 5 sec.

When a traffic light is green or amber for one direction, the other direction has a red light. When the traffic light is green, the corresponding WALK light is on, except that DON'T WALK flashes for 12 sec just before a green light turns to amber, as follows:

DON'T WALK $\frac{1}{2}$ sec ⎫
off $\frac{1}{2}$ sec ⎬ repeat 8 times;
DON'T WALK 4 sec (and remains on through amber and red cycles).

If the sensor is activated while the Berkeley light is green, the car or pedestrian will pass on that cycle. But if it is activated during the amber or red portions, another cycle will be necessary after the Del Mar traffic has passed.

Write a complete MMIX program that controls these lights, following the stated protocol. Assume that the special clock register rC increases by 1 exactly ρ times per second, where the integer ρ is a given constant.

35. [*37*] This exercise is designed to give some experience in the many applications of computers for which the output is to be displayed graphically rather than in the usual tabular form. The object is to "draw" a crossword puzzle diagram.

You are given as input a matrix of zeros and ones. An entry of zero indicates a white square; a one indicates a black square. The output should generate a diagram of the puzzle, with the appropriate squares numbered for words across and down.

For example, given the matrix

$$\begin{pmatrix} 1 & 0 & 0 & 0 & 0 & 1 \\ 0 & 0 & 1 & 0 & 0 & 0 \\ 0 & 0 & 0 & 0 & 1 & 0 \\ 0 & 1 & 0 & 0 & 0 & 0 \\ 0 & 0 & 0 & 1 & 0 & 0 \\ 1 & 0 & 0 & 0 & 0 & 1 \end{pmatrix},$$

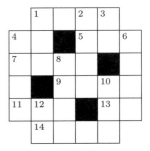

Fig. 18. Diagram corresponding to the matrix in exercise 35.

the corresponding puzzle diagram would be as shown in Fig. 18. A square is numbered if it is a white square and either (a) the square below it is white and there is no white square immediately above, or (b) the square to its right is white and there is no white square immediately to its left. If black squares occur at the edges, they should be removed from the diagram. This is illustrated in Fig. 18, where the black squares at the corners were dropped. A simple way to accomplish this is to artificially insert rows and columns of −1's at the top, bottom, and sides of the given input matrix, then to change every +1 that is adjacent to a −1 into a −1 until no +1 remains next to any −1.

Figure 18 was produced by the METAPOST program shown in Fig. 19. Simple changes to the uses of line and black, and to the coordinates in the for loop, will produce any desired diagram.

Write a complete MMIX program that reads a 25 × 25 matrix of zeros and ones in the standard input file and writes a suitable METAPOST program on the standard output file. The input should consist of 25 lines, each consisting of 25 digits followed by "newline"; for example, the first line corresponding to the matrix above would be '1000011111111111111111111', using extra 1s to extend the original 6 × 6 array. The diagram will not necessarily be symmetrical, and it might have long paths of black squares that are connected to the outside in strange ways.

```
beginfig(18)
transform t; t=identity rotated -90 scaled 17pt;
def line(expr i,j,ii,jj) =
 draw ((i,j)--(ii,jj)) transformed t;
enddef;
def black(expr i,j) =
 fill ((i,j)--(i+1,j)--(i+1,j+1)--(i,j+1)--cycle) transformed t;
enddef;
line (1,2,1,6); line (2,1,2,7); line (3,1,3,7); line (4,1,4,7);
line (5,1,5,7); line (6,1,6,7); line (7,2,7,6);
line (2,1,6,1); line (1,2,7,2); line (1,3,7,3); line (1,4,7,4);
line (1,5,7,5); line (1,6,7,6); line (2,7,6,7);
numeric n; n=0;
for p = (1,2),(1,4),(1,5), (2,1),(2,4),(2,6),
   (3,1),(3,3), (4,3),(4,5), (5,1),(5,2),(5,5), (6,2):
 n:=n+1; label.lrt(decimal n infont "cmr8", p transformed t);
endfor
black(2,3); black(3,5); black(4,2); black(5,4);
endfig;
```

Fig. 19. The METAPOST program that generated Fig. 18.

1.3.3′. Applications to Permutations

The MIX programs in the former Section 1.3.3 will all be converted to MMIX programs, and so will the MIX programs in Chapters 2, 3, 4, 5, and 6. Anyone who wishes to help with this instructive conversion project is invited to join the MMIXmasters (see page v).

1.4'. SOME FUNDAMENTAL PROGRAMMING TECHNIQUES

1.4.1'. Subroutines

WHEN A CERTAIN task is to be performed at several different places in a program, we usually don't want to repeat the coding over and over. To avoid this situation, the coding (called a *subroutine*) can be put into one place only, and a few extra instructions can be added to restart the main routine properly after the subroutine is finished. Transfer of control between subroutines and main programs is called *subroutine linkage*.

Each machine has its own peculiar way to achieve efficient subroutine linkage, usually by using special instructions. Our discussion will be based on MMIX machine language, but similar remarks will apply to subroutine linkage on most other general-purpose computers.

Subroutines are used to save space in a program. They do not save any time, other than the time implicitly saved by having less space — for example, less time to load the program, and better use of high-speed memory on machines with several grades of memory. The extra time taken to enter and leave a subroutine is usually negligible, except in critical innermost loops.

Subroutines have several other advantages. They make it easier to visualize the structure of a large and complex program; they form a logical segmentation of the entire problem, and this usually makes debugging of the program easier. Many subroutines have additional value because they can be used by people other than the programmer of the subroutine.

Most computer installations have built up a large library of useful subroutines, and such a library greatly facilitates the programming of standard computer applications that arise. A programmer should not think of this as the *only* purpose of subroutines, however; subroutines should not always be regarded as general-purpose programs to be used by the community. Special-purpose subroutines are just as important, even when they are intended to appear in only one program. Section 1.4.3' contains several typical examples.

The simplest subroutines are those that have only one entrance and one exit, such as the Maximum subroutine we have already considered (see Program M in Section 1.3.2' and exercise 1.3.2'–3). Let's look at that program again, recasting it slightly so that a fixed number of cells, 100, is searched for the maximum:

```
       * Maximum of X[1..100]
       j IS $0 ;m IS $1 ;kk IS $2 ;xk IS $3
       Max100 SETL  kk,100*8   M1. Initialize.
              LDO   m,x0,kk
              JMP   1F
       3H     LDO   xk,x0,kk   M3. Compare.
              CMP   t,xk,m
              PBNP  t,5F
       4H     SET   m,xk       M4. Change m.
       1H     SR    j,kk,3
       5H     SUB   kk,kk,8    M5. Decrease k.
              PBP   kk,3B      M2. All tested?
       6H     POP   2,0        Return to main program.
```

$$(1)$$

This subroutine is assumed to be part of a larger program in which the symbol t has been defined to stand for register \$255, and the symbol x0 has been defined to stand for a global register such that $X[k]$ appears in location $x0 + 8k$. In that larger program, the single instruction "PUSHJ \$1,Max100" will cause register \$1 to be set to the current maximum value of $\{X[1], \ldots, X[100]\}$, and the position of the maximum will appear in \$2. Linkage in this case is achieved by the PUSHJ instruction that invokes the subroutine, together with "POP 2,0" at the subroutine's end. These MMIX instructions cause local registers to be renumbered while the subroutine is active; furthermore, the PUSHJ inserts a return address into special register rJ, and the POP jumps to this location.

We can also accomplish subroutine linkage in a simpler, rather different way, by using MMIX's GO instruction instead of pushing and popping. We might, for instance, use the following code in place of (1):

```
* Maximum of X[1..100]
j GREG ;m GREG ;kk GREG ;xk GREG
         GREG    @          Base address
GoMax100 SETL    kk,100*8   M1. Initialize.
         LDO     m,x0,kk                          (2)
         JMP     1F
3H       ...                (Continue as in (1))
         PBP     kk,3B      M2. All tested?
6H       GO      kk,$0,0    Return to main program. ▮
```

Now the instruction "GO \$0,GoMax100" will transfer control to the subroutine, placing the address of the following instruction into \$0; the subsequent "GO kk,\$0,0" at the subroutine's end will return to this address. In this case the maximum value will appear in global register m, and its location will be in global register j. Two additional global registers, kk and xk, have also been set aside for use by this subroutine. Furthermore, the "GREG @" provides a base address so that we can GO to GoMax100 in a single instruction; otherwise a two-step sequence like "GETA \$0,GoMax100; GO \$0,\$0,0" would be necessary. Subroutine linkage like (2) is commonly used on machines that have no built-in register stack mechanism.

It is not hard to obtain *quantitative* statements about the amount of code saved and the amount of time lost when subroutines are used. Suppose that a piece of coding requires k tetrabytes and that it appears in m places in the program. Rewriting this as a subroutine, we need a PUSHJ or GO instruction in each of the m places where the subroutine is called, plus a single POP or GO instruction to return control. This gives a total of $m + k + 1$ tetrabytes, rather than mk, so the amount saved is

$$(m - 1)(k - 1) - 2. \tag{3}$$

If k is 1 or m is 1 we cannot possibly save any space by using subroutines; this, of course, is obvious. If k is 2, m must be greater than 3 in order to gain, etc.

The amount of time lost is the time taken for the PUSHJ, POP, and/or GO instructions in the linkage. If the subroutine is invoked t times during a run of the program, and if we assume that running time is governed by the approximations in Table 1.3.1'–1, the extra cost is $4tv$ in case (1), or $6tv$ in case (2).

These estimates must be taken with a grain of salt, because they were given for an idealized situation. Many subroutines cannot be called simply with a single PUSHJ or GO instruction. Furthermore, if code is replicated in many parts of a program without using a subroutine approach, each instance can be customized to take advantage of special characteristics of the particular part of the program in which it lies. With a subroutine, on the other hand, the code must be written for the most general case; this will often add several additional instructions.

When a subroutine is written to handle a general case, it is expressed in terms of *parameters*. Parameters are values that govern a subroutine's actions; they are subject to change from one call of the subroutine to another.

The coding in the outside program that transfers control to a subroutine and gets it properly started is known as the *calling sequence*. Particular values of parameters, supplied when the subroutine is called, are known as *arguments*. With our GoMax100 subroutine, the calling sequence is simply "GO $0,GoMax100", but a longer calling sequence is generally necessary when arguments must be supplied.

For example, we might want to generalize (2) to a subroutine that finds the maximum of the first n elements of an array, given *any* constant n, by placing n in the instruction stream with the two-step calling sequence

$$\text{GO \$0,GoMax; \quad TETRA } n. \tag{4}$$

The GoMax subroutine could then take the form

```
* Maximum of X[1..n]
j GREG ;m GREG ;kk GREG ;xk GREG
        GREG   @          Base address
GoMax   LDT    kk,$0,0    Fetch the argument.
        SL     kk,kk,3
        LDO    m,x0,kk
        JMP    1F
3H      ...               (Continue as in (1))
        PBP    kk,3B
6H      GO     kk,$0,4    Return to caller.  ▌
```

(5)

Still better would be to communicate the parameter n by putting it into a register. We could, for example, use the two-step calling sequence

$$\text{SET \$1,n; \quad GO \$0,GoMax} \tag{6}$$

together with a subroutine of the form

```
GoMax   SL     kk,$1,3    Fetch the argument.
        LDO    m,x0,kk
        ...
6H      GO     kk,$0,0    Return.  ▌
```

(7)

This variation is faster than (5), and it allows n to vary dynamically without modifying the instruction stream.

Notice that the address of array element $X[0]$ is also essentially a parameter to subroutines (1), (2), (5), and (7). The operation of putting this address into register x0 may be regarded as part of the calling sequence, in cases when the array is different each time.

If the calling sequence occupies c tetrabytes of memory, formula (3) for the amount of space saved changes to

$$(m - 1)(k - c) - \text{constant} \tag{8}$$

and the time lost for subroutine linkage is slightly increased.

A further correction to the formulas above can be necessary because certain registers might need to be saved and restored. For example, in the GoMax subroutine we must remember that by writing "SET \$1,n; GO \$0,GoMax" we are not only computing the maximum value in register m and its position in register j, we are also changing the values of global registers kk and xk. We have implemented (2), (5), and (7) with the implicit assumption that registers kk and xk are for the exclusive use of the maximum-finding routine, but many computers are not blessed with a large number of registers. Even MMIX will run out of registers if a lot of subroutines are present simultaneously. We might therefore want to revise (7) so that it will work with kk $\equiv$ \$2 and xk $\equiv$ \$3, say, without clobbering the contents of those registers. We could do this by writing

```
 j GREG  ;m GREG  ;kk IS $2  ;xk IS $3
         GREG    @            Base address
 GoMax   STO     kk,Tempkk    Save previous register contents.
         STO     xk,Tempxk
         SL      kk,$1,3      Fetch the argument.
         LDO     m,x0,kk                                         (9)
         ...
         LDO     kk,Tempkk    Restore previous register contents.
         LDO     xk,Tempxk
 6H      GO      $0,$0,0      Return.  ∎
```

and by setting aside two octabytes called Tempkk and Tempxk in the data segment. Of course this change adds potentially significant overhead cost to each use of the subroutine.

A subroutine may be regarded as an *extension* of the computer's machine language. For example, whenever the GoMax subroutine is present in memory we have a single machine instruction (namely, "GO \$0,GoMax") that is a maximum-finder. It is important to define the effect of each subroutine just as carefully as the machine language operators themselves have been defined; a programmer should therefore be sure to write down the relevant characteristics, even though nobody else will be making use of the routine or its specification. In the case of GoMax as given in (7) or (9), the characteristics are as follows:

> Calling sequence: GO \$0,GoMax.
> Entry conditions: $\$1 = n \geq 1$; x0 = address of $X[0]$.   (10)
> Exit conditions: $\text{m} = \max_{1 \leq k \leq n} X[k] = X[\text{j}]$.

A specification should mention all changes to quantities that are external to the subroutine. If registers kk and xk are not considered "private" to the variant of GoMax in (7), we should include the fact that those registers are affected, as part of that subroutine's exit conditions. The subroutine also changes register t, namely register \$255; but that register is conventionally used for temporary quantities of only momentary significance, so we needn't bother to list it explicitly.

Now let's consider *multiple entrances* to subroutines. Suppose we have a program that requires the general subroutine GoMax, but it usually wants to use the special case GoMax100 in which $n = 100$. The two can be combined as follows:

GoMax100 SET \$1,100   First entrance   (11)
GoMax   ...   Second entrance; continue as in (7) or (9). ∎

We could also add a *third* entrance, say GoMax50, by putting the code

GoMax50 SET \$1,50;   JMP GoMax

in some convenient place.

A subroutine might also have *multiple exits*, meaning that it is supposed to return to one of several different locations, depending on conditions that it has detected. For example, we can extend subroutine (11) yet again by assuming that an upper bound parameter is given in global register b; the subroutine is now supposed to exit to one of the two tetrabytes following the GO instruction that calls it:

Calling sequence for general n	Calling sequence for $n = 100$
SET \$1,n; GO \$0,GoMax	GO \$0,GoMax100
Exit here if m ≤ 0 or m ≥ b.	Exit here if m ≤ 0 or m ≥ b.
Exit here if $0 < m < b$.	Exit here if $0 < m < b$.

(In other words, we skip the tetrabyte after the GO when the maximum value is positive and less than the upper bound. A subroutine like this would be useful in a program that often needs to make such distinctions after computing a maximum value.) The implementation is easy:

```
* Maximum of X[1..n] with bounds check
j GREG ;m GREG ;kk GREG ;xk GREG
         GREG    @           Base address
GoMax100 SET     $1,100      Entrance for n = 100
GoMax    SL      kk,$1,3     Entrance for general n
         LDO     m,x0,kk
         JMP     1F
3H       ...                 (Continue as in (1))
         PBP     kk,3B
         BNP     m,1F        Branch if m ≤ 0.
         CMP     kk,m,b
         BN      kk,2F       Branch if m < b.
1H       GO      kk,$0,0     Take first exit if m ≤ 0 or m ≥ b.
2H       GO      kk,$0,4     Otherwise take second exit.  ∎
```

                                                                      (12)

Notice that this program combines the instruction-stream linking technique of (5) with the register-setting technique of (7). The location to which a subroutine exits is, strictly speaking, a parameter; hence the locations of multiple exits must be supplied as arguments. When a subroutine accesses one of its parameters all the time, the corresponding argument is best passed in a register, but when an argument is constant and not always needed it is best kept in the instruction stream.

Subroutines may call on other subroutines. Indeed, complicated programs often have subroutine calls nested more than five deep. The only restriction that must be followed when using the GO-type linkage described above is that all temporary storage locations and registers must be distinct; thus no subroutine may call on any other subroutine that is (directly or indirectly) calling on it. For example, consider the following scenario:

[Main program]	[Subroutine A]	[Subroutine B]	[Subroutine C]	
	A	B	C	
⋮	⋮	⋮	⋮	
GO $0,A	GO $1,B	GO $2,C	GO $0,A	(13)
⋮	⋮	⋮	⋮	
	GO $0,$0,0	GO $1,$1,0	GO $2,$2,0	

If the main program calls A, which calls B, which calls C, and then C calls on A, the address in $0 referring to the main program is destroyed, and there is no way to return to that program.

Using a memory stack. Recursive situations like (13) do not often arise in simple programs, but a great many important applications do have a natural recursive structure. Fortunately there is a straightforward way to avoid interference between subroutine calls, by letting each subroutine keep its local variables on a *stack*. For example, we can set aside a global register called sp (the "stack pointer") and use GO $0,Sub to invoke each subroutine. If the code for the subroutine has the form

$$
\begin{array}{lll}
\text{Sub} & \text{STO} & \$0,\text{sp},0 \\
 & \text{ADD} & \text{sp},\text{sp},8 \\
 & \cdots & \\
 & \text{SUB} & \text{sp},\text{sp},8 \\
 & \text{LDO} & \$0,\text{sp},0 \\
 & \text{GO} & \$0,\$0,0
\end{array} \qquad (14)
$$

register $0 will always contain the proper return address; the problem of (13) no longer arises. (Initially we set sp to an address in the data segment, following all other memory locations needed.) Moreover, the STO/ADD and SUB/LDO instructions of (14) can be omitted if Sub is a so-called *leaf subroutine* — a subroutine that doesn't call any other subroutines.

A stack can be used to hold parameters and other local variables besides the return addresses stored in (14). Suppose, for example, that subroutine Sub needs 20 octabytes of local data, in addition to the return address; then we can use a scheme like this:

```
Sub  STO   fp,sp,0     Save the old frame pointer.
     SET   fp,sp       Establish a new frame pointer.
     INCL  sp,8*22     Advance the stack pointer.
     STO   $0,fp,8     Save the return address.
     ...                                                      (15)
     LDO   $0,fp,8     Restore the return address.
     SET   sp,fp       Restore the stack pointer.
     LDO   fp,sp,0     Restore the frame pointer.
     GO    $0,$0,0     Return to caller.  ▮
```

Here fp is a global register called the *frame pointer*. Within the "..." part of the subroutine, local quantity number k is equivalent to the octabyte in memory location $fp + 8k + 8$, for $1 \le k \le 20$. The instructions at the beginning are said to "push" local quantities onto the "top" of the stack; the instructions at the end "pop" those quantities off, leaving the stack in the condition it had when the subroutine was entered.

Using the register stack. We have discussed GO-type subroutine linkage at length because many computers have no better alternative. But MMIX has built-in instructions PUSHJ and POP, which handle subroutine linkage in a more efficient way, avoiding most of the overhead in schemes like (9) and (15). These instructions allow us to keep most parameters and local variables entirely in registers, instead of storing them into a memory stack and loading them again later. With PUSHJ and POP, most of the details of stack maintenance are done automatically by the machine.

The basic idea is quite simple, once the general idea of a stack is understood. MMIX has a *register stack* consisting of octabytes $S[0]$, $S[1]$, ..., $S[\tau - 1]$ for some number $\tau \ge 0$. The topmost L octabytes in the stack (namely $S[\tau - L]$, $S[\tau - L + 1]$, ..., $S[\tau - 1]$) are the current *local registers* $\$0, \$1, ..., \$(L-1)$; the other $\tau - L$ octabytes of the stack are currently inaccessible to the program, and we say they have been "pushed down." The current number of local registers, L, is kept in MMIX's special register rL, although a programmer rarely needs to know this. Initially $L = 2$, $\tau = 2$, and local registers $\$0$ and $\$1$ represent the command line as in Program 1.3.2′H.

MMIX also has *global registers*, namely $\$G$, $\$(G+1)$, ..., $\$255$; the value of G is kept in special register rG, and we always have $0 \le L \le G \le 255$. (In fact, we also always have $G \ge 32$.) Global registers are *not* part of the register stack.

Registers that are neither local nor global are called *marginal*. These registers, namely $\$L$, $\$(L+1)$, ..., $\$(G-1)$, have the value zero whenever they are used as input operands to an MMIX instruction.

The register stack grows when a marginal register is given a value. This marginal register becomes local, and so do all marginal registers with smaller numbers. For example, if eight local registers are currently in use, the instruction ADD $\$10,\$20,5$ causes $\$8$, $\$9$, and $\$10$ to become local; more precisely, if rL = 8, the instruction ADD $\$10,\$20,5$ sets $\$8 \leftarrow 0$, $\$9 \leftarrow 0$, $\$10 \leftarrow 5$, and rL $\leftarrow 11$. (Register $\$20$ remains marginal.)

If $X is a local register, the instruction PUSHJ $X,Sub decreases the number of local registers and changes their effective register numbers: Local registers previously called $(X+1), $(X+2), ..., $(L−1) are called $0, $1, ..., $(L−X−2) inside the subroutine, and the value of L decreases by X + 1. Thus the register stack remains unchanged, but X + 1 of its entries have become inaccessible; the subroutine cannot damage those entries, and it has X+1 newly marginal registers to play with.

If X ≥ G, so that $X is a global register, the action of PUSHJ $X,Sub is similar, but a new entry is placed on the register stack and then $L+1$ registers are pushed down instead of X + 1. In this case L is zero when the subroutine begins; all of the formerly local registers have been pushed down, and the subroutine starts out with a clean slate.

The register stack shrinks only when a POP instruction is given, or when a program explicitly decreases the number of local registers with an instruction such as PUT rL,5. The purpose of POP X,YZ is to make the items pushed down by the most recent PUSHJ accessible again, as they were before, and to remove items from the register stack if they are no longer necessary. In general the X field of a POP instruction is the number of values "returned" by the subroutine, if X ≤ L. If X > 0, the main value returned is $(X − 1); this value is removed from the register stack, together with all entries above it, and the return value is placed in the position specified by the PUSHJ command that invoked the subroutine. The behavior of POP is similar when X > L, but in this case the register stack remains intact and zero is placed in the position of the PUSHJ.

The rules we have just stated are a bit complicated, because many different cases can arise in practice. A few examples will, however, make everything clear. Suppose we are writing a routine A and we want to call subroutine B; suppose further that routine A has 5 local registers that should not be accessible to B. These registers are $0, $1, $2, $3, and $4. We reserve the next register, $5, for the main result of subroutine B. If B has, say, three parameters, we set $6 ← arg0, $7 ← arg1, and $8 ← arg2, then issue the command PUSHJ $5,B; this invokes B and the arguments are now found in $0, $1, and $2.

If B returns no result, it will conclude with the command POP 0,YZ; this will restore $0, $1, $2, $3, and $4 to their former values and set $L ← 5$.

If B returns a single result x, it will place x in $0 and conclude with the command POP 1,YZ. This will restore $0, $1, $2, $3, and $4 as before; it will also set $5 ← x$ and $L ← 6$.

If B returns two results x and a, it will place the main result x in $1 and the auxiliary result a in $0. Then POP 2,YZ will restore $0 through $4 and set $5 ← x$, $6 ← a$, $L ← 7$. Similarly, if B returns ten results $(x, a_0, ..., a_8)$, it will place the main result x in $9 and the others in the first nine registers: $0 ← a_0$, $1 ← a_1$, ..., $8 ← a_8$. Then POP 10,YZ will restore $0 through $4 and set $5 ← x$, $6 ← a_0$, ..., $14 ← a_8$. (The curious permutation of registers that arises when two or more results are returned may seem strange at first. But it makes sense, because it leaves the register stack unchanged except for the main result. For example, if subroutine B wants arg0, arg1, and arg2 to reappear in

$6, $7, and $8 after it has finished its work, it can leave them as auxiliary results in $0, $1, and $2 and then say POP 4,YZ.)

The YZ field of a POP instruction is usually zero, but in general the instruction POP X,YZ returns to the instruction that is YZ+1 tetrabytes after the PUSHJ that invoked the current subroutine. This generality is useful for subroutines with multiple exits. More precisely, a PUSHJ subroutine in location @ sets special register rJ to @ + 4 before jumping to the subroutine; a POP instruction then returns to location rJ + 4YZ.

We can now recast the programs previously written with GO linkage so that they use PUSH/POP linkage instead. For example, the two-entrance, two-exit subroutine for maximum-finding in (12) takes the following form when MMIX's register stack mechanism is used:

```
* Maximum of X[1..n] with bounds check
j IS $0 ;m IS $1 ;kk IS $2 ;xk IS $3
Max100  SET    $0,100    Entrance for n = 100
Max     SL     kk,$0,3   Entrance for general n
        LDO    m,x0,kk
        JMP    1F                                               (16)
        ...              (Continue as in (12))
        BNZ    kk,2F
1H      POP    2,0       Take first exit if max ≤ 0 or max ≥ b.
2H      POP    2,1       Otherwise take second exit.  ∎
```

Calling sequence for general n	Calling sequence for $n = 100$
SET $A,$n$; PUSHJ $R,Max (A = R+1)	PUSHJ $R,Max100
Exit here if $R ≤ 0 or $R ≥ b.	Exit here if $R ≤ 0 or $R ≥ b.
Exit here if 0 < $R < b.	Exit here if 0 < $R < b.

The local result register $R in the PUSHJ of this calling sequence is arbitrary, depending on the number of local variables the caller wishes to retain. The local argument register $A is then $(R + 1). After the call, $R will contain the main result (the maximum value) and $A will contain the auxiliary result (the array index of that maximum). If there are several arguments and/or auxiliaries, they are conventionally called A0, A1, ..., and we conventionally assume that A0 = R+1, A1 = R+2, ... when PUSH/POP calling sequences are written down.

A comparison of (12) and (16) shows only mild advantages for (16): The new form does not need to allocate global registers for j, m, kk, and xk, nor does it need a global base register for the address of the GO command. (Recall from Section 1.3.1′ that GO takes an absolute address, while PUSHJ has a relative address.) A GO instruction is slightly slower than PUSHJ; it is no slower than POP, according to Table 1.3.1′–1, although high-speed implementations of MMIX could implement POP more efficiently. Programs (12) and (16) both have the same length.

The advantages of PUSH/POP linkage over GO linkage begin to manifest themselves when we have *nonleaf* subroutines (namely, subroutines that call other subroutines, possibly themselves). Then the GO-based code of (14) can be replaced by

```
Sub   GET   retadd,rJ
      ...
      PUT   rJ,retadd
      POP   X,0
```

(17)

where **retadd** is a local register. (For example, **retadd** might be $5; its register number is generally greater than or equal to the number of returned results X, so the POP instruction will automatically remove it from the register stack.) Now the costly memory references of (14) are avoided.

A nonleaf subroutine with many local variables and/or parameters is significantly better off with a register stack than with the memory stack scheme of (15), because we can often perform the computations entirely in registers. We should note, however, that MMIX's register stack applies only to local variables that are *scalar*, not to local array variables that must be accessed by address computation. Subroutines that need non-scalar local variables should use a scheme like (15) for all such variables, while keeping scalars on the register stack. Both approaches can be used simultaneously, with **fp** and **sp** updated only by subroutines that need a memory stack.

If the register stack becomes extremely large, MMIX will automatically store its bottom entries in the stack segment of memory, using a behind-the-scenes procedure that we will study in Section 1.4.3′. (Recall from Section 1.3.2′ that the stack segment begins at address #6000 0000 0000 0000.) MMIX stores register stack items in memory also when a SAVE command saves a program's entire current context. Saved stack items are automatically restored from memory when a POP command needs them or when an UNSAVE command restores a saved context. But in most cases MMIX is able to push and pop local registers without actually accessing memory, and without actually changing the contents of very many internal machine registers.

Stacks have many other uses in computer programs; we will study their basic properties in Section 2.2.1. We will get a further taste of nested subroutines and recursive procedures in Section 2.3, when we consider operations on trees. Chapter 8 studies recursion in detail.

*Assembly language features. The MMIX assembly language supports the writing of subroutines in three ways that were not mentioned in Section 1.3.2′. The most important of these is the PREFIX operation, which makes it easy to define "private" symbols that will not interfere with symbols defined elsewhere in a large program. The basic idea is that a symbol can have a structured form like **Sub:X** (meaning symbol X of subroutine **Sub**), possibly carried to several levels like **Lib:Sub:X** (meaning symbol X of subroutine **Sub** in library **Lib**).

Structured symbols are accommodated by extending rule 1 of MMIXAL in Section 1.3.2′ slightly, allowing the colon character ':' to be regarded as a "letter" that can be used to construct symbols. Every symbol that does not begin with a colon is implicitly extended by placing the *current prefix* in front of it. The current prefix is initially ':', but the user can change it with the

UNIVERSITY OF HERTFORDSHIRE LRC

PREFIX command. For example,

ADD	x,y,z	means	ADD :x,:y,:z
PREFIX	Foo:	current prefix is :Foo:	
ADD	x,y,z	means	ADD :Foo:x,:Foo:y,:Foo:z
PREFIX	Bar:	current prefix is :Foo:Bar:	
ADD	:x,y,:z	means	ADD :x,:Foo:Bar:y,:z
PREFIX	:	current prefix reverts to :	
ADD	x,Foo:Bar:y,Foo:z	means	ADD :x,:Foo:Bar:y,:Foo:z

One way to use this idea is to replace the opening lines of (16) by

```
            PREFIX Max:
    j IS $0 ;m IS $1 ;kk IS $2 ;xk IS $3
    x0 IS :x0 ;b IS :b ;t IS :t        External symbols
    :Max100 SET     $0,100   Entrance for n = 100
    :Max    SL      kk,$0,3  Entrance for general n
            LDO     m,x0,kk
            JMP     1F
            ...                (Continue as in (16))
```

$$(18)$$

and to add "PREFIX :" at the end. Then the symbols j, m, kk, and xk are free for use in the rest of the program or in the definition of other subroutines. Further examples of the use of prefixes appear in Section 1.4.3′.

MMIXAL also includes a pseudo-operation called LOCAL. The assembly command "LOCAL $40" means, for example, that an error message should be given at the end of assembly if GREG commands allocate so many registers that $40 will be global. (This feature is needed only when a subroutine uses more than 32 local registers, because "LOCAL $31" is always implicitly true.)

A third feature for subroutine support, BSPEC ... ESPEC, is also provided. It allows information to be passed to the object file so that debugging routines and other system programs know what kind of linkage is being used by each subroutine. This feature is discussed in the *MMIXware* document; it is primarily of interest in the output of compilers.

Strategic considerations. When ad hoc subroutines are written for special-purpose use, we can afford to use GREG instructions liberally, so that plenty of global registers are filled with basic constants that make our program run fast. Comparatively few local registers are needed, unless the subroutines are used recursively.

But when dozens or hundreds of general-purpose subroutines are written for inclusion in a large library, with the idea of allowing any user program to include whatever subroutines it needs, we obviously can't allow each subroutine to allocate a substantial number of globals. Even one global variable per subroutine might be too much.

Thus we want to use GREG generously when we have only a few subroutines, but we want to use it sparingly when the number of subroutines is potentially huge. In the latter case we probably can make good use of local variables without too much loss of efficiency.

Let's conclude this section by discussing briefly how we might go about writing a complex and lengthy program. How can we decide what kind of subroutines we will need? What calling sequences should be used? One successful way to determine this is to use an iterative procedure:

Step 0 (Initial idea). First we decide vaguely upon the general plan of attack that the program will use.

Step 1 (A rough sketch of the program). We start now by writing the "outer levels" of the program, in any convenient language. A somewhat systematic way to go about this has been described very nicely by E. W. Dijkstra, *Structured Programming* (Academic Press, 1972), Chapter 1, and by N. Wirth, *CACM* **14** (1971), 221–227. First we break the whole program into a small number of pieces, which might be thought of temporarily as subroutines although they are called only once. These pieces are successively refined into smaller and smaller parts, having correspondingly simpler jobs to do. Whenever some computational task arises that seems likely to occur elsewhere or that has already occurred elsewhere, we define a subroutine (a real one) to do that job. We do not write the subroutine at this point; we continue writing the main program, assuming that the subroutine has performed its task. Finally, when the main program has been sketched, we tackle the subroutines in turn, trying to take the most complex subroutines first and then their sub-subroutines, etc. In this manner we will come up with a list of subroutines. The actual function of each subroutine has probably already changed several times, so that the first parts of our sketch will by now be incorrect; but that is no problem, since we are merely making a sketch. We now have a reasonably good idea about how each subroutine will be called and how general-purpose it should be. We should consider extending the generality of each subroutine, at least a little.

Step 2 (First working program). The next step goes in the opposite direction from step 1. We now write in computer language, say MMIXAL or PL/MMIX or — most probably — a higher-level language. We start this time with the lowest level subroutines, and do the main program last. As far as possible, we try never to write any instructions that call a subroutine before the subroutine itself has been coded. (In step 1, we tried the opposite, never considering a subroutine until all of its calls had been written.)

As more and more subroutines are written during this process, our confidence gradually grows, since we are continually extending the power of the machine we are programming. After an individual subroutine is coded, we should immediately prepare a complete description of what it does, and what its calling sequences are, as in (10). It is also important to be sure that global variables are not used for two conflicting purposes at the same time; when preparing the sketch in step 1, we didn't have to worry about such problems.

Step 3 (Reexamination). The result of step 2 should be very nearly a working program, but we may be able to improve it. A good way is to reverse direction again, studying for each subroutine *all* of the places it is called. Perhaps the subroutine should be enlarged to do some of the more common things that are always done by the outside routine just before or after the subroutine is called. Perhaps several subroutines should be merged into one; or perhaps a subroutine is called only once and should not be a subroutine at all. Perhaps a subroutine is never called and can be dispensed with entirely.

At this point, it is often a good idea to scrap everything and start over again at step 1, or even at step 0! This is not intended to be a facetious remark; the time spent in getting this far has not been wasted, for we have learned a great deal about the problem. With hindsight, we will probably have discovered several improvements that could be made to the program's overall organization. There's no reason to be afraid to go back to step 1 — it will be much easier to go through steps 2 and 3 again, now that a similar program has been done already. Moreover, we will quite probably save as much debugging time later on as it will take to rewrite everything. Some of the best computer programs ever written owe much of their success to the fact that all the work was unintentionally lost, at about this stage, and the authors were forced to begin again.

On the other hand, there is probably never a point when a complex computer program cannot be improved somehow, so steps 1 and 2 should not be repeated indefinitely. When significant improvements can clearly be made, the additional time required to start over is well spent, but eventually a point of diminishing returns is reached.

Step 4 (Debugging). After a final polishing of the program, including perhaps the allocation of storage and other last-minute details, it is time to look at it in still another direction from the three that were used in steps 1, 2, and 3: Now we study the program in the order in which the computer will *perform* it. This may be done by hand or, of course, by machine. The author has found it quite helpful at this point to make use of system routines that trace each instruction the first two times it is executed; it is important to rethink the ideas underlying the program and to check that everything is actually taking place as expected.

Debugging is an art that needs much further study, and the way to approach it is highly dependent on the facilities available at each computer installation. A good start towards effective debugging is often the preparation of appropriate test data. The most successful debugging techniques are typically designed and built into the program itself: Many of today's best programmers devote nearly half of their programs to facilitating the debugging process in the other half. The first half, which usually consists of fairly straightforward routines that display relevant information in a readable format, will eventually be of little importance, but the net result is a surprising gain in productivity.

Another good debugging practice is to keep a record of every mistake made. Even though this will probably be quite embarrassing, such information is invaluable to anyone doing research on the debugging problem, and it will also help you learn how to cope with future errors.

Note: The author wrote most of the preceding comments in 1964, after he had successfully completed several medium-sized software projects but before he had developed a mature programming style. Later, during the 1980s, he learned that an additional technique, called *structured documentation* or *literate programming*, is probably even more important. A summary of his current beliefs about the best way to write programs of all kinds appears in the book *Literate Programming* (Cambridge University Press, first published in 1992). Incidentally, Chapter 11 of that book contains a detailed record of all bugs removed from the TeX program during the period 1978–1991.

> Up to a point it is better to let the snags [bugs] be there
> than to spend such time in design that there are none
> (how many decades would this course take?).
> — A. M. TURING, Proposals for ACE (1945)

EXERCISES

1. [*20*] Write a subroutine `GoMaxR` that generalizes Algorithm 1.2.10M by finding the maximum value of $\{X[a], X[a+r], X[a+2r], \ldots, X[n]\}$, where r and n are positive parameters and a is the smallest positive number with $a \equiv n$ (modulo r), namely $a = 1 + (n-1) \bmod r$. Give a special entrance `GoMax` for the case $r = 1$, using a GO-style calling sequence so that your subroutine is a generalization of (7).

2. [*20*] Convert the subroutine of exercise 1 from GO linkage to PUSHJ/POP linkage.

3. [*15*] How can scheme (15) be simplified when `Sub` is a leaf subroutine?

4. [*15*] The text in this section speaks often of PUSHJ, but Section 1.3.1′ mentions also a command called PUSHGO. What is the difference between PUSHJ and PUSHGO?

5. [*0*] True or false: The number of marginal registers is $G - L$.

6. [*10*] What is the effect of the instruction `DIVU $5,$5,$5` if $5 is a marginal register?

7. [*10*] What is the effect of the instruction `INCML $5,#abcd` if $5 is a marginal register?

8. [*15*] Suppose the instruction `SET $15,0` is performed when there are 10 local registers. This increases the number of local registers to 16; but the newly local registers (including $15) are all zero, so they still behave essentially as if they were marginal. Is the instruction `SET $15,0` therefore entirely redundant in such a case?

9. [*20*] When a trip interrupt has been been enabled for some exceptional condition like arithmetic overflow, the trip handler might be called into action at unpredictable times. We don't want to clobber any of the interrupted program's registers; yet a trip handler can't do much unless it has "elbow room." Explain how to use PUSHJ and POP so that plenty of local registers are safely available to a handler.

▶ **10.** [*20*] True or false: If an MMIX program never uses the instructions PUSHJ, PUSHGO, POP, SAVE, or UNSAVE, all 256 registers $0, $1, ..., $255 are essentially equivalent, in the sense that the distinction between local, global, and marginal registers is irrelevant.

11. [*20*] Guess what happens if a program issues more POP instructions than PUSH instructions.

▶ **12.** [*10*] True or false:
   a) The current prefix in an MMIXAL program always begins with a colon.
   b) The current prefix in an MMIXAL program always ends with a colon.
   c) The symbols : and :: are equivalent in MMIXAL programs.

▶ **13.** [*21*] Write two MMIX subroutines to calculate the Fibonacci number F_n mod 2^{64}, given n. The first subroutine should call itself recursively, using the definition

$$F_n = n \quad \text{if } n \le 1; \qquad F_n = F_{n-1} + F_{n-2} \quad \text{if } n > 1.$$

The second subroutine should *not* be recursive. Both subroutines should use PUSH/POP linkage and should avoid global variables entirely.

▶ **14.** [*M21*] What is the running time of the subroutines in exercise 13?

▶ **15.** [*21*] Convert the recursive subroutine of exercise 13 to GO-style linkage, using a memory stack as in (15) instead of MMIX's register stack. Compare the efficiency of the two versions.

▶ **16.** [*25*] (*Nonlocal **goto** statements*.) Sometimes we want to jump out of a subroutine, to a location that is not in the calling routine. For example, suppose subroutine A calls subroutine B, which calls subroutine C, which calls itself recursively a number of times before deciding that it wants to exit directly to A. Explain how to handle such situations when using MMIX's register stack. (We can't simply JMP from C to A; the stack must be properly popped.)

1.4.2'. Coroutines

Subroutines are special cases of more general program components, called *co-routines*. In contrast to the unsymmetric relationship between a main routine and a subroutine, there is complete symmetry between coroutines, which *call on each other*.

To understand the coroutine concept, let us consider another way of thinking about subroutines. The viewpoint adopted in the previous section was that a subroutine was merely an extension of the computer hardware, introduced to save lines of coding. This may be true, but another point of view is also possible: We may consider the main program and the subroutine as a *team* of programs, each member of the team having a certain job to do. The main program, in the course of doing its job, will activate the subprogram; the subprogram will perform its own function and then activate the main program. We might stretch our imagination to believe that, from the subroutine's point of view, when it exits *it* is calling the *main* routine; the main routine continues to perform its duty, then "exits" to the subroutine. The subroutine acts, then calls the main routine again.

This egalitarian philosophy may sound far-fetched, but it actually rings true with respect to coroutines. There is no way to distinguish which of two coroutines is subordinate to the other. Suppose a program consists of coroutines A and B; when programming A, we may think of B as our subroutine, but when programming B, we may think of A as our subroutine. Whenever a coroutine is activated, it resumes execution of its program at the point where the action was last suspended.

The coroutines A and B might, for example, be two programs that play chess. We can combine them so that they will play against each other.

Such coroutine linkage is easy to achieve with MMIX if we set aside two global registers, a and b. In coroutine A, the instruction "GO a,b,0" is used to activate coroutine B; in coroutine B, the instruction "GO b,a,0" is used to activate coroutine A. This scheme requires only $3u$ of time to transfer control each way.

The essential difference between routine-subroutine and coroutine-coroutine linkage can be seen by comparing the GO-type linkage of the previous section with the present scheme: A subroutine is always initiated *at its beginning*, which is usually a fixed place; the main routine or a coroutine is always initiated *at the place following* where it last terminated.

Coroutines arise most naturally in practice when they are connected with algorithms for input and output. For example, suppose it is the duty of coroutine A to read a file and to perform some transformation on the input, reducing it to a sequence of items. Another coroutine, which we will call B, does further processing of those items, and outputs the answers; B will periodically call for the successive input items found by A. Thus, coroutine B jumps to A whenever it wants the next input item, and coroutine A jumps to B whenever an input item has been found. The reader may say, "Well, B is the main program and A is merely a *subroutine* for doing the input." This, however, becomes less true when the process A is very complicated; indeed, we can imagine A as the main routine and B as a subroutine for doing the output, and the above description remains valid. The usefulness of the coroutine idea emerges midway between these two extremes, when both A and B are complicated and each one calls the other in numerous places. It is not easy to find short, simple examples of coroutines that illustrate the importance of the idea; the most useful coroutine applications are generally quite lengthy.

In order to study coroutines in action, let us consider a contrived example. Suppose we want to write a program that translates one code into another. The input code to be translated is a sequence of 8-bit characters terminated by a period, such as

$$\texttt{a2b5e3426fg0zyw3210pq89r.} \qquad (1)$$

This code appears on the standard input file, interspersed with whitespace characters in an arbitrary fashion. For our purposes a "whitespace character" will be any byte whose value is less than or equal to $^\#20$, the ASCII code for ' '. All whitespace characters in the input are ignored; the other characters should be interpreted as follows, when they are read in sequence: (1) If the next character is one of the decimal digits 0 or 1 or $\cdots$ or 9, say n, it indicates $(n+1)$ repetitions of the following character, whether the following character is a digit or not. (2) A nondigit simply denotes itself. The output of our program is to consist of the resulting sequence separated into groups of three characters each, until a period appears; the last group may have fewer than three characters. For example, (1) should be translated into

$$\texttt{abb bee eee e44 446 66f gzy w22 220 0pq 999 999 999 r.} \qquad (2)$$

Notice that 3426f does not mean 3427 repetitions of the letter f; it means 4 fours and 3 sixes followed by f. If the input sequence is '1.', the output is simply '.', not '..', because the first period terminates the output. The goal of our program is to produce a sequence of lines on the standard output file, with 16 three-character groups per line (except, of course, that the final line might be shorter). The three-character groups should be separated by blank spaces, and each line should end as usual with the ASCII newline character $^\#$a.

To accomplish this translation, we will write two coroutines and a subroutine. The program begins by giving symbolic names to three global registers, one for temporary storage and the others for coroutine linkage.

```
01  * An example of coroutines
02  t          IS     $255      Temporary data of short duration
03  in         GREG   0         Address for resuming the first coroutine
04  out        GREG   0         Address for resuming the second coroutine  ▌
```

The next step is to set aside the memory locations used for working storage.

```
05  * Input and output buffers
06             LOC    Data_Segment
07             GREG   @                   Base address
08  OutBuf     TETRA  "                      ",#a,0   (see exercise 3)
09  Period     BYTE   '.'
10  InArgs     OCTA   InBuf,1000
11  InBuf      LOC    #100                ▌
```

Now we turn to the program itself. The subroutine we need, called NextChar, is designed to find non-whitespace characters of the input, and to return the next such character:

```
12  * Subroutine for character input
13  inptr      GREG   0                   (the current input position)
14  1H         LDA    t,InArgs            Fill the input buffer.
15             TRAP   0,Fgets,StdIn
16             LDA    inptr,InBuf         Start at beginning of buffer.
17  0H         GREG   Period
18             CSN    inptr,t,0B          If error occurred, read a '.'.
19  NextChar   LDBU   $0,inptr,0          Fetch the next character.
20             INCL   inptr,1
21             BZ     $0,1B               Branch if at end of buffer.
22             CMPU   t,$0,' '
23             BNP    t,NextChar          Branch if character is whitespace.
24             POP    1,0                 Return to caller.  ▌
```

This subroutine has the following characteristics:

Calling sequence: PUSHJ $R,NextChar.
Entry conditions: inptr points to the first unread character.
Exit conditions: $R = next non-whitespace character of input;
                  inptr is ready for the next entry to NextChar.

The subroutine also changes register t, namely register $255; but we usually omit that register from such specifications, as we did in 1.4.1′–(10).

Our first coroutine, called In, finds the characters of the input code with the proper replication. It begins initially at location In1:

```
25  * First coroutine
26  count    GREG  0                    (the repetition counter)
27  1H       GO    in,out,0             Send a character to the Out coroutine.
28  In1      PUSHJ $0,NextChar          Get a new character.
29           CMPU  t,$0,'9'
30           PBP   t,1B                 Branch if it exceeds '9'.
31           SUB   count,$0,'0'
32           BN    count,1B             Branch if it is less than '0'.
33           PUSHJ $0,NextChar          Get another character.
34  1H       GO    in,out,0             Send it to Out.
35           SUB   count,count,1        Decrease the repetition counter.
36           PBNN  count,1B             Repeat if necessary.
37           JMP   In1                  Otherwise begin a new cycle.  ▌
```

This coroutine has the following characteristics:

Calling sequence (from Out): GO out,in,0.
Exit conditions (to Out): $0 = next input character with proper replication.
Entry conditions
     (upon return): $0 unchanged from its value at exit.

Register count is private to In and need not be mentioned.

The other coroutine, called Out, puts the code into three-character groups and sends them to the standard output file. It begins initially at Out1:

```
38  * Second coroutine
39  outptr   GREG  0                    (the current output position)
40  1H       LDA   t,OutBuf             Empty the output buffer.
41           TRAP  0,Fputs,StdOut
42  Out1     LDA   outptr,OutBuf        Start at beginning of buffer.
43  2H       GO    out,in,0             Get a new character from In.
44           STBU  $0,outptr,0          Store it as the first of three.
45           CMP   t,$0,'.'
46           BZ    t,1F                 Branch if it was '.'.
47           GO    out,in,0             Otherwise get another character.
48           STBU  $0,outptr,1          Store it as the second of three.
49           CMP   t,$0,'.'
50           BZ    t,2F                 Branch if it was '.'.
51           GO    out,in,0             Otherwise get another character.
52           STBU  $0,outptr,2          Store it as the third of three.
53           CMP   t,$0,'.'
54           BZ    t,3F                 Branch if it was '.'.
55           INCL  outptr,4             Otherwise advance to next group.
56  0H       GREG  OutBuf+4*16
57           CMP   t,outptr,0B
58           PBNZ  t,2B                 Branch if fewer than 16 groups.
59           JMP   1B                   Otherwise finish the line.
```

60	3H	INCL	outptr,1	Move past a stored character.
61	2H	INCL	outptr,1	Move past a stored character.
62	OH	GREG	#a	(newline character)
63	1H	STBU	OB,outptr,1	Store newline after period.
64	OH	GREG	0	(null character)
65		STBU	OB,outptr,2	Store null after newline.
66		LDA	t,OutBuf	
67		TRAP	0,Fputs,StdOut	Output the final line.
68		TRAP	0,Halt,0	Terminate the program. ∎

The characteristics of `Out` are designed to complement those of `In`:

Calling sequence (from `In`): `GO in,out,0.`
Exit conditions (to `In`): $0 unchanged from its value at entry.
Entry conditions
    (upon return): $0 = next input character with proper replication.

To complete the program, we need to get everything off to a good start. Initialization of coroutines tends to be a little tricky, although not really difficult.

69	* Initialization			
70	Main	LDA	inptr,InBuf	Initialize NextChar.
71		GETA	in,In1	Initialize In.
72		JMP	Out1	Start with Out (see exercise 2). ∎

This completes the program. The reader should study it carefully, noting in particular how each coroutine can be read and written independently as though the other coroutine were its subroutine.

We learned in Section 1.4.1′ that MMIX's PUSHJ and POP instructions are superior to the GO command with respect to subroutine linkage. But with coroutines the opposite is true: Pushing and popping are quite unsymmetrical, and MMIX's register stack can get hopelessly entangled if two or more coroutines try to use it simultaneously. (See exercise 6.)

There is an important relation between coroutines and *multipass algorithms*. For example, the translation process we have just described could have been done in two distinct passes: We could first have done just the `In` coroutine, applying it to the entire input and writing each character with the proper amount of replication into an intermediate file. After this was finished, we could have read that file and done just the `Out` coroutine, taking the characters in groups of three. This would be called a "two-pass" process. (Intuitively, a "pass" denotes a complete scan of the input. This definition is not precise, and in many algorithms the number of passes taken is not at all clear; but the intuitive concept of "pass" is useful in spite of its vagueness.)

Figure 22(a) illustrates a four-pass process. Quite often we will find that the same process can be done in just one pass, as shown in part (b) of the figure, if we substitute four coroutines A, B, C, D for the respective passes A, B, C, D. Coroutine A will jump to B when pass A would have written an item of output on File 1; coroutine B will jump to A when pass B would have read an item of input from File 1, and B will jump to C when pass B would have written an item of output on File 2; etc. UNIX® users will recognize this as a "pipe," denoted by "PassA | PassB | PassC | PassD". The programs for passes B, C, and D are sometimes referred to as "filters."

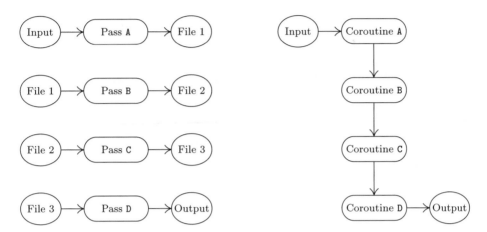

Fig. 22. Passes: (a) a four-pass algorithm, and (b) a one-pass algorithm.

Conversely, a process done by n coroutines can often be transformed into an n-pass process. Due to this correspondence it is worthwhile to compare multipass algorithms with one-pass algorithms.

a) *Psychological difference.* A multipass algorithm is generally easier to create and to understand than a one-pass algorithm for the same problem. A process that has been broken into a sequence of small steps, which happen one after the other, is easier to comprehend than an involved process in which many transformations take place simultaneously.

Also, if a very large problem is being tackled and if many people are supposed to cooperate in producing a computer program, a multipass algorithm provides a natural way to divide up the job.

These advantages of a multipass algorithm are present in coroutines as well, since each coroutine can be written essentially separate from the others. The linkage makes an apparently multipass algorithm into a single-pass process.

b) *Time difference.* The time required to pack, write, read, and unpack the intermediate data that flows between passes (for example, the information in the files of Fig. 22) is avoided in a one-pass algorithm. For this reason, a one-pass algorithm will be faster.

c) *Space difference.* The one-pass algorithm requires space to hold all the programs in memory simultaneously, while a multipass algorithm requires space for only one at a time. This requirement may affect the speed, even to a greater extent than indicated in statement (b). For example, many computers have a limited amount of "fast memory" and a larger amount of slower memory; if each pass just barely fits into the fast memory, the result will be considerably faster than if we use coroutines in a single pass (since the use of coroutines would presumably force most of the program to appear in the slower memory or to be repeatedly swapped in and out of fast memory).

Occasionally there is a need to design algorithms for several computer configurations at once, some of which have larger memory capacity than others. In such cases it is possible to write the program in terms of coroutines, and to let the memory size govern the number of passes: Load together as many coroutines as feasible, and supply input or output subroutines for the missing links.

Although this relationship between coroutines and passes is important, we should keep in mind that coroutine applications cannot always be split into multipass algorithms. If coroutine B gets input from A and also sends back crucial information to A, as in the example of chess play mentioned earlier, the sequence of actions can't be converted into pass A followed by pass B.

Conversely, it is clear that some multipass algorithms cannot be converted to coroutines. Some algorithms are inherently multipass; for example, the second pass may require cumulative information from the first pass, like the total number of occurrences of a certain word in the input. There is an old joke worth noting in this regard:

> *Little old lady, riding a bus.* "Little boy, can you tell me how to get off at Pasadena Street?"
> *Little boy.* "Just watch me, and get off two stops before I do."

(The joke is that the little boy gives a two-pass algorithm.)

So much for multipass algorithms. Coroutines also play an important role in discrete system simulation; see Section 2.2.5. When several more-or-less independent coroutines are controlled by a master process, they are often called *threads* of a computation. We will see further examples of coroutines in numerous places throughout this series of books. The important idea of *replicated coroutines* is discussed in Chapter 8, and some interesting applications of this idea may be found in Chapter 10.

EXERCISES

1. [*10*] Explain why short, simple examples of coroutines are hard for the author of a textbook to find.

▸ **2.** [*20*] The program in the text starts up the Out coroutine first. What would happen if In were the first to be executed instead — that is, if lines 71 and 72 were changed to "GETA out,Out1; JMP In1"?

3. [*15*] Explain the TETRA instruction on line 08 of the program in the text. (There are exactly fifteen blank spaces between the double-quote marks.)

4. [*20*] Suppose two coroutines A and B want to treat MMIX's remainder register rR as if it were their private property, although both coroutines do division. (In other words, when one coroutine jumps to the other, it wants to be able to assume that the contents of rR will not have been altered when the other coroutine returns.) Devise a coroutine linkage that allows them this freedom.

5. [*20*] Could MMIX do reasonably efficient coroutine linkage by using its PUSH and POP instructions, without any GO commands?

6. [*20*] The program in the text uses MMIX's register stack only in a very limited way, namely when In calls NextChar. Discuss to what extent two cooperating coroutines could both make use of the register stack.

▶ **7.** [*30*] Write an MMIX program that *reverses* the translation done by the program in the text. That is, your program should convert a file containing three-character groups like (2) into a file containing code like (1). The output should be as short a string of characters as possible, except for newlines; thus, for example, the zero before the z in (1) would not really be produced from (2).

1.4.3′. Interpretive Routines

In this section we will investigate a common type of program known as an *interpretive routine*, often called an *interpreter* for short. An interpretive routine is a computer program that performs the instructions of another program, where the other program is written in some machine-like language. By a machine-like language, we mean a way of representing instructions, where the instructions typically have operation codes, addresses, etc. (This definition, like most definitions of today's computer terms, is not precise, nor should it be; we cannot draw the line exactly and say just which programs are interpreters and which are not.)

Historically, the first interpreters were built around machine-like languages designed specially for simple programming; such languages were easier to use than a real machine language. The rise of symbolic languages for programming soon eliminated the need for interpretive routines of that kind, but interpreters have by no means begun to die out. On the contrary, their use has continued to grow, to the extent that an effective use of interpretive routines may be regarded as one of the essential characteristics of modern programming. The new applications of interpreters are made chiefly for the following reasons:

a) a machine-like language is able to represent a complicated sequence of decisions and actions in a compact, efficient manner; and

b) such a representation provides an excellent way to communicate between passes of a multipass process.

In such cases, special purpose machine-like languages are developed for use in a particular program, and programs in those languages are often generated only by computers. (Today's expert programmers are also good machine designers: They not only create an interpretive routine, they also define a *virtual machine* whose language is to be interpreted.)

The interpretive technique has the further advantage of being relatively machine-independent, since only the interpreter must be revised when changing computers. Furthermore, helpful debugging aids can readily be built into an interpretive system.

Examples of type (a) interpreters appear in several places later in this series of books; see, for example, the recursive interpreter in Chapter 8 and the "Parsing

Machine" in Chapter 10. We typically need to deal with situations in which a great many special cases arise, all similar, but having no really simple pattern.

For example, consider writing an algebraic compiler in which we want to generate efficient machine-language instructions that add two quantities together. There might be ten classes of quantities (constants, simple variables, subscripted variables, fixed or floating point, signed or unsigned, etc.) and the combination of all pairs yields 100 different cases. A long program would be required to do the proper thing in each case. The interpretive solution to this problem is to make up an ad hoc language whose "instructions" fit in one byte. Then we simply prepare a table of 100 "programs" in this language, where each program ideally fits in a single word. The idea is then to pick out the appropriate table entry and to perform the program found there. This technique is simple and efficient.

An example interpreter of type (b) appears in the article "Computer-Drawn Flowcharts" by D. E. Knuth, *CACM* **6** (1963), 555–563. In a multipass program, the earlier passes must transmit information to the later passes. This information is often transmitted most efficiently in a machine-like language, as a set of instructions for the later pass; the later pass is then nothing but a special purpose interpretive routine, and the earlier pass is a special purpose "compiler." This philosophy of multipass operation may be characterized as *telling* the later pass what to do, whenever possible, rather than simply presenting it with a lot of facts and asking it to *figure out* what to do.

Another example of a type-(b) interpreter occurs in connection with compilers for special languages. If the language includes many features that are not easily done on the machine except by subroutine, the resulting object programs will be very long sequences of subroutine calls. This would happen, for example, if the language were concerned primarily with multiple precision arithmetic. In such a case the object program would be considerably shorter if it were expressed in an interpretive language. See, for example, the book *ALGOL 60 Implementation*, by B. Randell and L. J. Russell (New York: Academic Press, 1964), which describes a compiler to translate from ALGOL 60 into an interpretive language, and which also describes the interpreter for that language; and see "An ALGOL 60 Compiler," by Arthur Evans, Jr., *Ann. Rev. Auto. Programming* **4** (1964), 87–124, for examples of interpretive routines used *within* a compiler. The rise of microprogrammed machines and of special-purpose integrated circuit chips has made this interpretive approach even more valuable.

The TEX program, which produced the pages of the book you are now reading, converted a file that contained the text of this section into an interpretive language called DVI format, designed by D. R. Fuchs in 1979. [See D. E. Knuth, *TEX: The Program* (Reading, Mass.: Addison–Wesley, 1986), Part 31.] The DVI file that TEX produced was then processed by an interpreter called dvips, written by T. G. Rokicki, and converted to a file of instructions in another interpretive language called PostScript® [Adobe Systems Inc., *PostScript Language Reference*, 3rd edition (Reading, Mass.: Addison–Wesley, 1999)]. The PostScript file was sent to the publisher, who sent it to a commercial printer, who used a PostScript interpreter to produce printing plates. This three-pass operation illustrates interpreters of type (b); TEX itself also includes a small interpreter of type (a) to process the so-called ligature and kerning information for characters that are being printed [*TEX: The Program*, §545].

There is another way to look at a program written in interpretive language: It may be regarded as a series of subroutine calls, one after another. Such a program may in fact be expanded into a long sequence of calls on subroutines, and, conversely, such a sequence can usually be packed into a coded form that is readily interpreted. The advantages of interpretive techniques are the compactness of representation, the machine independence, and the increased diagnostic capability. An interpreter can often be written so that the amount of time spent in interpretation of the code itself and branching to the appropriate routine is negligible.

*An MMIX simulator. When the language presented to an interpretive routine is the machine language of another computer, the interpreter is often called a *simulator* (or sometimes an *emulator*).

In the author's opinion, entirely too much programmers' time has been spent in writing such simulators and entirely too much computer time has been wasted in using them. The motivation for simulators is simple: A computer installation buys a new machine and still wants to run programs written for the old machine (rather than rewriting the programs). However, this usually costs more and gives poorer results than if a special task force of programmers were given temporary employment to do the reprogramming. For example, the author once participated in such a reprogramming project, and a serious error was discovered in the original program, which had been in use for several years; the new program worked at five times the speed of the old, besides giving the right answers for a change! (Not all simulators are bad; for example, it is usually advantageous for a computer manufacturer to simulate a new machine before it has been built, so that software for the new machine may be developed as soon as possible. But that is a very specialized application.) An extreme example of the inefficient use of computer simulators is the true story of machine A simulating machine B running a program that simulates machine C. This is the way to make a large, expensive computer give poorer results than its cheaper cousin.

In view of all this, why should such a simulator rear its ugly head in this book? There are three reasons:

a) The simulator we will describe below is a good example of a typical interpretive routine; the basic techniques employed in interpreters are illustrated here. It also illustrates the use of subroutines in a moderately long program.

b) We will describe a simulator of the MMIX computer, written in (of all things) the MMIX language. This will reinforce our knowledge of the machine. It also will facilitate the writing of MMIX simulators for other computers, although we will not plunge deeply into the details of 64-bit integer or floating point arithmetic.

c) Our simulation of MMIX explains how the register stack can be implemented efficiently in hardware, so that pushing and popping are accomplished with very little work. Similarly, the simulator presented here clarifies the SAVE and UNSAVE operators, and it provides details about the behavior of trip interrupts. Such things are best understood by looking at a reference implementation, so that we can see how the machine really works.

Computer simulators as described in this section should be distinguished from *discrete system simulators*. Discrete system simulators are important programs that will be discussed in Section 2.2.5.

Now let's turn to the task of writing an MMIX simulator. We begin by making a tremendous simplification: Instead of attempting to simulate all the things that happen simultaneously in a pipelined computer, we will interpret only one instruction at a time. Pipeline processing is extremely instructive and important, but it is beyond the scope of this book; interested readers can find a complete program for a full-fledged pipeline "meta-simulator" in the *MMIXware* document. We will content ourselves here with a simulator that is blithely unaware of such things as cache memory, virtual address translation, dynamic instruction scheduling, reorder buffers, etc., etc. Moreover, we will simulate only the instructions that ordinary MMIX user programs can do; privileged instructions like LDVTS, which are reserved for the operating system, will be considered erroneous if they arise. Trap interrupts will not be simulated by our program unless they perform rudimentary input or output as described in Section 1.3.2′.

The input to our program will be a binary file that specifies the initial contents of memory, just as the memory would be set up by an operating system when running a user program (including command line data). We want to mimic the behavior of MMIX's hardware, pretending that MMIX itself is interpreting the instructions that begin at symbolic location Main; thus, we want to implement the specifications that were laid down in Section 1.3.1′, in the run-time environment that was discussed in Section 1.3.2′. Our program will, for example, maintain an array of 256 octabytes g[0], g[1], ..., g[255] for the simulated global registers. The first 32 elements of this array will be the special registers listed in Table 1.3.1′–2; one of those special registers will be the simulated clock, rC. We will assume that each instruction takes a fixed amount of time, as specified by Table 1.3.1′–1; the simulated rC will increase by 2^{32} for each μ and by 1 for each v. Thus, for example, after we have simulated Program 1.3.2′P, the simulated rC will contain #00003228000bb091, which represents $12840\mu + 766097v$.

The program is rather long, but it has many points of interest and we will study it in short easy pieces. It begins as usual by defining a few symbols and by specifying the contents of the data segment. We put the array of 256 simulated global registers first in that segment; for example, the simulated \$255 will be the octabyte g[255], in memory location Global+8*255. This global array is followed by a similar array called the *local register ring*, where we will keep the top items of the simulated register stack. The size of this ring is set to 256, although 512 or any higher power of 2 would also work. (A large ring of local registers costs more, but it might be noticeably faster when a program uses the register stack heavily. One of the purposes of a simulator is to find out whether additional hardware would be worth the expense.) The main portion of the data segment, starting at Chunk0, will be devoted to the simulated memory.

```
001  * MMIX Simulator (Simplified)
002  t        IS    $255              Volatile register for temporary info
003  lring_size IS 256                Size of the local register ring
004           LOC   Data_Segment      Start at location #2000 0000 0000 0000
005  Global   LOC   @+8*256           256 octabytes for global registers
006  g        GREG  Global            Base address for globals
007  Local    LOC   @+8*lring_size    lring_size octabytes for local registers
008  l        GREG  Local             Base address for locals
009           GREG  @                 Base address for IOArgs and Chunk0
010  IOArgs   OCTA  0,BinaryRead      (See exercise 20)
011  Chunk0   IS    @                 Beginning of simulated memory area
012           LOC   #100              Put everything else in the text segment. ▮
```

One of the key subroutines we will need is called MemFind. Given a 64-bit address A, this subroutine returns the resulting address R where the simulated contents of $M_8[A]$ can be found. Of course 2^{64} bytes of simulated memory cannot be squeezed into a 2^{61}-byte data segment; but the simulator remembers all addresses that have occurred before, and it assumes that all locations not yet encountered are equal to zero.

Memory is divided into "chunks" of 2^{12} bytes each. MemFind looks at the leading $64 - 12 = 52$ bits of A to see what chunk it belongs to, and extends the list of known chunks, if necessary. Then it computes R by adding the trailing 12 bits of A to the starting address of the relevant simulated chunk. (The chunk size could be any power of 2, as long as each chunk contains at least one octabyte. Small chunks cause MemFind to search through longer lists of chunks-in-hand; large chunks cause MemFind to waste space for bytes that will never be accessed.)

Each simulated chunk is encapsulated in a "node," which occupies $2^{12} + 24$ bytes of memory. The first octabyte of such a node, called the KEY, identifies the simulated address of the first byte in the chunk. The second octabyte, called the LINK, points to the next node on MemFind's list; it is zero on the last node of the list. The LINK is followed by 2^{12} bytes of simulated memory called the DATA. Finally, each node ends with eight all-zero bytes, which are used as padding in the implementation of input-output (see exercises 15–17).

MemFind maintains its list of chunk nodes in order of use: The first node, pointed to by head, is the one that MemFind found on the previous call, and it links to the next-most-recently-used chunk, etc. If the future is like the past, MemFind will therefore not have to search far down its list. (Section 6.1 discusses such "self-organizing" list searches in detail.) Initially head points to Chunk0, whose KEY and LINK and DATA are all zero. The allocation pointer alloc is set initially to the place where the next chunk node will appear when it is needed, namely Chunk0+nodesize.

We implement MemFind with the PREFIX operation of MMIXAL discussed in Section 1.4.1′, so that the private symbols head, key, addr, etc., will not conflict with any symbols in the rest of the program. The calling sequence will be

$$\text{SET arg}, A; \quad \text{PUSHJ res}, \text{MemFind} \tag{1}$$

after which the resulting address R will appear in register res.

013		PREFIX	:Mem:	(Begin private symbols for MemFind)
014	head	GREG	0	Address of first chunk
015	curkey	GREG	0	KEY(head)
016	alloc	GREG	0	Address of next chunk to allocate
017	Chunk	IS	#1000	Bytes per chunk, must be a power of 2
018	addr	IS	$0	The given address A
019	key	IS	$1	Its chunk address
020	test	IS	$2	Temporary register for key search
021	newlink	IS	$3	The second most recently used node
022	p	IS	$4	Temporary pointer register
023	t	IS	:t	External temporary register
024	KEY	IS	0	
025	LINK	IS	8	
026	DATA	IS	16	
027	nodesize	GREG	Chunk+3*8	
028	mask	GREG	Chunk-1	
029	:MemFind	ANDN	key,addr,mask	
030		CMPU	t,key,curkey	
031		PBZ	t,4F	Branch if head is the right chunk.
032		BN	addr,:Error	Disallow negative addresses A.
033		SET	newlink,head	Prepare for the search loop.
034	1H	SET	p,head	p ← head.
035		LDOU	head,p,LINK	head ← LINK(p).
036		PBNZ	head,2F	Branch if head ≠ 0.
037		SET	head,alloc	Otherwise allocate a new node.
038		STOU	key,head,KEY	
039		ADDU	alloc,alloc,nodesize	
040		JMP	3F	
041	2H	LDOU	test,head,KEY	
042		CMPU	t,test,key	
043		BNZ	t,1B	Loop back if KEY(head) ≠ key.
044	3H	LDOU	t,head,LINK	Adjust pointers: t ← LINK(head),
045		STOU	newlink,head,LINK	LINK(head) ← newlink,
046		SET	curkey,key	curkey ← key,
047		STOU	t,p,LINK	LINK(p) ← t.
048	4H	SUBU	t,addr,key	t ← chunk offset.
049		LDA	$0,head,DATA	$0 ← address of DATA(head).
050		ADDU	$0,t,$0	
051		POP	1,0	Return R.
052		PREFIX	:	(End of the ':Mem:' prefix)
053	res	IS	$2	Result register for PUSHJ
054	arg	IS	res+1	Argument register for PUSHJ ▌

We come next to the most interesting aspect of the simulator, the implementation of MMIX's register stack. Recall from Section 1.4.1′ that the register stack is conceptually a list of τ items $S[0]$, $S[1]$, ..., $S[\tau - 1]$. The final item $S[\tau - 1]$ is said to be at the "top" of the stack, and MMIX's local registers $0, $1, ..., $(L-1)$ are the topmost L items $S[\tau - L]$, $S[\tau - L + 1]$, ..., $S[\tau - 1]$; here L is the value of special register rL. We could simulate the stack by simply keeping it entirely in the simulated memory; but an efficient machine wants its registers to be instantly accessible, not in a relatively slow memory unit. Therefore we will simulate an efficient design that keeps the topmost stack items in an array of internal registers called the *local register ring*.

The basic idea is quite simple. Suppose the local register ring has ρ elements, $l[0], l[1], \ldots, l[\rho-1]$. Then we keep local register \$$k$ in $l[(\alpha+k) \bmod \rho]$, where α is an appropriate offset. (The value of ρ is chosen to be a power of 2, so that remainders mod ρ require no expensive computation. Furthermore we want ρ to be at least 256, so that there is room for all of the local registers.) A PUSH operation, which renumbers the local registers so that what once was, say, \$3 is now called \$0, simply increases the value of α by 3; a POP operation restores the previous state by decreasing α. Although the registers change their numbers, no data actually needs to be pushed down or popped up.

Of course we need to use memory as a backup when the register stack gets large. The status of the ring at any time is best visualized in terms of three variables, α, β, and γ:

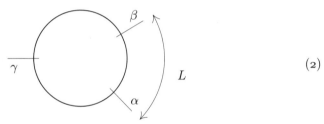

$$(2)$$

Elements $l[\alpha], l[\alpha+1], \ldots, l[\beta-1]$ of the ring are the current local registers \$0, \$1, \ldots, \$$(L-1)$; elements $l[\beta], l[\beta+1], \ldots, l[\gamma-1]$ are currently unused; and elements $l[\gamma], l[\gamma+1], \ldots, l[\alpha-1]$ contain items of the register stack that have been pushed down. If $\gamma \neq \alpha$, we can increase γ by 1 if we first store $l[\gamma]$ in memory. If $\gamma \neq \beta$, we can decrease γ by 1 if we then load $l[\gamma]$. MMIX has two special registers called the *stack pointer* rS and the *stack offset* rO, which hold the memory addresses where $l[\gamma]$ and $l[\alpha]$ will be stored, if necessary. The values of α, β, and γ are related to rL, rS, and rO by the formulas

$$\alpha = (\text{rO}/8) \bmod \rho, \quad \beta = (\alpha + \text{rL}) \bmod \rho, \quad \gamma = (\text{rS}/8) \bmod \rho. \quad (3)$$

The simulator keeps most of MMIX's special registers in the first 32 positions of the global register array. For example, the simulated remainder register rR is the octabyte in location `Global+8*rR`. But eight of the special registers, including rS, rO, rL, and rG, are potentially relevant to every simulated instruction, so the simulator maintains them separately in its own global registers. Thus, for example, register `ss` holds the simulated value of rS, and register `ll` holds eight times the simulated value of rL:

055	ss	GREG 0	The simulated stack pointer, rS
056	oo	GREG 0	The simulated stack offset, rO
057	ll	GREG 0	The simulated local threshold register, rL, times 8
058	gg	GREG 0	The simulated global threshold register, rG, times 8

```
059 aa   GREG  0    The simulated arithmetic status register, rA
060 ii   GREG  0    The simulated interval counter, rI
061 uu   GREG  0    The simulated usage counter, rU
062 cc   GREG  0    The simulated cycle counter, rC  ▌
```

Here is a subroutine that obtains the current value of the simulated register k, given k. The calling sequence is

$$\text{SLU arg}, k, 3; \quad \text{PUSHJ res}, \text{GetReg} \tag{4}$$

after which the desired value will be in res.

```
063 lring_mask GREG  8*lring_size-1
064 :GetReg    CMPU  t,$0,gg            Subroutine to get $k:
065            BN    t,1F               Branch if k < G.
066            LDOU  $0,g,$0            Otherwise $k is global; load g[k].
067            POP   1,0                Return the result.
068 1H         CMPU  t,$0,ll            t ← [$k is local].
069            ADDU  $0,$0,oo
070            AND   $0,$0,lring_mask
071            LDOU  $0,1,$0            Load l[(α + k) mod ρ].
072            CSNN  $0,t,0             Zero it if $k is marginal.
073            POP   1,0                Return the result.  ▌
```

Notice the colon in the label field of line 064. This colon is redundant, because the current prefix is ':' (see line 052); the colon on line 029 was, however, necessary for the external symbol MemFind, because at that time the current prefix was ':Mem:'. Colons in the label field, redundant or not, give us a handy way to advertise the fact that a subroutine is being defined.

The next subroutines, StackStore and StackLoad, simulate the operations of increasing γ by 1 and decreasing γ by 1 in the diagram (2). They return no result. StackStore is called only when $\gamma \neq \alpha$; StackLoad is called only when $\gamma \neq \beta$. Both of them must save and restore rJ, because they are not leaf subroutines.

```
074 :StackStore GET   $0,rJ            Save the return address.
075             AND   t,ss,lring_mask
076             LDOU  $1,1,t           $1 ← l[γ].
077             SET   arg,ss
078             PUSHJ res,MemFind
079             STOU  $1,res,0         M₈[rS] ← $1.
080             ADDU  ss,ss,8          Increase rS by 8.
081             PUT   rJ,$0            Restore the return address.
082             POP   0                Return to caller.

083 :StackLoad  GET   $0,rJ            Save the return address.
084             SUBU  ss,ss,8          Decrease rS by 8.
085             SET   arg,ss
086             PUSHJ res,MemFind
087             LDOU  $1,res,0         $1 ← M₈[rS].
088             AND   t,ss,lring_mask
```

```
089              STOU   $1,1,t              l[γ] ← $1.
090              PUT    rJ,$0               Restore the return address.
091              POP    0                   Return to caller.  ▌
```

(Register rJ on lines 074, 081, 083, and 090 is, of course, the *real* rJ, not the simulated rJ. When we simulate a machine on itself, we have to remember to keep such things straight!)

The `StackRoom` subroutine is called when we have just increased β. It checks whether $\beta = \gamma$ and, if so, it increases γ.

```
092  :StackRoom SUBU   t,ss,oo
093              SUBU   t,t,ll
094              AND    t,t,lring_mask
095              PBNZ   t,1F                Branch if (rS−rO)/8 ≢ rL (modulo ρ).
096              GET    $0,rJ               Oops, we're not a leaf subroutine.
097              PUSHJ  res,StackStore      Advance rS.
098              PUT    rJ,$0               Restore the return address.
099  1H          POP    0                   Return to caller.  ▌
```

Now we come to the heart of the simulator, its main simulation loop. An interpretive routine generally has a central control section that is called into action between interpreted instructions. In our case, the program transfers to location `Fetch` when it is ready to simulate a new command. We keep the address @ of the next simulated instruction in the global register `inst_ptr`. `Fetch` usually sets `loc` ← `inst_ptr` and advances `inst_ptr` by 4; but if we are simulating a `RESUME` command that inserts the simulated rX into the instruction stream, `Fetch` sets `loc` ← `inst_ptr` − 4 and leaves `inst_ptr` unchanged. This simulator considers an instruction to be ineligible for execution unless its location `loc` is in the text segment (that is, `loc` < #2000 0000 0000 0000).

```
100  * The main loop
101  loc       GREG  0    Where the simulator is at
102  inst_ptr  GREG  0    Where the simulator will be next
103  inst      GREG  0    The current instruction being simulated
104  resuming  GREG  0    Are we resuming an instruction in rX?
105  Fetch  PBZ    resuming,1F       Branch if not resuming.
106         SUBU   loc,inst_ptr,4    loc ← inst_ptr − 4.
107         LDTU   inst,g,8*rX+4     inst ← right half of rX.
108         JMP    2F
109  1H     SET    loc,inst_ptr      loc ← inst_ptr.
110         SET    arg,loc
111         PUSHJ  res,MemFind
112         LDTU   inst,res,0        inst ← M₄[loc].
113         ADDU   inst_ptr,loc,4    inst_ptr ← loc + 4.
114  2H     CMPU   t,loc,g
115         BNN    t,Error           Branch if loc ≥ Data_Segment.  ▌
```

The main control routine does the things common to all instructions. It unpacks the current instruction into its various parts and puts the parts into

convenient registers for later use. Most importantly, it sets global register f to
64 bits of "info" corresponding to the current opcode. A master table, which
starts at location Info, contains such information for each of MMIX's 256 opcodes.
(See Table 1 on page 88.) For example, f is set to an odd value if and only if the
Z field of the current opcode is an "immediate" operand or the opcode is JMP;
similarly $f \wedge {}^{\#}40$ is nonzero if and only if the instruction has a relative address.
Later steps of the simulator will be able to decide quickly what needs to be done
with respect to the current instruction because most of the relevant information
appears in register f.

116	op	GREG	0	Opcode of the current instruction
117	xx	GREG	0	X field of the current instruction
118	yy	GREG	0	Y field of the current instruction
119	zz	GREG	0	Z field of the current instruction
120	yz	GREG	0	YZ field of the current instruction
121	f	GREG	0	Packed information about the current opcode
122	xxx	GREG	0	X field times 8
123	x	GREG	0	X operand and/or result
124	y	GREG	0	Y operand
125	z	GREG	0	Z operand
126	xptr	GREG	0	Location where x should be stored
127	exc	GREG	0	Arithmetic exceptions

128	Z_is_immed_bit	IS	#1	Flag bits possibly set in f
129	Z_is_source_bit	IS	#2	
130	Y_is_immed_bit	IS	#4	
131	Y_is_source_bit	IS	#8	
132	X_is_source_bit	IS	#10	
133	X_is_dest_bit	IS	#20	
134	Rel_addr_bit	IS	#40	
135	Mem_bit	IS	#80	

136	Info	IS	#1000	
137	Done	IS	Info+8*256	
138	info	GREG	Info	(Base address for the master info table)
139	c255	GREG	8*255	(A handy constant)
140	c256	GREG	8*256	(Another handy constant)
141		MOR	op,inst,#8	$op \leftarrow inst \gg 24$.
142		MOR	xx,inst,#4	$xx \leftarrow (inst \gg 16) \wedge {}^{\#}ff$.
143		MOR	yy,inst,#2	$yy \leftarrow (inst \gg 8) \wedge {}^{\#}ff$.
144		MOR	zz,inst,#1	$zz \leftarrow inst \wedge {}^{\#}ff$.
145	OH GREG -#10000			
146		ANDN	yz,inst,OB	
147		SLU	xxx,xx,3	
148		SLU	t,op,3	
149		LDOU	f,info,t	$f \leftarrow Info[op]$.
150		SET	x,0	$x \leftarrow 0$ (default value).
151		SET	y,0	$y \leftarrow 0$ (default value).
152		SET	z,0	$z \leftarrow 0$ (default value).
153		SET	exc,0	$exc \leftarrow 0$ (default value). ▮

The first thing we do, after having unpacked the instruction into its various fields, is convert a relative address to an absolute address if necessary.

154		AND	t,f,Rel_addr_bit
155		PBZ	t,1F	Branch if not a relative address.
156		PBEV	f,2F	Branch if op isn't JMP or JMPB.
157	9H	GREG	-#1000000
158		ANDN	yz,inst,9B	$yz \leftarrow inst \wedge$ #ffffff (namely XYZ).
159		ADDU	t,yz,9B	$t \leftarrow XYZ - 2^{24}$.
160		JMP	3F
161	2H	ADDU	t,yz,0B	$t \leftarrow YZ - 2^{16}$.
162	3H	CSOD	yz,op,t	Set $yz \leftarrow t$ if op is odd ("backward").
163		SL	t,yz,2
164		ADDU	yz,loc,t	$yz \leftarrow loc + yz \ll 2$. ∎

The next task is critical for most instructions: We install the operands specified by the Y and Z fields into global registers y and z. Sometimes we also install a third operand into global register x, specified by the X field or coming from a special register like the simulated rD or rM.

165	1H		PBNN	resuming,Install_X	Branch unless resuming < 0.
		...			(See exercise 14.)
174	Install_X	AND	t,f,X_is_source_bit
175		PBZ	t,1F	Branch unless $X is a source.
176		SET	arg,xxx
177		PUSHJ	res,GetReg
178		SET	x,res	$x \leftarrow \$X$.
179	1H	SRU	t,f,5
180		AND	t,t,#f8	$t \leftarrow$ special register number, times 8.
181		PBZ	t,Install_Z
182		LDOU	x,g,t	If $t \neq 0$, set $x \leftarrow g[t]$.
183	Install_Z	AND	t,f,Z_is_source_bit
184		PBZ	t,1F	Branch unless $Z is a source.
185		SLU	arg,zz,3
186		PUSHJ	res,GetReg
187		SET	z,res	$z \leftarrow \$Z$.
188		JMP	Install_Y
189	1H	CSOD	z,f,zz	If Z is immediate, $z \leftarrow Z$.
190		AND	t,op,#f0
191		CMPU	t,t,#e0
192		PBNZ	t,Install_Y	Branch unless #e0 ≤ op < #f0.
193		AND	t,op,#3
194		NEG	t,3,t
195		SLU	t,t,4
196		SLU	z,yz,t	$z \leftarrow yz \ll (48, 32, 16, \text{ or } 0)$.
197		SET	y,x	$y \leftarrow x$.
198	Install_Y	AND	t,f,Y_is_immed_bit
199		PBZ	t,1F	Branch unless Y is immediate.
200		SET	y,yy	$y \leftarrow Y$.
201		SLU	t,yy,40
202		ADDU	f,f,t	Insert Y into left half of f.

```
203  1H       AND    t,f,Y_is_source_bit
204           BZ     t,1F                        Branch unless $Y is a source.
205           SLU    arg,yy,3
206           PUSHJ  res,GetReg
207           SET    y,res                       y ← $Y.  ∎
```

When the X field specifies a destination register, we set xptr to the memory address where we will eventually store the simulated result; this address will be either in the Global array or the Local ring. The simulated register stack grows at this point if the destination register must be changed from marginal to local.

```
208  1H       AND    t,f,X_is_dest_bit
209           BZ     t,1F                        Branch unless $X is a destination.
210  XDest    CMPU   t,xxx,gg
211           BN     t,3F                        Branch if $X is not global.
212           LDA    xptr,g,xxx                  xptr ← address of g[X].
213           JMP    1F
214  2H       ADDU   t,oo,ll
215           AND    t,t,lring_mask
216           STCO   0,1,t                       l[(α + L) mod ρ] ← 0.
217           INCL   ll,8                        L ← L + 1.   ($L becomes local.)
218           PUSHJ  res,StackRoom               Make sure β ≠ γ.
219  3H       CMPU   t,xxx,ll
220           BNN    t,2B                        Branch if $X is not local.
221           ADD    t,xxx,oo
222           AND    t,t,lring_mask
223           LDA    xptr,l,t                    xptr ← address of l[(α + X) mod ρ].  ∎
```

Finally we reach the climax of the main control cycle: We simulate the current instruction by essentially doing a 256-way branch, based on the current opcode. The left half of register f is, in fact, an MMIX instruction that we *perform* at this point, by inserting it into the instruction stream via a RESUME command. For example, if we are simulating an ADD command, we put "ADD x,y,z" into the right half of rX and clear the exception bits of rA; the RESUME command will then cause the sum of registers y and z to be placed in register x, and rA will record whether overflow occurred. After the RESUME, control will pass to location Done, unless the inserted instruction was a branch or jump.

```
224  1H       AND    t,f,Mem_bit
225           PBZ    t,1F                        Branch unless inst accesses memory.
226           ADDU   arg,y,z
227           CMPU   t,op,#A0                     t ← [op is a load instruction].
228           BN     t,2F
229           CMPU   t,arg,g
230           BN     t,Error                     Error if storing into the text segment.
231  2H       PUSHJ  res,MemFind                 res ← address of M[y + z].
232  1H       SRU    t,f,32
233           PUT    rX,t                        rX ← left half of f.
234           PUT    rM,x                        rM ← x  (prepare for MUX).
235           PUT    rE,x                        rE ← x  (prepare for FCMPE, FUNE, FEQLE).
```

236	OH GREG	#30000	
237	AND	t,aa,0B	t ← current rounding mode.
238	ORL	t,U_BIT<<8	Enable underflow trip (see below).
239	PUT	rA,t	Prepare rA for arithmetic.
240	OH GREG	Done	
241	PUT	rW,0B	rW ← Done.
242	RESUME	0	Execute the instruction in rX. ∎

Some instructions can't be simulated by simply "performing themselves" like an ADD command and jumping to Done. For example, a MULU command must insert the high half of its computed product into the simulated rH. A branch command must change inst_ptr if the branch is taken. A PUSHJ command must push the simulated register stack, and a POP command must pop it. SAVE, UNSAVE, RESUME, TRAP, etc., all need special care; therefore the next part of the simulator deals with all cases that don't fit the nice "x equals y op z" pattern.

Let's start with multiplication and division, since they are easy:

243	MulU	MULU	x,y,z	Multiply y by z, unsigned.
244		GET	t,rH	Set t ← upper half of the product.
245		STOU	t,g,8*rH	g[rH] ← upper half product.
246		JMP	XDone	Finish by storing x.
247	Div	DIV	x,y,z	
	...			(For division, see exercise 6.) ∎

If the simulated instruction was a branch command, say "BZ \$X,RA", the main control routine will have converted the relative address RA to an absolute address in register yz (line 164), and it will also have placed the contents of the simulated \$X into register x (line 178). The RESUME command will then execute the instruction "BZ x,BTaken" (line 242); and control will pass to BTaken instead of Done if the simulated branch is taken. BTaken adds $2v$ to the simulated running time, changes inst_ptr, and jumps to Update.

254	BTaken	ADDU	cc,cc,4	Increase rC by $4v$.
255	PBTaken	SUBU	cc,cc,2	Decrease rC by $2v$.
256		SET	inst_ptr,yz	inst_ptr ← branch address.
257		JMP	Update	Finish the command.
258	Go	SET	x,inst_ptr	GO instruction: Set x ← loc + 4.
259		ADDU	inst_ptr,y,z	inst_ptr ← $(y + z) \bmod 2^{64}$.
260		JMP	XDone	Finish by storing x. ∎

(Line 257 could have jumped to Done, but that would be slower; a shortcut to Update is justified because a branch command doesn't store x and cannot cause an arithmetic exception. See lines 500–541 below.)

A PUSHJ or PUSHGO command pushes the simulated register stack down by increasing the α pointer of (2); this means increasing the simulated rO, namely register oo. If the command is "PUSHJ \$X,RA" and if \$X is local, we push $X + 1$ octabytes down by first setting \$X ← X and then increasing oo by $8(X + 1)$. (The value we have put in \$X will be used later by POP to determine how to restore oo to its former value. Simulated register \$X will then be set to the

result of the subroutine, as explained in Section 1.4.1′.) If $X is global, we push
rL + 1 octabytes down in a similar way.

261	PushGo	ADDU	yz,y,z	$yz \leftarrow (y+z) \bmod 2^{64}$.
262	PushJ	SET	inst_ptr,yz	$inst\_ptr \leftarrow yz$.
263		CMPU	t,xxx,gg	
264		PBN	t,1F	Branch if $X is local.
265		SET	xxx,ll	Pretend that X = rL.
266		SRU	xx,xxx,3	
267		INCL	ll,8	Increase rL by 1.
268		PUSHJ	0,StackRoom	Make sure $\beta \neq \gamma$ in (2).
269	1H	ADDU	t,xxx,oo	
270		AND	t,t,lring_mask	
271		STOU	xx,l,t	$l[(\alpha+X) \bmod \rho] \leftarrow X$.
272		ADDU	t,loc,4	
273		STOU	t,g,8*rJ	$g[rJ] \leftarrow loc + 4$.
274		INCL	xxx,8	
275		SUBU	ll,ll,xxx	Decrease rL by X + 1.
276		ADDU	oo,oo,xxx	Increase rO by 8(X + 1).
277		JMP	Update	Finish the command. ∎

Special routines are needed also to simulate POP, SAVE, UNSAVE, and several
other opcodes including RESUME. Those routines deal with interesting details
about MMIX, and we will consider them in the exercises; but we'll skip them for
now, since they do not involve any techniques related to interpretive routines
that we haven't seen already.

We might as well present the code for SYNC and TRIP, however, since those
routines are so simple. (Indeed, there's nothing to do for "SYNC XYZ" except to
check that XYZ ≤ 3, since we aren't simulating cache memory.) Furthermore,
we will take a look at the code for TRAP, which is interesting because it illustrates
the important technique of a jump table for multiway switching:

278	Sync	BNZ	xx,Error	Branch if X ≠ 0.
279		CMPU	t,yz,4	
280		BNN	t,Error	Branch if YZ ≥ 4.
281		JMP	Update	Finish the command.
282	Trip	SET	xx,0	Initiate a trip to location 0.
283		JMP	TakeTrip	(See exercise 13.)
284	Trap	STOU	inst_ptr,g,8*rWW	$g[rWW] \leftarrow inst\_ptr$.
285	OH GREG	#8000000000000000		
286		ADDU	t,inst,0B	
287		STOU	t,g,8*rXX	$g[rXX] \leftarrow inst + 2^{63}$.
288		STOU	y,g,8*rYY	$g[rYY] \leftarrow y$.
289		STOU	z,g,8*rZZ	$g[rZZ] \leftarrow z$.
290		SRU	y,inst,6	
291		CMPU	t,y,4*ll	
292		BNN	t,Error	Branch if X ≠ 0 or Y > Ftell.
293		LDOU	t,g,c255	$t \leftarrow g[255]$.

```
294   OH GREG @+4
295            GO     y,0B,y              Jump to @ + 4 + 4Y.
296            JMP    SimHalt             Y = Halt: Jump to SimHalt.
297            JMP    SimFopen            Y = Fopen: Jump to SimFopen.
298            JMP    SimFclose           Y = Fclose: Jump to SimFclose.
299            JMP    SimFread            Y = Fread: Jump to SimFread.
300            JMP    SimFgets            Y = Fgets: Jump to SimFgets.
301            JMP    SimFgetws           Y = Fgetws: Jump to SimFgetws.
302            JMP    SimFwrite           Y = Fwrite: Jump to SimFwrite.
303            JMP    SimFputs            Y = Fputs: Jump to SimFputs.
304            JMP    SimFputws           Y = Fputws: Jump to SimFputws.
305            JMP    SimFseek            Y = Fseek: Jump to SimFseek.
306            JMP    SimFtell            Y = Ftell: Jump to SimFtell.
307   TrapDone STO    t,g,8*rBB           Set g[rBB] ← t.
308            STO    t,g,c255            A trap ends with g[255] ← g[rBB].
309            JMP    Update              Finish the command.  ∎
```

(See exercises 15–17 for SimFopen, SimFclose, SimFread, etc.)

Now let's look at the master Info table (Table 1), which allows the simulator to deal rather painlessly with 256 different opcodes. Each table entry is an octabyte consisting of (i) a four-byte MMIX instruction, which will be invoked by the RESUME instruction on line 242; (ii) two bytes that define the simulated running time, one byte for μ and one byte for v; (iii) a byte that names a special register, if such a register ought to be loaded into x on line 182; and (iv) a byte that is the sum of eight 1-bit flags, expressing special properties of the opcode. For example, the info for opcode FIX is

$$\text{FIX x,0,z; \quad BYTE 0,4,0,\#26;}$$

it means that (i) the instruction FIX x,0,z should be performed, to round a floating point number to a fixed point integer; (ii) the simulated running time should be increased by $0\mu + 4v$; (iii) no special register is needed as an input operand; and (iv) the flag byte

$$\#26 = \text{X\_is\_dest\_bit} + \text{Y\_is\_immed\_bit} + \text{Z\_is\_source\_bit}$$

determines the treatment of registers x, y, and z. (The Y_is_immed_bit actually causes the Y field of the simulated instruction to be inserted into the Y field of "FIX x,0,z"; see line 202.)

One interesting aspect of the Info table is that the RESUME command of line 242 executes the instruction as if it were in location Done-4, since rW = Done. Therefore, if the instruction is a JMP, the address must be relative to Done-4; but MMIXAL always assembles JMP commands with an address relative to the assembled location @. We trick the assembler into doing the right thing by writing, for example, "JMP Trap+@-O", where O is defined to equal Done-4. Then the RESUME command will indeed jump to location Trap as desired.

After we have executed the special instruction inserted by RESUME, we normally get to location Done. From here on everything is anticlimactic; but

Table 1

MASTER INFORMATION TABLE FOR SIMULATOR CONTROL

```
O IS Done-4                                      LDB x,res,0; BYTE 1,1,0,#aa      (LDB)
LOC Info                                         LDB x,res,0; BYTE 1,1,0,#a9      (LDBI)
JMP Trap+@-O; BYTE 0,5,0,#0a      (TRAP)         ...
FCMP x,y,z; BYTE 0,1,0,#2a        (FCMP)         JMP Cswap+@-O; BYTE 2,2,0,#ba    (CSWAP)
FUN x,y,z; BYTE 0,1,0,#2a         (FUN)          JMP Cswap+@-O; BYTE 2,2,0,#b9    (CSWAPI)
FEQL x,y,z; BYTE 0,1,0,#2a        (FEQL)         LDUNC x,res,0; BYTE 1,1,0,#aa    (LDUNC)
FADD x,y,z; BYTE 0,4,0,#2a        (FADD)         LDUNC x,res,0; BYTE 1,1,0,#a9    (LDUNCI)
FIX x,0,z; BYTE 0,4,0,#26         (FIX)          JMP Error+@-O; BYTE 0,1,0,#2a    (LDVTS)
FSUB x,y,z; BYTE 0,4,0,#2a        (FSUB)         JMP Error+@-O; BYTE 0,1,0,#29    (LDVTSI)
FIXU x,0,z; BYTE 0,4,0,#26        (FIXU)         SWYM 0; BYTE 0,1,0,#0a           (PRELD)
FLOT x,0,z; BYTE 0,4,0,#26        (FLOT)         SWYM 0; BYTE 0,1,0,#09           (PRELDI)
FLOT x,0,z; BYTE 0,4,0,#25        (FLOTI)        SWYM 0; BYTE 0,1,0,#0a           (PREGO)
FLOTU x,0,z; BYTE 0,4,0,#26       (FLOTU)        SWYM 0; BYTE 0,1,0,#09           (PREGOI)
...                                              JMP Go+@-O; BYTE 0,3,0,#2a       (GO)
FMUL x,y,z; BYTE 0,4,0,#2a        (FMUL)         JMP Go+@-O; BYTE 0,3,0,#29       (GOI)
FCMPE x,y,z; BYTE 0,4,rE,#2a      (FCMPE)        STB x,res,0; BYTE 1,1,0,#9a      (STB)
FUNE x,y,z; BYTE 0,1,rE,#2a       (FUNE)         STB x,res,0; BYTE 1,1,0,#99      (STBI)
FEQLE x,y,z; BYTE 0,4,rE,#2a      (FEQLE)        ...
FDIV x,y,z; BYTE 0,40,0,#2a       (FDIV)         STO xx,res,0; BYTE 1,1,0,#8a     (STCO)
FSQRT x,0,z; BYTE 0,40,0,#26      (FSQRT)        STO xx,res,0; BYTE 1,1,0,#89     (STCOI)
FREM x,y,z; BYTE 0,4,0,#2a        (FREM)         STUNC x,res,0; BYTE 1,1,0,#9a    (STUNC)
FINT x,0,z; BYTE 0,4,0,#26        (FINT)         STUNC x,res,0; BYTE 1,1,0,#99    (STUNCI)
MUL x,y,z; BYTE 0,10,0,#2a        (MUL)          SWYM 0; BYTE 0,1,0,#0a           (SYNCD)
MUL x,y,z; BYTE 0,10,0,#29        (MULI)         SWYM 0; BYTE 0,1,0,#09           (SYNCDI)
JMP MulU+@-O; BYTE 0,10,0,#2a     (MULU)         SWYM 0; BYTE 0,1,0,#0a           (PREST)
JMP MulU+@-O; BYTE 0,10,0,#29     (MULUI)        SWYM 0; BYTE 0,1,0,#09           (PRESTI)
JMP Div+@-O; BYTE 0,60,0,#2a      (DIV)          SWYM 0; BYTE 0,1,0,#0a           (SYNCID)
JMP Div+@-O; BYTE 0,60,0,#29      (DIVI)         SWYM 0; BYTE 0,1,0,#09           (SYNCIDI)
JMP DivU+@-O; BYTE 0,60,rD,#2a    (DIVU)         JMP PushGo+@-O; BYTE 0,3,0,#2a   (PUSHGO)
JMP DivU+@-O; BYTE 0,60,rD,#29    (DIVUI)        JMP PushGo+@-O; BYTE 0,3,0,#29   (PUSHGOI)
ADD x,y,z; BYTE 0,1,0,#2a         (ADD)          OR x,y,z; BYTE 0,1,0,#2a         (OR)
ADD x,y,z; BYTE 0,1,0,#29         (ADDI)         OR x,y,z; BYTE 0,1,0,#29         (ORI)
ADDU x,y,z; BYTE 0,1,0,#2a        (ADDU)         ...
...                                              SET x,z; BYTE 0,1,0,#20          (SETH)
CMPU x,y,z; BYTE 0,1,0,#29        (CMPUI)        SET x,z; BYTE 0,1,0,#20          (SETMH)
NEG x,0,z; BYTE 0,1,0,#26         (NEG)          ...
NEG x,0,z; BYTE 0,1,0,#25         (NEGI)         ANDN x,x,z; BYTE 0,1,0,#30       (ANDNL)
NEGU x,0,z; BYTE 0,1,0,#26        (NEGU)         SET inst_ptr,yz; BYTE 0,1,0,#41  (JMP)
NEGU x,0,z; BYTE 0,1,0,#25        (NEGUI)        SET inst_ptr,yz; BYTE 0,1,0,#41  (JMPB)
SL x,y,z; BYTE 0,1,0,#2a          (SL)           JMP PushJ+@-O; BYTE 0,1,0,#60    (PUSHJ)
...                                              JMP PushJ+@-O; BYTE 0,1,0,#60    (PUSHJB)
BN x,BTaken+@-O; BYTE 0,1,0,#50   (BN)           SET x,yz; BYTE 0,1,0,#60         (GETA)
BN x,BTaken+@-O; BYTE 0,1,0,#50   (BNB)          SET x,yz; BYTE 0,1,0,#60         (GETAB)
BZ x,BTaken+@-O; BYTE 0,1,0,#50   (BZ)           JMP Put+@-O; BYTE 0,1,0,#02      (PUT)
...                                              JMP Put+@-O; BYTE 0,1,0,#01      (PUTI)
PBNP x,PBTaken+@-O; BYTE 0,3,0,#50  (PBNPB)      JMP Pop+@-O; BYTE 0,3,rJ,#00     (POP)
PBEV x,PBTaken+@-O; BYTE 0,3,0,#50  (PBEV)       JMP Resume+@-O; BYTE 0,5,0,#00   (RESUME)
PBEV x,PBTaken+@-O; BYTE 0,3,0,#50  (PBEVB)      JMP Save+@-O; BYTE 20,1,0,#20    (SAVE)
CSN x,y,z; BYTE 0,1,0,#3a         (CSN)          JMP Unsave+@-O; BYTE 20,1,0,#02  (UNSAVE)
CSN x,y,z; BYTE 0,1,0,#39         (CSNI)         JMP Sync+@-O; BYTE 0,1,0,#01     (SYNC)
...                                              SWYM x,y,z; BYTE 0,1,0,#00       (SWYM)
ZSEV x,y,z; BYTE 0,1,0,#2a        (ZSEV)         JMP Get+@-O; BYTE 0,1,0,#20      (GET)
ZSEV x,y,z; BYTE 0,1,0,#29        (ZSEVI)        JMP Trip+@-O; BYTE 0,5,0,#0a     (TRIP)
```

Entries not shown here explicitly follow a pattern that is easily deduced from the examples shown. (See, for example, exercise 1.)

we can take satisfaction in the fact that an instruction has been simulated successfully and the current cycle is nearly finished. Only a few details still need to be wrapped up: We must store the result x in the appropriate place, if the X_is_dest_bit flag is present, and we must check if an arithmetic exception has triggered a trip interrupt:

```
500  Done    AND    t,f,X_is_dest_bit
501          BZ     t,1F                Branch unless $X is a destination.
502  XDone  .STOU   x,xptr,0            Store x in simulated $X.
503  1H      GET    t,rA
504          AND    t,t,#ff             t ← new arithmetic exceptions.
505          OR     exc,exc,t           exc ← exc ∨ t.
506          AND    t,exc,U_BIT+X_BIT
507          CMPU   t,t,U_BIT
508          PBNZ   t,1F                Branch unless underflow is exact.
509  OH GREG U_BIT<<8
510          AND    t,aa,0B
511          BNZ    t,1F                Branch if underflow is enabled.
512          ANDNL  exc,U_BIT           Ignore U if exact and not enabled.
513  1H      PBZ    exc,Update
514          SRU    t,aa,8
515          AND    t,t,exc
516          PBZ    t,4F                Branch unless trip interrupt needed.
        . . .                           (See exercise 13.)
539  4H      OR     aa,aa,exc           Record new exceptions in rA.   ∎
```

Line number 500 is used here for convenience, although several hundred instructions and the entire Info table actually intervene between line 309 and this part of the program. Incidentally, the label Done on line 500 does not conflict with the label Done on line 137, because both of them define the same equivalent value for this symbol.

After line 505, register exc contains the bit codes for all arithmetic exceptions triggered by the instruction just simulated. At this point we must deal with a curious asymmetry in the rules for IEEE standard floating point arithmetic: An underflow exception (U) is suppressed unless the underflow trip has been enabled in rA or unless an inexact exception (X) has also occurred. (We had to enable the underflow trip in line 238 for precisely this reason; the simulator ends with the commands

$$\text{LOC U\_Handler;} \quad \text{ORL exc,U\_BIT;} \quad \text{JMP Done} \qquad (5)$$

so that exc will properly record underflow exceptions in cases where a floating point computation was exact but produced a denormal result.)

Finally — Hurray! — we are able to close the cycle of operations that began long ago at location Fetch. We update the runtime clocks, take a deep breath, and return to Fetch again:

```
540  OH GREG #0000000800000004
541  Update  MOR    t,f,0B              2³²mems + oops
```

542		ADDU	cc,cc,t	Increase the simulated clock, rC.
543		ADDU	uu,uu,1	Increase the usage counter, rU.
544		SUBU	ii,ii,1	Decrease the interval counter, rI.
545	AllDone	PBZ	resuming,Fetch	Go to Fetch if resuming = 0.
546		CMPU	t,op,#F9	Otherwise set t ← [op = RESUME].
547		CSNZ	resuming,t,0	Clear resuming if not resuming,
548		JMP	Fetch	and go to Fetch. ∎

Our simulation program is now complete, except that we still must initialize everything properly. We assume that the simulator will be run with a command line that names a binary file. Exercise 20 explains the simple format of that file, which specifies what should be loaded into the simulated memory before simulation begins. Once the program has been loaded, we launch it as follows: At line 576 below, register loc will contain a location from which a simulated UNSAVE command will get the program off to a good start. (In fact, we simulate an UNSAVE that is being simulated by a simulated RESUME. The code is tricky, perhaps, but it works.)

549	Infile	IS	3	(Handle for binary input file)
550	Main	LDA	Mem:head,Chunk0	Initialize MemFind.
551		ADDU	Mem:alloc,Mem:head,Mem:nodesize	
552		GET	t,rN	
553		INCL	t,1	
554		STOU	t,g,8*rN	g[rN] ← (our rN) + 1.
555		LDOU	t,$1,8	t ← binary file name ($argv$[1]).
556		STOU	t,IOArgs	
557		LDA	t,IOArgs	(See line 010)
558		TRAP	0,Fopen,Infile	Open the binary file.
559		BN	t,Error	
	...			Now load the file (see exercise 20).
576		STOU	loc,g,c255	g[255] ← place to UNSAVE.
577		SUBU	arg,loc,8*13	arg ← place where $255 appears.
578		PUSHJ	res,MemFind	
579		LDOU	inst_ptr,res,0	inst_ptr ← Main.
580		SET	arg,#90	
581		PUSHJ	res,MemFind	
582		LDTU	x,res,0	x ← $M_4[^\#90]$.
583		SET	resuming,1	resuming ← 1.
584		CSNZ	inst_ptr,x,#90	If x ≠ 0, set inst_ptr ← $^\#90$.
585	0H	GREG	#FB<<24+255	
586		STOU	0B,g,8*rX	g[rX] ← "UNSAVE $255".
587		SET	gg,c255	G ← 255.
588		JMP	Fetch	Start the ball rolling.
589	Error	NEG	t,22	t ← −22 for error exit.
590	Exit	TRAP	0,Halt,0	End of simulation.
591		LOC Global+8*rK; OCTA −1		
592		LOC Global+8*rT; OCTA #8000000500000000		
593		LOC Global+8*rTT; OCTA #8000000600000000		
594		LOC Global+8*rV; OCTA #369c200400000000 ∎		

The simulated program's Main starting address will be in the simulated register $255 after the simulated UNSAVE. Lines 580–584 of this code implement a feature that wasn't mentioned in Section 1.3.2′: If an instruction is loaded into location #90, the program begins there instead of at Main. (This feature allows a subroutine library to initialize itself before starting a user program at Main.)

Lines 591–594 initialize the simulated rK, rT, rTT, and rV to appropriate constant values. Then the program is finished; it ends with the trip-handler instructions of (5).

Whew! Our simulator has turned out to be pretty long — longer, in fact, than any other program that we will encounter in this book. But in spite of its length, the program above is incomplete in several respects because the author did not want to make it even longer:

a) Several parts of the code have been left as exercises.

b) The program simply branches to Error and quits, when it detects a problem. A decent simulator would distinguish between different types of error, and would have a way to keep going.

c) The program doesn't gather any statistics, except for the total running time (cc) and the total number of instructions simulated (uu). A more complete program would, for example, remember how often the user guessed correctly with respect to branches versus probable branches; it would also record the number of times the StackLoad and StackStore subroutines need to access simulated memory. It might also analyze its own algorithms, studying for example the efficiency of the self-organizing search technique used by MemFind.

d) The program has no diagnostic facilities. A useful simulator would, for example, allow interactive debugging, and would output selected snapshots of the simulated program's execution; such features would not be difficult to add. The ability to monitor a program easily is, in fact, one of the main reasons for the importance of interpretive routines in general.

EXERCISES

1. [*20*] Table 1 shows the Info entries only for selected opcodes. What entries are appropriate for (a) opcode #3F (SRUI)? (b) opcode #55 (PBPB)? (c) opcode #D9 (MUXI)? (d) opcode #E6 (INCML)?

▶ **2.** [*26*] How much time does it take the simulator to simulate the instructions (a) ADDU $255,$Y,$Z; (b) STHT $X,$Y,0; (c) PBNZ $X,@-4?

3. [*23*] Explain why $\gamma \neq \alpha$ when StackRoom calls StackStore on line 097.

▶ **4.** [*20*] Criticize the fact that MemFind never checks to see if alloc has gotten too large. Is this a serious blunder?

▶ **5.** [*20*] If the MemFind subroutine branches to Error, it does not pop the register stack. How many items might be on the register stack at such a time?

6. [*20*] Complete the simulation of DIV and DIVU instructions, by filling in the missing code of lines 248–253.

7. [*21*] Complete the simulation of CSWAP instructions, by writing appropriate code.

8. [*22*] Complete the simulation of GET instructions, by writing appropriate code.

9. [*23*] Complete the simulation of PUT instructions, by writing appropriate code.

10. [*24*] Complete the simulation of POP instructions, by writing appropriate code. *Note:* If the normal action of POP as described in Section 1.4.1′ would leave rL > rG, MMIX will pop entries off the top of the register stack so that rL = rG. For example, if the user pushes 250 registers down with PUSHJ and then says "PUT rG,32; POP", only 32 of the pushed-down registers will survive.

11. [*25*] Complete the simulation of SAVE instructions, by writing appropriate code. *Note:* SAVE pushes all the local registers down and stores the entire register stack in memory, followed by $G, $(G + 1), ..., $255, followed by rB, rD, rE, rH, rJ, rM, rR, rP, rW, rX, rY, and rZ (in that order), followed by the octabyte 2^{56}rG + rA.

12. [*26*] Complete the simulation of UNSAVE instructions, by writing appropriate code. *Note:* The very first simulated UNSAVE is part of the initial loading process (see lines 583–588), so it should not update the simulated clocks.

13. [*27*] Complete the simulation of trip interrupts, by filling in the missing code of lines 517–538.

14. [*28*] Complete the simulation of RESUME instructions, by writing appropriate code. *Note:* When rX is nonnegative, its most significant byte is called the "ropcode"; ropcodes 0, 1, 2 are available for user programs. Line 242 of the simulator uses ropcode 0, which simply inserts the lower half of rX into the instruction stream. Ropcode 1 is similar, but the instruction in rX is performed with y ← rY and z ← rZ in place of the normal operands; this variant is allowed only when the first hexadecimal digit of the inserted opcode is #0, #1, #2, #3, #6, #7, #C, #D, or #E. Ropcode 2 sets $X ← rZ and exc ← Q, where X is the third byte from the right of rX and Q is the third byte from the left; this makes it possible to set the value of a register and simultaneously raise any subset of the arithmetic exceptions DVWIOUZX. Ropcodes 1 and 2 can be used only when $X is not marginal. Your solution to this exercise should cause RESUME to set resuming ← 0 if the simulated rX is negative, otherwise resuming ← (1, −1, −2) for ropcodes (0, 1, 2). You should also supply the code that is missing from lines 166–173.

▸ **15.** [*25*] Write the routine SimFputs, which simulates the operation of outputting a string to the file corresponding to a given handle.

▸ **16.** [*25*] Write the routine SimFopen, which opens a file corresponding to a given handle. (The simulator can use the same handle number as the user program.)

▸ **17.** [*25*] Continuing the previous exercises, write the routine SimFread, which reads a given number of bytes from a file corresponding to a given handle.

▸ **18.** [*21*] Would this simulator be of any use if lring_size were less than 256, for example if lring_size = 32?

19. [*14*] Study all the uses of the StackRoom subroutine (namely in line 218, line 268, and in the answer to exercise 11). Can you suggest a better way to organize the code? (See step 3 in the discussion at the end of Section 1.4.1′.)

20. [*20*] The binary files input by the simulator consist of one or more groups of octabytes each having the simple form

$$\lambda, \; x_0, \; x_1, \; ..., \; x_{l-1}, \; 0$$

for some $l \geq 0$, where x_0, x_1, ..., and x_{l-1} are nonzero; the meaning is

$$M_8[\lambda + 8k] \leftarrow x_k, \qquad \text{for } 0 \leq k < l.$$

The file ends after the last group. Complete the simulator by writing MMIX code to load such input (lines 560–575 of the program). The final value of register loc should be the location of the last octabyte loaded, namely $\lambda + 8(l-1)$.

▶ **21.** [20] Is the simulation program of this section able to simulate itself? If so, is it able to simulate itself simulating itself? And if so, is it $\cdots$?

▶ **22.** [40] Implement an efficient *jump trace* routine for MMIX. This is a program that records all transfers of control in the execution of another given program by recording a sequence of pairs (x_1, y_1), (x_2, y_2), ..., meaning that the given program jumped from location x_1 to y_1, then (after performing the instructions in locations y_1, y_1+1, ..., x_2) it jumped from x_2 to y_2, etc. [From this information it is possible for a subsequent routine to reconstruct the flow of the program and to deduce how frequently each instruction was performed.]

A trace routine differs from a simulator because it allows the traced program to occupy its normal memory locations. A jump trace modifies the instruction stream in memory, but does so only to the extent necessary to retain control. Otherwise it allows the machine to execute arithmetic and memory instructions at full speed. Some restrictions are necessary; for example, the program being traced shouldn't modify itself. But you should try to keep such restrictions to a minimum.

ANSWERS TO EXERCISES

SECTION 1.3.1′

1. #7d9 or #7D9.

2. (a) $\{B, D, F, b, d, f\}$. (b) $\{A, C, E, a, c, e\}$. An odd fact of life.

3. (Solution by Gregor N. Purdy.) 2 bits = 1 nyp; 2 nyps = 1 nybble; 2 nybbles = 1 byte. Incidentally, the word "byte" was coined in 1956 by members of IBM's Stretch computer project; see W. Buchholz, *BYTE* **2**, 2 (February 1977), 144.

4. 1000 MB = 1 gigabyte (GB), 1000 GB = 1 terabyte (TB), 1000 TB = 1 petabyte (PB), 1000 PB = 1 exabyte (EB), 1000 EB = 1 zettabyte (ZB), 1000 ZB = 1 yottabyte (YB), according to the 19th Conférence Générale des Poids et Mesures (1990).

(Some people, however, use 2^{10} instead of 1000 in these formulas, claiming for example that a kilobyte is 1024 bytes. To resolve the ambiguity, such units should preferably be called *large kilobytes*, *large megabytes*, etc., and denoted by KKB, MMB, ... to indicate their binary nature.)

> *We can think of 1024 as a "computer's thousand" — rather in the way that 13 is (or was) a "baker's dozen".*
> — T. H. O'BEIRNE (1962)

5. If $-2^{n-1} \leq x < 2^{n-1}$, then $-2^n < x - s(\alpha) < 2^n$; hence $x \neq s(\alpha)$ implies that $x \not\equiv s(\alpha)$ (modulo 2^n). But $s(\alpha) = u(\alpha) - 2^n[\alpha$ begins with 1$] \equiv u(\alpha)$ (modulo 2^n).

6. Using the notation of the previous exercise, we have $u(\bar{\alpha}) = 2^n - 1 - u(\alpha)$; hence $u(\bar{\alpha}) + 1 \equiv -u(\alpha)$ (modulo 2^n), and it follows that $s(\bar{\alpha}) + 1 = -s(\alpha)$. Overflow might occur, however, when adding 1. In that case $\alpha = 10\ldots0$, $s(\alpha) = -2^{n-1}$, and $-s(\alpha)$ is not representable.

7. Yes. (See the discussion of shifting.)

8. The radix point now falls between rH and $X. (In general, if the binary radix point is m positions from the end of $Y and n positions from the end of $Z, it is $m + n$ positions from the end of the product.)

9. Yes, except when X = Y, or X = Z, or overflow occurs.

10. $Y = #8000 0000 0000 0000, $Z = #ffff ffff ffff ffff is the *only* example!

11. (a) True, because $s(\$Y) \equiv u(\$Y)$ and $s(\$Z) \equiv u(\$Z)$ (modulo 2^{64}) by exercise 5. (b) Clearly true if $s(\$Y) \geq 0$ and $s(\$Z) \geq 0$, because $s(\$Y) = u(\$Y)$ and $s(\$Z) = u(\$Z)$ in such a case. Also true if $Z = 0 or $Z = 1 or $Z = $Y or $Y = 0. Otherwise false.

12. If X ≠ Y, say 'ADDU $X,$Y,$Z; CMPU carry,$X,$Y; ZSN carry,carry,1'. But if X = Y = Z, say 'ZSN carry,$X,1; ADDU $X,$X,$X'.

13. Overflow occurs on signed addition if and only if $Y and $Z have the same sign but their unsigned sum has the opposite sign. Thus

XOR $0,$Y,$Z; ADDU $X,$Y,$Z; XOR $1,$X,$Y; ANDN $1,$1,$0; ZSN ovfl,$1,1

determines the presence or absence of overflow when X ≠ Y.

14. Interchange X and Y in the previous answer. (Overflow occurs when computing $x = y - z$ if and only if it occurs when computing $y = x + z$.)

15. Let $\dot{y}$ and $\dot{z}$ be the sign bits of y and z, so that $s(y) = y - 2^{64}\dot{y}$ and $s(z) = z - 2^{64}\dot{z}$; we want to calculate $s(y)s(z) \bmod 2^{128} = (yz - 2^{64}(\dot{y}z + y\dot{z})) \bmod 2^{128}$. Thus the program MULU $X,$Y,$Z; GET $0,rH; ZSN $1,$Y,$Z; SUBU $0,$0,$1; ZSN $1,$Z,$Y; SUBU $0,$0,$1 puts the desired octabyte in $0.

16. After the instructions in the previous answer, check that the upper half is the sign extension of the lower half, by saying 'SR $1,$X,63; CMP $1,$0,$1; ZSNZ ovfl,$1,1'.

17. Let a be the stated constant, which is $(2^{65}+1)/3$. Then $ay/2^{65} = y/3 + y/(3 \cdot 2^{65})$, so $\lfloor ay/2^{65} \rfloor = \lfloor y/3 \rfloor$ for $0 \le y < 2^{65}$.

18. By a similar argument, $\lfloor ay/2^{66} \rfloor = \lfloor y/5 \rfloor$ for $0 \le y < 2^{66}$ when $a = (2^{66}+1)/5 = $ #cccc cccc cccc cccd.

19. This statement is widely believed, and it has been implemented by compiler writers who did not check the math. But it is *false* when $z = 7, 21, 23, 25, 29, 31, 39, 47, 49, 53, 55, 61, 63, 71, 81, 89, \ldots$, and in fact for 189 odd divisors z less than 1000!

Let $\epsilon = ay/2^{64+e} - y/z = (z-r)y/(2^{64+e}z)$, where $r = 2^{64+e} \bmod z$. Then $0 < \epsilon < 2/z$, hence trouble can arise only when $y \equiv -1$ (modulo z) and $\epsilon \ge 1/z$. It follows that the formula $\lfloor ay/2^{64+e} \rfloor = \lfloor y/z \rfloor$ holds for all unsigned octabytes y, $0 \le y < 2^{64}$, if and only if it holds for the single value $y = 2^{64} - 1 - (2^{64} \bmod z)$.

(The formula is, however, always correct in the restricted range $0 \le y < 2^{63}$. And Michael Yoder observes that high-multiplication by $\lceil 2^{64+e+1}/z \rceil - 2^{64}$, followed by addition of y and right-shift by $e + 1$, does work in general.)

20. 4ADDU $X,$Y,$Y; 4ADDU $X,$X,$X.

21. SL sets $X to zero, overflowing if $Y was nonzero. SLU and SRU set $X to zero. SR sets $X to 64 copies of the sign bit of $Y, namely to $-[\$Y < 0]$. (Notice that shifting left by -1 does *not* shift right.)

22. Dull's program takes the wrong branch when the SUB instruction causes overflow. For example, it treats *every* nonnegative number as less than -2^{63}; it treats $2^{63} - 1$ as less than every negative number. Although no error arises when $1 and $2 have the same sign, or when the numbers in $1 and $2 are both less than 2^{62} in absolute value, the correct formulation 'CMP $0,$1,$2; BN $0,Case1' is much better. (Similar errors have been made by programmers and compiler writers since the 1950s, often causing significant and mysterious failures.)

23. CMP $0,$1,$2; BNP $0,Case1.

24. ANDN.

25. XOR $X,$Y,$Z; SADD $X,$X,0.

26. ANDN $X,$Y,$Z.

27. BDIF $W,$Y,$Z; ADDU $X,$Z,$W; SUBU $W,$Y,$W.

28. BDIF $0,$Y,$Z; BDIF $X,$Z,$Y; OR $X,$0,$X.

29. NOR $0,$Y,0; BDIF $0,$0,$Z; NOR $X,$0,0. (This sequence computes $2^n - 1 - \max(0, (2^n - 1 - y) - z)$ in each byte position.)

30. XOR $1,$0,$2; BDIF $1,$3,$1; SADD $1,$1,0 when $2 = $ #2020202020202020 and $3 = $ #0101010101010101.

31. MXOR $1,$4,$0; SADD $1,$1,0 when $4 = $ #0101010101010101.

32. $C^T_{ji} = C_{ij} = (A^T_{1i} \bullet B^T_{j1}) \circ \cdots \circ (A^T_{ni} \bullet B^T_{jn}) = (B^T \overset{\circ}{\underset{\bullet}{}} A^T)_{ji}$ if $\bullet$ is commutative.

33. MOR (or MXOR) with the constant $^\#01\,80\,40\,20\,10\,08\,04\,02$.

34. MOR $X,$Z,[#0080004000200010]; MOR $Y,$Z,[#0008000400020001]. (Here we use brackets to denote registers that contain auxiliary constants.)

To go back, also checking that an 8-bit code is sufficient:

```
PUT   rM,[#00ff00ff00ff00ff]
MOR   $0,$X,[#4020100804020180]
MUX   $1,$0,$Y
BNZ   $1,BadCase
MUX   $1,$Y,$0
MOR   $Z,$1,[#8020080240100401]   ▮
```

35. MOR $X,$Y,$Z; MOR $X,$Z,$X; here $Z is the constant (14).

36. XOR $0,$Y,$Z; MOR $0,[-1],$0. *Notes:* Changing XOR to BDIF gives a mask for the bytes where $Y *exceeds* $Z. Given such a mask, AND it with $^\#8040201008040201$ and MOR with $^\#$ff to get a one-byte encoding of the relevant byte positions.

37. Let the elements of the field be polynomials in the Boolean matrix

$$\begin{pmatrix} 0 & 1 & 0 & 0 & 0 & 0 & 0 & 0 \\ 0 & 0 & 1 & 0 & 0 & 0 & 0 & 0 \\ 0 & 0 & 0 & 1 & 0 & 0 & 0 & 0 \\ 0 & 0 & 0 & 0 & 1 & 0 & 0 & 0 \\ 0 & 0 & 0 & 0 & 0 & 1 & 0 & 0 \\ 0 & 0 & 0 & 0 & 0 & 0 & 1 & 0 \\ 0 & 0 & 0 & 0 & 0 & 0 & 0 & 1 \\ 1 & 0 & 0 & 0 & 1 & 1 & 1 & 0 \end{pmatrix}.$$

For example, this matrix is m($^\#40\,20\,10\,08\,04\,02\,01\,8e$), and if we square it with MXOR we get the matrix m($^\#20\,10\,08\,04\,02\,01\,8e\,47$). The sum and product of such field elements are then obtained by XOR and MXOR, respectively.

(A field with 2^k elements for $2 \le k \le 7$ is obtained in a similar way from polynomials in the matrices $^\#0103$, $^\#020105$, $^\#04020109$, $^\#0804020112$, $^\#100804020121$, $^\#20100804020141$. Matrices of size up to 16×16 can be represented as four octabytes; then multiplication requires eight MXORs and four XORs. We can, however, do multiplication in a field of 2^{16} elements by performing only five MXORs and three XORs, if we represent the large field as a quadratic extension of the field of 2^8 elements.)

38. It sets $1 to the sum of the eight signed bytes initially in $0; it also sets $2 to the rightmost nonzero such byte, or zero; and it sets $0 to zero. (Changing SR to SRU would treat the bytes as unsigned. Changing SLU to SL would often overflow.)

39. The assumed running times are (a) $(3v$ or $2v)$ versus $2v$; (b) $(4v$ or $3v)$ versus $2v$; (c) $(4v$ or $3v)$ versus $3v$; (d) $(v$ or $4v)$ versus $2v$; (e) $(2v$ or $5v)$ versus $2v$; (f) $(2v$ or $5v)$ versus $3v$. So we should use the conditional instructions in cases (a, d) and (c, f), unless $0 is negative with probability $> 2/3$; in the latter case we should use the PBN variants, (d) and (f). The conditionals always win in cases (b, e).

If the ADDU commands had been ADD, the instructions would not have been equivalent, because of possible overflows.

40. Suppose you GO to address $^\#101$; this sets @ $\leftarrow$ $^\#101$. The tetrabyte $M_4[^\#101]$ is the same as the tetrabyte $M_4[^\#100]$. If the opcode of that instruction is, say, PUSHJ, register rJ will be set to $^\#105$. Similarly, if that instruction is GETA $0,@, register $0 will be set to $^\#101$. In such situations the value for @ in MMIX assembly language is slightly different from the actual value during program execution.

Programmers could use these principles to send some sort of signal to a subroutine, based on the two trailing bits of @. (Tricky, but hey, why not use the bits we've got?)

41. (a) True. (b) True. (c) True. (d) False, but true with SRU in place of SR.

42. (a) NEGU $1,$0; CSNN $1,$0,$0. (b) ANDN $1,$0,[#8000000000000000].

43. Trailing zeros (solution by J. Dallos): SUBU $0,$Z,1; SADD $0,$0,$Z.

Leading zeros: FLOTU $0,1,$Z; SRU $0,$0,52; SUB $0,[1086],$0. (If $Z could be zero, add the command CSZ $0,$Z,64.) This is the shortest program, but not the fastest; we save $2v$ if we reverse all bits (exercise 35) and count *trailing* zeros.

44. Use "high tetra arithmetic," in which each 32-bit number appears in the *left* half of a register. LDHT and STHT load and store such quantities (see exercise 7); SETMH loads an immediate constant. To add, subtract, multiply, or divide high tetras $Y and $Z, producing a high tetra $X with correct attention to integer overflow and divide check, the following commands work perfectly: (a) ADD $X,$Y,$Z. (b) SUB $X,$Y,$Z. (c) SR $X,$Z,32; MUL $X,$Y,$X (assuming that we have X ≠ Y). (d) DIV $X,$Y,$Z; SL $X,$X,32; now rR is the high tetra remainder.

46. It causes a trip to location 0.

47. #DF is MXORI ("multiple exclusive-or immediate"); #55 is PBPB ("probable branch positive backward"). But in a program we use the names MXOR and PBP; the assembler silently adds the I and B when required.

48. STO and STOU; also the "immediate" variants LDOI and LDOUI, STOI and STOUI; also NEGI and NEGUI, although NEG is not equivalent to NEGU; also any two of the four opcodes FLOTI, FLOTUI, SFLOTI, and SFLOTUI.

(Every MMIX operation on signed numbers has a corresponding operation on unsigned numbers, obtained by adding 2 to the opcode. This consistency makes the machine design easier to learn, the machine easier to build, and the compilers easier to write. But of course it also makes the machine less versatile, because it leaves no room for other operations that might be desired.)

49. Octabyte $M_8[0]$ is set to #0000 0100 0000 0001; rH is set to #0000 0123 4321 0000; M_2[#0244 4200 0000 0122] is set to #0121; rA is set to #00041 (because overflow occurs on the STW); rB is set to f(7) = #401c 0000 0000 0000; and $1 ← #6ff8 ffff ffff ffff. (Also rL ← 2, if rL was originally 0 or 1.) We assume that the program is not located in such a place that the STCO, STB, or STW instructions could clobber it.

50. $4\mu + 34v = v + (\mu+v) + v + (\mu+v) + (\mu+v) + v + v + 10v + v + (\mu+v) + v + 4v + v + v + v + v + 3v + v + v + v.$

51.

35010001	a0010101	2e010101	a5010101	f6000001	c4010101
b5010101	8e010101	1a010101	db010101	c7010101	3d010101
33010101	e4010001	f7150001	08010001	5701ffff	3f010101

52. Opcodes ADDI, ADDUI, SUBI, SUBUI, SLI, SLUI, SRI, SRUI, ORI, XORI, ANDNI, BDIFI, WDIFI, TDIFI, ODIFI: X = Y = 255, Z = 0. Opcode MULI: X = Y = 255, Z = 1. Opcodes INCH, INCMH, INCML, INCL, ORH, ORMH, ORML, ORL, ANDNH, ANDNMH, ANDNML, ANDNL: X = 255, Y = Z = 0. Opcodes OR, AND, MUX: X = Y = Z = 255. Opcodes CSN, CSZ, ..., CSEV: X = Z = 255, Y arbitrary. Opcodes BN, BZ, ..., PBEV: X arbitrary, Y = 0, Z = 1. Opcode JMP: X = Y = 0, Z = 1. Opcodes PRELD, PRELDI, PREGO, PREGOI, SWYM: X, Y, Z arbitrary. (Subtle point: An instruction that sets register $X is not a no-op when X is marginal, because it causes rL to increase; and all registers except $255 are marginal when rL = 0 and rG = 255.)

53. MULU, MULUI, PUT, PUTI, UNSAVE.

54. FCMP, FADD, FIX, FSUB, ..., FCMPE, FEQLE, ..., FINT, MUL, MULI, DIV, DIVI, ADD, ADDI, SUB, SUBI, NEG, SL, SLI, STB, STBI, STW, STWI, STT, STTI, STSF, STSFI, PUT, PUTI, UNSAVE. (This was not quite a fair question, because the complete rules for floating point operations appear only elsewhere. One fine point is that FCMP might change the I_BIT of rA, if $Y or $Z is Not-a-Number, but FEQL and FUN never cause exceptions.)

55. FCMP, FUN, ..., SRUI, CSN, CSNI, ..., LDUNCI, GO, GOI, PUSHGO, PUSHGOI, OR, ORI, ..., ANDNL, PUSHJ, PUSHJB, GETA, GETAB, PUT, PUTI, POP, SAVE, UNSAVE, GET.

56. *Minimum space:*

LDO	$1,x		MUL	$0,$0,$1	
SET	$0,$1		SUB	$2,$2,1	
SETL	$2,12		PBP	$2,@-4*2	∎

Space $= 6 \times 4 = 24$ bytes, time $= \mu + 149v$. Faster solutions are possible.

Minimum time: The assumption that $|x^{13}| \le 2^{63}$ implies that $|x| < 2^5$ and $x^8 < 2^{39}$. The following solution, based on an idea of Y. N. Patt, exploits this fact.

LDO	$0,x	$0 = x$
MUL	$1,$0,$0	$1 = x^2$
MUL	$1,$1,$1	$1 = x^4$
SL	$2,$1,25	$2 = 2^{25}x^4$
SL	$3,$0,39	$3 = 2^{39}x$
ADD	$3,$3,$1	$3 = 2^{39}x + x^4$
MULU	$1,$3,$2	u($1) $= 2^{25}x^8$, rH $= x^5 + 2^{25}x^4 \, [x < 0]$
GET	$2,rH	$2 \equiv x^5$ (modulo 2^{25})
PUT	rM,[#1ffffff]	
MUX	$2,$2,$0	$2 = x^5$
SRU	$1,$1,25	$1 = x^8$
MUL	$0,$1,$2	$0 = x^{13}$ ∎

Space $= 12 \times 4 = 48$ bytes, time $= \mu + 48v$. At least five multiplications are "necessary," according to the theory developed in Section 4.6.3; yet this program uses only four! And in fact there is a way to avoid multiplication altogether.

True minimum time: As R. W. Floyd points out, we have $|x| \le 28$, so the minimum execution time is achieved by referring to a table (unless $\mu > 45v$):

	LDO	$0,x	$0 = x$
	8ADDU	$0,$0,[Table]	
	LDO	$0,$0,8*28	$0 = x^{13}$
	. . .		
Table	OCTA	-28*28*28*28*28*28*28*28*28*28*28*28*28	
	OCTA	-27*27*27*27*27*27*27*27*27*27*27*27*27	
	. . .		
	OCTA	28*28*28*28*28*28*28*28*28*28*28*28*28	∎

Space $= 3 \times 4 + 57 \times 8 = 468$ bytes, time $= 2\mu + 3v$.

57. (1) An operating system can allocate high-speed memory more efficiently if program blocks are known to be "read-only." (2) An instruction cache in hardware will be faster and less expensive if instructions cannot change. (3) Same as (2), with "pipeline" in place of "cache." If an instruction is modified after entering a pipeline, the pipeline needs to be flushed; the circuitry needed to check this condition is complex and time-consuming. (4) Self-modifying code cannot be used by more than one process at once. (5) Self-modifying code can defeat techniques for "profiling" (that is, for computing the number of times each instruction is executed).

SECTION 1.3.2′

1. (a) It refers to the label of line 24. (b) No indeed. Line 23 would refer to line 24 instead of line 38; line 31 would refer to line 24 instead of line 21.

2. The current value of 9B will be a running count of the number of such lines that have appeared earlier.

3. Read in 100 octabytes from standard input; exchange their maximum with the last of them; exchange the maximum of the remaining 99 with the last of those; etc. Eventually the 100 octabytes will become completely sorted into nondecreasing order. The result is then written to the standard output. (Compare with Algorithm 5.2.3S.)

4. $^{\#}2233445566778899$. (Large values are reduced mod 2^{64}.)

5. BYTE "silly"; but this trick is not recommended.

6. False; TETRA @,@ is not the same as TETRA @; TETRA @.

7. He forgot that relative addresses are to tetrabyte locations; the two trailing bits are ignored.

8. LOC 16*((@+15)/16) or LOC -@/16*-16 or LOC (@+15)&-16, etc.

9. Change 500 to 600 on line 02; change Five to Six on line 35. (Five-digit numbers are not needed unless 1230 or more primes are to be printed. Each of the first 6542 primes will fit in a single wyde.)

10. $M_2[^{\#}2000000000000000] = {}^{\#}0002$, and the following nonzero data goes into the text segment:

$^{\#}$100:	$^{\#}$e3 fe 00 03	$^{\#}$15c: $^{\#}$23 ff f6 00
$^{\#}$104:	$^{\#}$c1 fb f7 00	$^{\#}$160: $^{\#}$00 00 07 01
$^{\#}$108:	$^{\#}$a6 fe f8 fb	$^{\#}$164: $^{\#}$35 fa 00 02
$^{\#}$10c:	$^{\#}$e7 fb 00 02	$^{\#}$168: $^{\#}$20 fa fa f7
$^{\#}$110:	$^{\#}$42 fb 00 13	$^{\#}$16c: $^{\#}$23 ff f6 1b
$^{\#}$114:	$^{\#}$e7 fe 00 02	$^{\#}$170: $^{\#}$00 00 07 01
$^{\#}$118:	$^{\#}$c1 fa f7 00	$^{\#}$174: $^{\#}$86 f9 f8 fa
$^{\#}$11c:	$^{\#}$86 f9 f8 fa	$^{\#}$178: $^{\#}$af f5 f8 00
$^{\#}$120:	$^{\#}$1c fd fe f9	$^{\#}$17c: $^{\#}$23 ff f8 04
$^{\#}$124:	$^{\#}$fe fc 00 06	$^{\#}$180: $^{\#}$1d f9 f9 0a
$^{\#}$128:	$^{\#}$43 fc ff fb	$^{\#}$184: $^{\#}$fe fc 00 06
$^{\#}$12c:	$^{\#}$30 ff fd f9	$^{\#}$188: $^{\#}$e7 fc 00 30
$^{\#}$130:	$^{\#}$4d ff ff f6	$^{\#}$18c: $^{\#}$a3 fc ff 00
$^{\#}$134:	$^{\#}$e7 fa 00 02	$^{\#}$190: $^{\#}$25 ff ff 01
$^{\#}$138:	$^{\#}$f1 ff ff f9	$^{\#}$194: $^{\#}$5b f9 ff fb
$^{\#}$13c:	$^{\#}$46 69 72 73	$^{\#}$198: $^{\#}$23 ff f8 00
$^{\#}$140:	$^{\#}$74 20 46 69	$^{\#}$19c: $^{\#}$00 00 07 01
$^{\#}$144:	$^{\#}$76 65 20 48	$^{\#}$1a0: $^{\#}$e7 fa 00 64
$^{\#}$148:	$^{\#}$75 6e 64 72	$^{\#}$1a4: $^{\#}$51 fa ff f4
$^{\#}$14c:	$^{\#}$65 64 20 50	$^{\#}$1a8: $^{\#}$23 ff f6 19
$^{\#}$150:	$^{\#}$72 69 6d 65	$^{\#}$1ac: $^{\#}$00 00 07 01
$^{\#}$154:	$^{\#}$73 0a 00 20	$^{\#}$1b0: $^{\#}$31 ff fa 62
$^{\#}$158:	$^{\#}$20 20 00 00	$^{\#}$1b4: $^{\#}$5b ff ff ed

(Notice that SET becomes SETL in $^{\#}$100, but ORI in $^{\#}$104. The current location @ is aligned to $^{\#}$15c at line 38, according to rule 7(a).) When the program begins, rG will be $^{\#}$f5, and we will have \$248 = $^{\#}$20000000000003e8, \$247 = $^{\#}$ffffffffffffc1a, \$246 = $^{\#}$13c, \$245 = $^{\#}$2030303030000000.

11. (a) If n is not prime, by definition n has a divisor d with $1 < d < n$. If $d > \sqrt{n}$, then n/d is a divisor with $1 < n/d < \sqrt{n}$. (b) If n is not prime, n has a *prime* divisor d with $1 < d \leq \sqrt{n}$. The algorithm has verified that n has no prime divisors $\leq p = \text{PRIME}[k]$; also $n = pq + r < pq + p \leq p^2 + p < (p+1)^2$. Any prime divisor of n is therefore greater than $p + 1 > \sqrt{n}$.

We must also prove that there will be a sufficiently large prime less than n when n is prime, namely that the $(k+1)$st prime p_{k+1} is less than $p_k^2 + p_k$; otherwise k would exceed j and $\text{PRIME}[k]$ would be zero when we needed it to be large. The necessary proof follows from "Bertrand's postulate": If p is prime there is a larger prime less than $2p$.

12. We could move Title, NewLn, and Blank to the data segment following BUF, where they could use ptop as their base address. Or we could change the LDA instructions on lines 38, 42, and 58 to SETL, knowing that the string addresses happen to fit in two bytes because this program is short. Or we could change LDA to GETA; but in that case we would have to align each string modulo 4, for example by saying

```
Title    BYTE    "First Five Hundred Primes",#a,0
         LOC     (@+3)&-4
NewLn    BYTE    #a,0
         LOC     (@+3)&-4
Blanks   BYTE    "   ",0    ▌
```

(See exercises 7 and 8.)

13. Line 35 gets the new title; change BYTE to WYDE on lines 35–37. Change Fputs to Fputws in lines 39, 43, 55, 59. Change the constant in line 45 to #0020066006600660. Change BUF+4 to BUF+2*4 on line 47. And change lines 50–52 to

$$\text{INCL r,'··'; \quad STWU r,t,0; \quad SUB t,t,2}.$$

Incidentally, the new title line might look like

```
Title    WYDE    "أول خمس ميات ألأرقام ألأولية"
```

when it is printed bidirectionally, but in the computer file the individual characters actually appear in "logical" order without ligatures. Thus a spelled-out sequence like

```
Title    WYDE    'أ','و','ل',' ','خ','م','س',' ',...,'ل','ي','ة'
```

would give an equivalent result, by the rule for string constants (rule 2).

14. We can, for example, replace lines 26–30 of Program P by

```
fn       GREG    0
sqrtn    GREG    0
         FLOT    fn,n
         FSQRT   sqrtn,fn
6H       LDWU    pk,ptop,kk
         FLOT    t,pk
         FREM    r,fn,t
         BZ      r,4B
7H       FCMP    t,sqrtn,t    ▌
```

The new FREM instruction is performed 9597 times, not 9538, because the new test in step P7 is not quite as effective as before. In spite of this, the floating point calculations reduce the running time by $426192\upsilon - 59\mu$, a notable improvement (unless of course

$\mu/\upsilon > 7000$). An additional savings of 38169υ can be achieved if the primes are stored as short floats instead of as unsigned wydes.

The number of divisibility tests can actually be reduced to 9357 if we replace q by $\sqrt{n} - 1.9999$ in step P7 (see the answer to exercise 11). But the extra subtractions cost more than they save, unless $\mu/\upsilon > 15$.

15. It prints a string consisting of a blank space followed by an asterisk followed by two blanks followed by an asterisk ... followed by k blanks followed by an asterisk ... followed by 74 blanks followed by an asterisk; a total of $2+3+\cdots+75 = \binom{76}{2} - 1 = 2849$ characters. The total effect is one of OP art.

17. The following subroutine returns zero if and only if the instruction is OK.

```
a         IS      #ffffffff            Table entry when anything goes
b         IS      #ffff04ff            Table entry when Y ≤ ROUND_NEAR
c         IS      #001f00ff            Table entry for PUT and PUTI
d         IS      #ff000000            Table entry for RESUME
e         IS      #ffff0000            Table entry for SAVE
f         IS      #ff0000ff            Table entry for UNSAVE
g         IS      #ff000003            Table entry for SYNC
h         IS      #ffff001f            Table entry for GET
table     GREG    @
          TETRA   a,a,a,a,a,b,a,b,b,b,b,b,b,b,b,b    0x
          TETRA   a,a,a,a,a,b,a,b,a,a,a,a,a,a,a,a    1x
          TETRA   a,a,a,a,a,a,a,a,a,a,a,a,a,a,a,a    2x
          TETRA   a,a,a,a,a,a,a,a,a,a,a,a,a,a,a,a    3x
          TETRA   a,a,a,a,a,a,a,a,a,a,a,a,a,a,a,a    4x
          TETRA   a,a,a,a,a,a,a,a,a,a,a,a,a,a,a,a    5x
          TETRA   a,a,a,a,a,a,a,a,a,a,a,a,a,a,a,a    6x
          TETRA   a,a,a,a,a,a,a,a,a,a,a,a,a,a,a,a    7x
          TETRA   a,a,a,a,a,a,a,a,a,a,a,a,a,a,a,a    8x
          TETRA   a,a,a,a,a,a,a,a,0,0,a,a,a,a,a,a    9x
          TETRA   a,a,a,a,a,a,a,a,a,a,a,a,a,a,a,a    Ax
          TETRA   a,a,a,a,a,a,a,a,a,a,a,a,a,a,a,a    Bx
          TETRA   a,a,a,a,a,a,a,a,a,a,a,a,a,a,a,a    Cx
          TETRA   a,a,a,a,a,a,a,a,a,a,a,a,a,a,a,a    Dx
          TETRA   a,a,a,a,a,a,a,a,a,a,a,a,a,a,a,a    Ex
          TETRA   a,a,a,a,a,a,c,c,a,d,e,f,g,a,h,a    Fx
tetra     IS      $1
maxXYZ    IS      $2
InstTest  BN      $0,9F                Invalid if address is negative.
          LDTU    tetra,$0,0           Fetch the tetrabyte.
          SR      $0,tetra,22          Extract its opcode (times 4).
          LDT     maxXYZ,table,$0      Get Xmax, Ymax, Zmax.
          BDIF    $0,tetra,maxXYZ      Check if any max is exceeded.
          PBNP    maxXYZ,9F            If not a PUT, we are done.
          ANDNML  $0,#ff00             Zero out the OP byte.
          BNZ     $0,9F                Branch if any max is exceeded.
          MOR     tetra,tetra,#4       Extract the X byte.
          CMP     $0,tetra,18
          CSP     tetra,$0,0           Set X ← 0 if 18 < X < 32.
```

```
              ODIF    $0,tetra,7        Set $0 ← X ÷ 7.
      9H      POP     1,0               Return $0 as the answer.  ∎
```

This solution does not consider a tetrabyte to be invalid if it would jump to a negative address, nor is 'SAVE $0,0' called invalid (although $0 can never be a global register).

18. The catch to this problem is that there may be several places in a row or column where the minimum or maximum occurs, and each is a potential saddle point.

Solution 1: In this solution we run through each row in turn, making a list of all columns in which the row minimum occurs and then checking each column on the list to see if the row minimum is also a column maximum. Notice that in all cases the terminating condition for a loop is that a register is ≤ 0.

```
      * Solution 1
      t       IS      $255
      a00     GREG    Data_Segment      Address of "a₀₀"
      a10     GREG    Data_Segment+8    Address of "a₁₀"
      ij      IS      $0                Element index and return register
      j       GREG    0                 Column index
      k       GREG    0                 Size of list of minimum indices
      x       GREG    0                 Current minimum value
      y       GREG    0                 Current element
      Saddle  SET     ij,9*8
      RowMin  SET     j,8
              LDB     x,a10,ij          Candidate for row minimum
      2H      SET     k,0               Set list empty.
      4H      INCL    k,1
              STB     j,a00,k           Put column index in list.
      1H      SUB     ij,ij,1           Go left one.
              SUB     j,j,1
              BZ      j,ColMax          Done with row?
      3H      LDB     y,a10,ij
              SUB     t,x,y
              PBN     t,1B              Is x still minimum?
              SET     x,y
              PBP     t,2B              New minimum?
              JMP     4B                Remember another minimum.
      ColMax  LDB     $1,a00,k          Get column from list.
              ADD     j,$1,9*8-8
      1H      LDB     y,a10,j
              CMP     t,x,y
              PBN     t,No              Is row min < column element?
              SUB     j,j,8
              PBP     j,1B              Done with column?
      Yes     ADD     ij,ij,$1          Yes; ij ← index of saddle.
              LDA     ij,a10,ij
              POP     1,0
      No      SUB     k,k,1             Is list empty?
              BP      k,ColMax          If not, try again.
              PBP     ij,RowMin         Have all rows been tried?
              POP     1,0               Yes; $0 = 0, no saddle.  ∎
```

Solution 2: An infusion of mathematics gives a different algorithm.

Theorem. *Let* $R(i) = \min_j a_{ij}$, $C(j) = \max_i a_{ij}$. *The element* $a_{i_0 j_0}$ *is a saddle point if and only if* $R(i_0) = \max_i R(i) = C(j_0) = \min_j C(j)$.

Proof. If $a_{i_0 j_0}$ is a saddle point, then for any fixed i, $R(i_0) = C(j_0) \geq a_{i j_0} \geq R(i)$; so $R(i_0) = \max_i R(i)$. Similarly $C(j_0) = \min_j C(j)$. Conversely, we have $R(i) \leq a_{ij} \leq C(j)$ for all i and j; hence $R(i_0) = C(j_0)$ implies that $a_{i_0 j_0}$ is a saddle point. ∎

(This proof shows that we always have $\max_i R(i) \leq \min_j C(j)$. So there is no saddle point if and only if all the R's are less than all the C's.)

According to the theorem, it suffices to find the smallest column maximum, then to search for an equal row minimum.

```
* Solution 2
t        IS     $255
a00      GREG   Data_Segment        Address of "a00"
a10      GREG   Data_Segment+8      Address of "a10"
a20      GREG   Data_Segment+8*2    Address of "a20"
ij       GREG   0                   Element index
ii       GREG   0                   Row index times 8
j        GREG   0                   Column index
x        GREG   0                   Current maximum
y        GREG   0                   Current element
z        GREG   0                   Current min max
ans      IS     $0                  Return register

Phase1   SET    j,8                 Start at column 8.
         SET    z,1000              z ← ∞ (more or less).
3H       ADD    ij,j,9*8-2*8
         LDB    x,a20,ij
1H       LDB    y,a10,ij
         CMP    t,x,y               Is x < y?
         CSN    x,t,y               If so, update the maximum.
2H       SUB    ij,ij,8             Move up one.
         PBP    ij,1B
         STB    x,a10,ij            Store column maximum.
         CMP    t,x,z               Is x < z?
         CSN    z,t,x               If so, update the min max.
         SUB    j,j,1               Move left a column.
         PBP    j,3B

Phase2   SET    ii,9*8-8            (At this point z = min_j C(j).)
3H       ADD    ij,ii,8             Prepare to search a row.
         SET    j,8
1H       LDB    x,a10,ij
         SUB    t,z,x               Is z > a_{ij}?
         PBP    t,No                There's no saddle in this row.
         PBN    t,2F
         LDB    x,a00,j             Is a_{ij} = C(j)?
         CMP    t,x,z
         CSZ    ans,t,ij            If so, remember a possible saddle point.
```

```
2H      SUB     j,j,1           Move left in row.
        SUB     ij,ij,1
        PBP     j,1B
        LDA     ans,a10,ans     A saddle point was found here.
        POP     1,0
No      SUB     ii,ii,8
        PBP     ii,3B           Try another row.
        SET     ans,0
        POP     1,0             ans = 0; no saddle.   ▮
```

We leave it to the reader to invent a still better solution in which Phase 1 records all possible rows that are candidates for the row search in Phase 2. It is not necessary to search all rows, just those i_0 for which $C(j_0) = \min_j C(j)$ implies $a_{i_0 j_0} = C(j_0)$. Usually there is at most one such row.

In some trial runs with elements selected at random from $\{-2, -1, 0, 1, 2\}$, Solution 1 required approximately $147\mu + 863v$ to run, while Solution 2 took about $95\mu + 510v$. Given a matrix of all zeros, Solution 1 found a saddle point in $26\mu + 188v$, Solution 2 in $96\mu + 517v$.

If an $m \times n$ matrix has *distinct* elements, and $m \geq n$, we can solve the problem by looking at only $O(m + n)$ of them and doing $O(m \log n)$ auxiliary operations. See Bienstock, Chung, Fredman, Schäffer, Shor, and Suri, *AMM* **98** (1991), 418–419.

19. Assume an $m \times n$ matrix. (a) By the theorem in the answer to exercise 18, all saddle points of a matrix have the same value, so (under our assumption of distinct elements) there is at most one saddle point. By symmetry the desired probability is mn times the probability that a_{11} is a saddle point. This latter is $1/(mn)!$ times the number of permutations with $a_{12} > a_{11}, \ldots, a_{1n} > a_{11}, a_{11} > a_{21}, \ldots, a_{11} > a_{m1}$; and this is $1/(m+n-1)!$ times the number of permutations of $m+n-1$ elements in which the first is greater than the next $(m - 1)$ and less than the remaining $(n - 1)$, namely $(m - 1)! \, (n - 1)!$. The answer is therefore

$$mn(m - 1)! \, (n - 1)!/(m + n - 1)! = (m + n) \Big/ \binom{m+n}{n}.$$

In our case this is $17/\binom{17}{8}$, only one chance in 1430. (b) Under the second assumption, an entirely different method must be used since there can be multiple saddle points; in fact either a whole row or whole column must consist entirely of saddle points. The probability equals the probability that there is a saddle point with value zero plus the probability that there is a saddle point with value one. The former is the probability that there is at least one column of zeros; the latter is the probability that there is at least one row of ones. The answer is $(1 - (1 - 2^{-m})^n) + (1 - (1 - 2^{-n})^m)$; in our case, $924744796234036231/18446744073709551616$, about 1 in 19.9. An approximate answer is $n2^{-m} + m2^{-n}$.

20. M. Hofri and P. Jacquet [*Algorithmica* **22** (1998), 516–528] have analyzed the case when the $m \times n$ matrix entries are distinct and in random order. The running times of the two MMIX programs are then $\big(mn + mH_n + 2m + 1 + (m + 1)/(n - 1)\big)\mu + \big(6mn + 7mH_n + 5m + 11 + 7(m + 1)/(n - 1)\big)v + O\big((m+n)^2/\binom{m+n}{m}\big)$ and $(m + 1)n\mu + \big(5mn + 6m + 4n + 7H_n + 8\big)v + O(1/n) + O\big((\log n)^2/m\big)$, respectively, as $m \to \infty$ and $n \to \infty$, assuming that $(\log n)/m \to 0$.

21. Farey SET y,1; ... POP.

This answer is the first of many in Volumes 1–3 for which MMIXmasters are being asked to contribute elegant solutions. (See the website information on page ii.) The fourth edition of this book will present the best parts of the best programs submitted. Note: Please reveal your full name, including all middle names, if you enter this competition, so that proper credit can be given!

22. (a) Induction. (b) Let $k \geq 0$ and $X = ax_{k+1} - x_k$, $Y = ay_{k+1} - y_k$, where $a = \lfloor (y_k + n)/y_{k+1} \rfloor$. By part (a) and the fact that $0 < Y \leq n$, we have $X \perp Y$ and $X/Y > x_{k+1}/y_{k+1}$. So if $X/Y \neq x_{k+2}/y_{k+2}$ we have, by definition, $X/Y > x_{k+2}/y_{k+2}$. But this implies that

$$\frac{1}{Yy_{k+1}} = \frac{Xy_{k+1} - Yx_{k+1}}{Yy_{k+1}} = \frac{X}{Y} - \frac{x_{k+1}}{y_{k+1}}$$

$$= \left(\frac{X}{Y} - \frac{x_{k+2}}{y_{k+2}}\right) + \left(\frac{x_{k+2}}{y_{k+2}} - \frac{x_{k+1}}{y_{k+1}}\right)$$

$$\geq \frac{1}{Yy_{k+2}} + \frac{1}{y_{k+1}y_{k+2}} = \frac{y_{k+1} + Y}{Yy_{k+1}y_{k+2}}$$

$$> \frac{n}{Yy_{k+1}y_{k+2}} \geq \frac{1}{Yy_{k+1}}.$$

Historical notes: C. Haros gave a (more complicated) rule for constructing such sequences, in *J. de l'École Polytechnique* **4**, 11 (1802), 364–368; his method was correct, but his proof was inadequate. Several years later, the geologist John Farey independently conjectured that x_k/y_k is always equal to $(x_{k-1} + x_{k+1})/(y_{k-1} + y_{k+1})$ [*Philos. Magazine and Journal* **47** (1816), 385–386]; a proof was supplied shortly afterwards by A. Cauchy [*Bull. Société Philomathique de Paris* (3) **3** (1816), 133–135], who attached Farey's name to the series. For more of its interesting properties, see G. H. Hardy and E. M. Wright, *An Introduction to the Theory of Numbers*, Chapter 3.

23. The following routine should do reasonably well on most pipeline and cache configurations.

```
a      IS    $0              SUB    n,n,8           STCO   0,a,56
n      IS    $1              ADD    a,a,8           ADD    a,a,64
z      IS    $2        3H    AND    t,a,63          PBNN   t,4B
t      IS    $255           PBNZ   t,2B        5H   CMP    t,n,8
                            CMP    t,n,64           BN     t,7F
1H     STB   z,a,0           BN     t,5F        6H   STCO   0,a,0
       SUB   n,n,1     4H    PREST  63,a,0           SUB    n,n,8
       ADD   a,a,1           SUB    n,n,64           ADD    a,a,8
Zero   BZ    n,9F            CMP    t,n,64           CMP    t,n,8
       SET   z,0             STCO   0,a,0            PBNN   t,6B
       AND   t,a,7           STCO   0,a,8       7H   BZ     n,9F
       BNZ   t,1B            STCO   0,a,16      8H   STB    z,a,0
       CMP   t,n,64          STCO   0,a,24           SUB    n,n,1
       PBNN  t,3F            STCO   0,a,32           ADD    a,a,1
       JMP   5F              STCO   0,a,40           PBNZ   n,8B
2H     STCO  0,a,0           STCO   0,a,48      9H   POP
```

24. The following routine merits careful study; comments are left to the reader. A faster program would be possible if we treated $\$0 \equiv \$1$ (modulo 8) as a special case.

```
in      IS    $2                                  SUB   $1,$1,8
out     IS    $3                                  SRU   out,out,1
r       IS    $4                                  MUX   in,in,out
l       IS    $5                                  BDIF  t,ones,in
m       IS    $6                                  AND   t,t,m
t       IS    $7                                  SRU   mm,mm,r
mm      IS    $8                                  PUT   rM,mm
tt      IS    $9                                  PBZ   t,2F
flip    GREG  #0102040810204080                   JMP   5F
ones    GREG  #0101010101010101          3H  MUX   out,tt,out
        LOC   #100                           STOU  out,$0,$1
StrCpy  AND   in,$0,#7                  2H  SLU   out,in,l
        SLU   in,in,3                        LDOU  in,$0,8
        AND   out,$1,#7                      INCL  $0,8
        SLU   out,out,3                      BDIF  t,ones,in
        SUB   r,out,in                   4H  SRU   tt,in,r
        LDOU  out,$1,0                       PBZ   t,3B
        SUB   $1,$1,$0                       SRU   mm,t,r
        NEG   m,0,1                          MUX   out,tt,out
        SRU   m,m,in                         BNZ   mm,1F
        LDOU  in,$0,0                        STOU  out,$0,$1
        PUT   rM,m                        5H  INCL  $0,8
        NEG   mm,0,1                         SLU   out,in,l
        BN    r,1F                           SLU   mm,t,l
        NEG   l,64,r                      1H  LDOU  in,$0,$1
        SLU   tt,out,r                       MOR   mm,mm,flip
        MUX   in,in,tt                       SUBU  t,mm,1
        BDIF  t,ones,in                      ANDN  mm,mm,t
        AND   t,t,m                          MOR   mm,mm,flip
        SRU   mm,mm,r                        SUBU  mm,mm,1
        PUT   rM,mm                          PUT   rM,mm
        JMP   4F                             MUX   in,in,out
1H      NEG   l,0,r                          STOU  in,$0,$1
        INCL  r,64                           POP   0
```

The running time, approximately $(n/4 + 4)\mu + (n + 40)\upsilon$ plus the time to POP, is less than the cost of the trivial code when $n \geq 8$ and $\mu \geq \upsilon$.

25. We assume that register p initially contains the address of the first byte, and that this address is a multiple of 8. Other local or global registers a, b, ... have also been declared. The following solution starts by counting the wyde frequencies first, since this requires only half as many operations as it takes to count byte frequencies. Then the byte frequencies are obtained as row and column sums of a 256×256 matrix.

```
* Cryptanalysis Problem (CLASSIFIED)
        LOC    Data_Segment
count   GREG   @                    Base address for wyde counts
        LOC    @+8*(1<<16)          Space for the wyde frequencies
freq    GREG   @                    Base address for byte counts
        LOC    @+8*(1<<8)           Space for the byte frequencies
p       GREG   @
        BYTE   "abracadabraa",0,"abc"     Trivial test data
```

```
ones    GREG    #0101010101010101
        LOC     #100
2H      SRU     b,a,45          Isolate next wyde.      ⎱ main
        LDO     c,count,b       Load old count.         ⎱ loop,
        INCL    c,1                                     ⎱ should
        STO     c,count,b       Store new count.        ⎱ run as
        SLU     a,a,16          Delete one wyde.        ⎱ fast as
        PBNZ    a,2B            Done with octabyte?     ⎱ possible
Phase1  LDOU    a,p,0           Start here: Fetch the next eight bytes.
        INCL    p,8
        BDIF    t,ones,a        Test if there's a zero byte.
        PBZ     t,2B            Do main loop, unless near the end.
2H      SRU     b,a,45          Isolate next wyde.
        LDO     c,count,b       Load old count.
        INCL    c,1
        STO     c,count,b       Store new count.
        SRU     b,t,48
        SLU     a,a,16
        BDIF    t,ones,a
        PBZ     b,2B            Continue unless done.
Phase2  SET     p,8*255         Now get ready to sum rows and columns.
1H      SL      a,p,8
        LDA     a,count,a       a ← address of row p.
        SET     b,8*255
        LDO     c,a,0
        SET     t,p
2H      INCL    t,#800
        LDO     x,count,t       Element of column p
        LDO     y,a,b           Element of row p
        ADD     c,c,x
        ADD     c,c,y
        SUB     b,b,8
        PBP     b,2B
        STO     c,freq,p
        SUB     p,p,8
        PBP     p,1B
        POP     ▌
```

How long is "long"? This two-phase method is inferior to a simple one-phase approach when the string length n is less than 2^{17}, but it takes only about $10/17$ as much time as the one-phase scheme when $n \approx 10^6$. A slightly faster routine can be obtained by "unrolling" the inner loop, as in the next answer.

Another approach, which uses a jump table and keeps the counts in 128 registers, is worthy of consideration when μ/ν is large.

[This problem has a long history. See, for example, Charles P. Bourne and Donald F. Ford, "A study of the statistics of letters in English words," *Information and Control* **4** (1961), 48–67.]

26. The wyde-counting trick in the previous solution will backfire if the machine's primary cache holds fewer than 2^{19} bytes, unless comparatively few of the wyde counts are nonzero. Therefore the following program computes only one-byte frequencies. This code avoids stalls, in a conventional pipeline, by never using the result of a LDO in the immediately following instruction.

```
Start   LDOU  a,p,0               INCL  c,1
        INCL  p,8                 SRU   bb,bb,53
        BDIF  t,ones,a            STO   c,freq,b
        BNZ   t,3F                LDO   c,freq,bb
2H      SRU   b,a,53              LDOU  a,p,0
        LDO   c,freq,b            INCL  p,8
        SLU   bb,a,8              INCL  c,1
        INCL  c,1                 BDIF  t,ones,a
        SRU   bb,bb,53            STO   c,freq,bb
        STO   c,freq,b            PBZ   t,2B
        LDO   c,freq,bb       3H  SRU   b,a,53
        SLU   b,a,16              LDO   c,freq,b
        INCL  c,1                 INCL  c,1
        SRU   b,b,53              STO   c,freq,b
        STO   c,freq,bb           SRU   b,b,3
        LDO   c,freq,b            SLU   a,a,8
        ...                       PBNZ  b,3B
        SLU   bb,a,56             POP        ▌
```

Another solution works better on a superscalar machine that issues two instructions simultaneously:

```
Start   LDOU  a,p,0               SLU   bbb,a,48
        INCL  p,8                 SLU   bbbb,a,56
        BDIF  t,ones,a            INCL  c,1
        SLU   bb,a,8              INCL  cc,1
        BNZ   t,3F                SRU   bbb,bbb,53
2H      SRU   b,a,53              SRU   bbbb,bbbb,53
        SRU   bb,bb,53            STO   c,freq,b
        LDO   c,freq,b            STO   cc,freqq,bb
        LDO   cc,freqq,bb         LDO   c,freq,bbb
        SLU   bbb,a,16            LDO   cc,freqq,bbbb
        SLU   bbbb,a,24           LDOU  a,p,0
        INCL  c,1                 INCL  p,8
        INCL  cc,1                INCL  c,1
        SRU   bbb,bbb,53          INCL  cc,1
        SRU   bbbb,bbbb,53        BDIF  t,ones,a
        STO   c,freq,b            SLU   bb,a,8
        STO   cc,freqq,bb         STO   c,freq,bbb
        LDO   c,freq,bbb          STO   cc,freqq,bbbb
        LDO   cc,freqq,bbbb       PBZ   t,2B
        SLU   b,a,32          3H  SRU   b,a,53
        SLU   bb,a,40             ...        ▌
        ...
```

In this case we must keep two separate frequency tables (and combine them at the end); otherwise an "aliasing" problem would lead to incorrect results in cases where b and bb both represent the same character.

27.   (a)   (b)

```
     t    IS    $255                    t    IS    $255
     n    IS    $0                      n    IS    $0
   new    GREG                        new    GREG
   old    GREG                        old    GREG
   phi    GREG                       phii    GREG    #9e3779b97f4a7c16
   rt5    GREG                         lo    GREG
   acc    GREG                         hi    GREG
     f    GREG                       hihi    GREG
          LOC   #100                        LOC   #100
  Main FLOT    t,5                   Main SET     n,2
       FSQRT   rt5,t                      SET     old,1
       FLOT    t,1                        SET     new,1
       FADD    phi,t,rt5           1H     ADDU    new,new,old
       INCH    phi,#fff0                  INCL    n,1
       FDIV    acc,phi,rt5                CMPU    t,new,old
       SET     n,1                        BN      t,9F
       SET     new,1                      SUBU    old,new,old
  1H   ADDU    new,new,old                MULU    lo,old,phii
       INCL    n,1                        GET     hi,rH
       CMPU    t,new,old                  ADDU    hi,hi,old
       BN      t,9F                       ADDU    hihi,hi,1
       SUBU    old,new,old                CSN     hi,lo,hihi
       FMUL    acc,acc,phi                CMP     t,hi,new
       FIXU    f,acc                      PBZ     t,1B
       CMP     t,f,new                    SET     t,1
       PBZ     t,1B               9H      TRAP    0,Halt,0    ▌
       SET     t,1
  9H   TRAP    0,Halt,0   ▌
```

Program (a) halts with $t = 1$ and $n = 71$; the floating point representation of ϕ is slightly high, hence errors ultimately accumulate until $\phi^{71}/\sqrt{5}$ is approximated by $F_{71} + .7$, which rounds to $F_{71} + 1$. Program (b) halts with $t = -1$ and $n = 94$; unsigned overflow occurs before the approximation fails. (Indeed, $F_{93} < 2^{64} < F_{94}$.)

29. The last man is in position 15. The total time before output is ...

MMIXmasters, please help! What is the neatest program that is analogous to the solution to exercise 1.3.2–22 in the third edition? Also, what would D. Ingalls do in the new situation? (Find a trick analogous to his previous scheme, but do not use self-modifying code.)

An asymptotically faster method appears in exercise 5.1.1–5.

30. Work with scaled numbers, $R_n = 10^n r_n$. Then $R_n(1/m) = R$ if and only if $10^n/(R + \frac{1}{2}) \le m < 10^n/(R - \frac{1}{2})$; thus we find $m_{k+1} = \lfloor (2 \cdot 10^n - 1)/(2R - 1) \rfloor$.

```
  * Sum of Rounded Harmonic Series
  MaxN IS    10
  a    GREG  0              Accumulator
  c    GREG  0              2 · 10^n
  d    GREG  0              Divisor or digit
  r    GREG  0              Scaled reciprocal
```

```
    s    GREG   0                      Scaled sum
    m    GREG   0                      m_k
    mm   GREG   0                      m_{k+1}
    nn   GREG   0                      n − MaxN
         LOC    Data_Segment
    dec  GREG   @+3                    Decimal point location
         BYTE   "   ."
         LOC    #100
    Main NEG    nn,MaxN-1     n ← 1.
         SET    c,20
    1H   SET    m,1
         SR     s,c,1         S ← 10^n.
         JMP    2F
    3H   SUB    a,c,1
         SL     d,r,1
         SUB    d,d,1
         DIV    mm,a,d
    4H   SUB    a,mm,m
         MUL    a,r,a
         ADD    s,s,a
         SET    m,mm          k ← k + 1.
    2H   ADD    a,c,m
         2ADDU  d,m,2
         DIV    r,a,d
         PBNZ   r,3B
    5H   ADD    a,nn,MaxN+1
         SET    d,#a          Newline
         JMP    7F
    6H   DIV    s,s,10        Convert digits.
         GET    d,rR
         INCL   d,'0'
    7H   STB    d,dec,a
         SUB    a,a,1
         BZ     a,@-4
         PBNZ   s,6B
    8H   SUB    $255,dec,3
         TRAP   0,Fputs,StdOut
    9H   INCL   nn,1          n ← n + 1.
         MUL    c,c,10
         PBNP   nn,1B
         TRAP   0,Halt,0      ▌
```

The outputs are respectively 3.7, 6.13, 8.445, 10.7504, 13.05357, 15.356255, 17.6588268, 19.96140681, 22.263991769, 24.5665766342, in $82\mu + 40659359\upsilon$. The calculation would work for n up to 17 without overflow, but the running time is of order $10^{n/2}$. (We could save about half the time by calculating $R_n(1/m)$ directly when $m < 10^{n/2}$, and by using the fact that $R_n(m_{k+1}) = R_n(m_k - 1)$ for larger values of m.)

31. Let $N = \lfloor 2 \cdot 10^n/(2m+1) \rfloor$. Then $S_n = H_N + O(N/10^n) + \sum_{k=1}^{m} (\lceil 2 \cdot 10^n/(2k-1) \rceil - \lceil 2 \cdot 10^n/(2k+1) \rceil) k/10^n = H_N + O(m^{-1}) + O(m/10^n) - 1 + 2H_{2m} - H_m = n \ln 10 + 2\gamma - 1 + 2\ln 2 + O(10^{-n/2})$ if we sum by parts and set $m \approx 10^{n/2}$.

Our approximation to S_{10} is ≈ 24.5665766209, which is closer than predicted.

32. To make the problem more challenging, the following ingenious solution due in part to ———— uses a lot of *trickery* in order to reduce execution time. Can the reader squeeze out any more nanoseconds?

> *MMIXmasters: Please help fill in the blanks! Note, for example, that remainders mod 7, 19, and 30 are most rapidly computed by* FREM; *division by 100 can be reduced to multiplication by 1//100+1 (see exercise 1.3.1′–19); etc.*

[To calculate Easter in years ≤ 1582, see *CACM* **5** (1962), 209–210. The first systematic algorithm for calculating the date of Easter was the *canon paschalis* due to Victorius of Aquitania (A.D. 457). There are many indications that the sole nontrivial application of arithmetic in Europe during the Middle Ages was the calculation of Easter date, hence such algorithms are historically significant. See *Puzzles and Paradoxes* by T. H. O'Beirne (London: Oxford University Press, 1965), Chapter 10, for further commentary; and see the book *Calendrical Calculations* by E. M. Reingold and N. Dershowitz (Cambridge Univ. Press, 2001) for date-oriented algorithms of all kinds.]

33. The first such year is A.D. 10317, although the error *almost* leads to failure in A.D. $10108 + 19k$ for $0 \leq k \leq 10$.

Incidentally, T. H. O'Beirne pointed out that the date of Easter repeats with a period of exactly 5,700,000 years. Calculations by Robert Hill show that the most common date is April 19 (220400 times per period), while the earliest and least common is March 22 (27550 times); the latest, and next-to-least common, is April 25 (42000 times). Hill found a nice explanation for the curious fact that the number of times any particular day occurs in the period is always a multiple of 25.

34. The following program follows the protocol to within a dozen or so v; this is more than sufficiently accurate, since ρ is typically more than 10^8, and $\rho v = 1\,\text{sec}$. All computation takes place in registers, except when a byte is input.

```
* Traffic Signal Problem
rho          GREG   250000000              Assume 250 MHz clock rate
t            IS     $255
Sensor_Buf   IS     Data_Segment
             GREG   Sensor_Buf
             LOC    #100
Lights       IS     3                      Handle for /dev/lights
Sensor       IS     4                      Handle for /dev/sensor
Lights_Name  BYTE   "/dev/lights",0
Sensor_Name  BYTE   "/dev/sensor",0
Lights_Args  OCTA   Lights_Name,BinaryWrite
Sensor_Args  OCTA   Sensor_Name,BinaryRead
Read_Sensor  OCTA   Sensor_Buf,1
Boulevard    BYTE   #77,0                  Green/red, WALK/DON'T
             BYTE   #7f,0                  Green/red, DON'T/DON'T
             BYTE   #73,0                  Green/red, off/DON'T
             BYTE   #bf,0                  Amber/red, DON'T/DON'T
Avenue       BYTE   #dd,0                  Red/green, DON'T/WALK
             BYTE   #df,0                  Red/green, DON'T/DON'T
             BYTE   #dc,0                  Red/green, DON'T/off
             BYTE   #ef,0                  Red/amber, DON'T/DON'T
```

```
goal        GREG    0                         Transition time for lights
Main        GETA    t,Lights_Args             Open the files: Fopen(Lights,
            TRAP    0,Fopen,Lights              "/dev/lights",BinaryWrite)
            GETA    t,Sensor_Args             Fopen(Sensor,
            TRAP    0,Fopen,Sensor              "/dev/sensor",BinaryRead)
            GET     goal,rC
            JMP     2F

            GREG    @
delay_go    GREG
Delay       GET     t,rC                      Subroutine for busy-waiting:
            SUBU    t,t,goal                  (N.B. Not CMPU; see below)
            PBN     t,Delay                   Repeat until rC passes goal.
            GO      delay_go,delay_go,0        Return to caller.

flash_go    GREG
n           GREG    0                         Iteration counter
green       GREG    0                         Boulevard or Avenue
temp        GREG
Flash       SET     n,8                       Subroutine to flash the lights:
1H          ADD     t,green,2*1
            TRAP    0,Fputs,Lights            DON'T WALK
            ADD     temp,goal,rho
            SR      t,rho,1
            ADDU    goal,goal,t
            GO      delay_go,Delay
            ADD     t,green,2*2
            TRAP    0,Fputs,Lights            (off)
            SET     goal,temp
            GO      delay_go,Delay
            SUB     n,n,1
            PBP     n,1B                      Repeat eight times.
            ADD     t,green,2*1
            TRAP    0,Fputs,Lights            DON'T WALK
            MUL     t,rho,4
            ADDU    goal,goal,t
            GO      delay_go,Delay            Hold for 4 sec.
            ADD     t,green,2*3
            TRAP    0,Fputs,Lights            DON'T WALK, amber
            GO      flash_go,flash_go,0        Return to caller.
Wait        GET     goal,rC                   Extend the 18 sec green.
1H          GETA    t,Read_Sensor
            TRAP    0,Fread,Sensor
            LDB     t,Sensor_Buf
            BZ      t,Wait                    Repeat until sensor is nonzero.
            GETA    green,Boulevard
            GO      flash_go,Flash            Finish the boulevard cycle.
            MUL     t,rho,8
            ADDU    goal,goal,t
            GO      delay_go,Delay            Amber for 8 sec.
```

```
              GETA    t,Avenue
              TRAP    0,Fputs,Lights           Green light for Berkeley.
              MUL     t,rho,8
              ADDU    goal,goal,t
              GO      delay_go,Delay
              GETA    green,Avenue
              GO      flash_go,Flash           Finish the avenue cycle.
              GETA    t,Read_Sensor
              TRAP    0,Fread,Sensor           Ignore sensor during green time.
              MUL     t,rho,5
              ADDU    goal,goal,t
              GO      delay_go,Delay           Amber for 5 sec.
      2H      GETA    t,Boulevard
              TRAP    0,Fputs,Lights           Green light for Del Mar.
              MUL     t,rho,18
              ADDU    goal,goal,t
              GO      delay_go,Delay           At least 18 sec to WALK.
              JMP     1B                       ▌
```

The SUBU instruction in the Delay subroutine is an interesting example of a case where the comparison should be done with SUBU, *not* with CMPU, in spite of the comments in exercise 1.3.1′–22. The reason is that the two quantities being compared, rC and goal, "wrap around" modulo 2^{64}.

SECTION 1.4.1′

1. j GREG ;m GREG ;kk GREG ;xk GREG ;rr GREG

```
              GREG    @                 Base address
      GoMax   SET     $2,1              Special entrance for r = 1
      GoMaxR  SL      rr,$2,3           Multiply arguments by 8.
              SL      kk,$1,3
              LDO     m,x0,kk
              ...                       (Continue as in (1))
      5H      SUB     kk,kk,rr          k ← k − r.
              PBP     kk,3B             Repeat if k > 0.
      6H      GO      kk,$0,0           Return to caller.  ▌
```

The calling sequence for the general case is SET $2,$r$; SET $1,$n$; GO $0,GoMaxR.

2. j IS $0 ;m IS $1 ;kk IS $2 ;xk IS $3 ;rr IS $4

```
      Max100  SET     $0,100            Special entrance for n = 100 and r = 1
      Max     SET     $1,1              Special entrance for r = 1
      MaxR    SL      rr,$1,3           Multiply arguments by 8.
              SL      kk,$0,3
              LDO     m,x0,kk
              ...                       (Continue as in (1))
      5H      SUB     kk,kk,rr          k ← k − r.
              PBP     kk,3B             Repeat if k > 0.
      6H      POP     2,0               Return to caller.  ▌
```

In this case the general calling sequence is SET $A1,$r$; SET $A0,$n$; PUSHJ $R,MaxR, where A0 = R + 1 and A1 = R + 2.

3. Just Sub ...; GO $0,$0,0. The local variables can be kept entirely in registers.

4. PUSHJ $X,RA has a relative address, allowing us to jump to any subroutine within $\pm 2^{18}$ bytes of our current location. PUSHGO $X,$Y,$Z or PUSHGO $X,A has an absolute address, allowing us to jump to any desired place.

5. True. There are $256 - G$ globals and L locals.

6. $5 ← rD and rR ← 0 and rL ← 6. All other newly local registers are also set to zero; for example, if rL was 3, this DIVU instruction would set $3 ← 0 and $4 ← 0.

7. $L ← 0, \ldots,$ $4 ← 0, $5 ← #abcd0000, rL ← 6.

8. Usually such an instruction has no essential impact, except that context switching with SAVE and UNSAVE generally take longer when fewer marginal registers are present. However, an important difference can arise in certain scenarios. For example, a subsequent PUSHJ $255,Sub followed by POP 1,0 would leave a result in $16 instead of $10.

9. PUSHJ $255,Handler will make at least 32 marginal registers available (because $G \geq 32$); then POP 0 will restore the previous local registers, and two additional instructions "GET $255,rB; RESUME" will restart the program as if nothing had happened.

10. Basically true. MMIX will start a program with rG set to 255 minus the number of assembled GREG operations, and with rL set to 2. Then, in the absence of PUSHJ, PUSHGO, POP, SAVE, UNSAVE, GET, and PUT, the value of rG will never change. The value of rL will increase if the program puts anything into $2, $3, $\ldots$, or $(rG − 1)$, but the effect will be the same as if all registers were equivalent. The only register with slightly different behavior is $255, which is affected by trip interrupts and used for communication in I/O traps. We could permute register numbers $2, $3, $\ldots$, $254 arbitrarily in any PUSH/POP/SAVE/UNSAVE/RESUME-free program that does not GET rL or PUT anything into rL or rG; the permuted program would produce identical results.

The distinction between local, global, and marginal is irrelevant also with respect to SAVE, UNSAVE, and RESUME, in the absence of PUSH and POP, except that the destination register of SAVE must be global and the destination register of certain instructions inserted by RESUME mustn't be marginal (see exercise 1.4.3′–14).

11. The machine tries to access virtual address #5fff ffff ffff fff8, which is just below the stack segment. Nothing has been stored there, so a "page fault" occurs and the operating system aborts the program.

(The behavior is, however, much more bizarre if a POP is given just after a SAVE, because SAVE essentially begins a new register stack immediately following the saved context. Anybody who tries such things is asking for trouble.)

12. (a) True. (Similarly, the name of the current "working directory" in a UNIX shell always begins with a slash.) (b) False. But confusion can arise if such prefixes are defined, so their use is discouraged. (c) False. (In this respect MMIXAL's structured symbols are *not* analogous to UNIX directory names.)

13.

Fib	CMP	$1,$0,2	Fib1	CMP	$1,$0,2	Fib2	CMP	$1,$0,1
	PBN	$1,1F		BN	$1,1F		BNP	$1,1F
	GET	$1,rJ		SUB	$2,$0,1		SUB	$2,$0,1
	SUB	$3,$0,1		SET	$0,1		SET	$0,0
	PUSHJ	$2,Fib		SET	$1,0	2H	ADDU	$0,$0,$1
	SUB	$4,$0,2	2H	ADDU	$0,$0,$1		ADDU	$1,$0,$1
	PUSHJ	$3,Fib		SUBU	$1,$0,$1		SUB	$2,$2,2
	ADDU	$0,$2,$3		SUB	$2,$2,1		PBP	$2,2B
	PUT	rJ,$1		PBNZ	$2,2B		CSZ	$0,$2,$1
1H	POP	1,0 ∎	1H	POP	1,0 ∎	1H	POP	1,0 ∎

Here Fib2 is a faster alternative to Fib1. In each case the calling sequence has the form "SET \$A,n; PUSHJ \$R,Fib...", where $A = R + 1$.

14. Mathematical induction shows that the POP instruction in Fib is executed exactly $2F_{n+1} - 1$ times and the ADDU instruction is executed $F_{n+1} - 1$ times. The instruction at 2H is performed $n - [n \neq 0]$ times in Fib1, $\lfloor n/2 \rfloor$ times in Fib2. Thus the total cost, including the two instructions in the calling sequence, comes to $(19F_{n+1} - 12)\upsilon$ for Fib, $(4n + 8)\upsilon$ for Fib1, and $(4\lfloor n/2 \rfloor + 12)\upsilon$ for Fib2, assuming that $n > 1$.

(The recursive subroutine Fib is a *terrible* way to compute Fibonacci numbers, because it forgets the values it has already computed. It spends more than $10^{22}\upsilon$ units of time just to compute F_{100}.)

15.
```
n    GREG                        GO    $0,Fib
  fn IS    n                     STO   fn,fp,24
     GREG  @                     LDO   n,fp,16
 Fib CMP   $1,n,2                SUB   n,n,2
     PBN   $1,1F                 GO    $0,Fib
     STO   fp,sp,0               LDO   $0,fp,24
     SET   fp,sp                 ADDU  fn,fn,$0
     INCL  sp,8*4                LDO   $0,fp,8
     STO   $0,fp,8               SET   sp,fp
     STO   n,fp,16               LDO   fp,sp,0
     SUB   n,n,1          1H     GO    $0,$0,0    ▮
```

The calling sequence is SET n,n; GO \$0,Fib; the answer is returned in global register fn. The running time comes to $(8F_{n+1} - 8)\mu + (32F_{n+1} - 23)\upsilon$, so the ratio between this version and the register stack subroutine of exercise 13 is approximately $(8\mu/\upsilon + 32)/19$. (Although exercise 14 points out that we shouldn't really calculate Fibonacci numbers recursively, this analysis does demonstrate the advantage of a register stack. Even if we are generous and assume that $\mu = \upsilon$, the memory stack costs more than twice as much in this example. A similar behavior occurs with respect to other subroutines, but the analysis for Fib is particularly simple.)

In the special case of Fib we can do without the frame pointer, because fp is always a fixed distance from sp. A memory-stack subroutine based on this observation runs about $(6\mu/\upsilon + 29)/19$ slower than the register-stack version; it's better than the version with general frames, but still not very good.

16. This is an ideal setup for a subroutine with two exits. Let's assume for convenience that B and C do not return any value, and that they each save rJ in \$1 (because they are not leaf subroutines). Then we can proceed as follows: A calls B by saying PUSHJ \$R,B as usual. B calls C by saying PUSHJ \$R,C; PUT rJ,\$1; POP 0,0 (with perhaps a different value of R than used by subroutine A). C calls itself by saying PUSHJ \$R,C; PUT rJ,\$1; POP 0,0 (with perhaps a different value of R than used by B). C jumps to A by saying PUT rJ,\$1; POP 0,0. C exits normally by saying PUT rJ,\$1; POP 0,2.

Extensions of this idea, in which values are returned and an arbitrary jump address can be part of the returned information, are clearly possible. Similar schemes apply to the GO-oriented memory stack protocol of (15).

SECTION 1.4.2′

1. If one coroutine calls the other only once, it is nothing but a subroutine; so we need an application in which each coroutine calls the other in at least two distinct places. Even then, it is often easy to set some sort of switch or to use some property of the data, so that upon entry to a fixed place within one coroutine it is possible to branch to one of two desired places; again, nothing more than a subroutine would be required. Coroutines become correspondingly more useful as the number of references between them grows larger.

2. The first character found by In would be lost.

3. This is an MMIXAL trick to make OutBuf contain fifteen tetrabytes TETRA ' ', followed by TETRA #a, followed by zero; and TETRA ' ' is equivalent to BYTE 0,0,0,' '. The output buffer is therefore set up to receive a line of 16 three-character groups separated by blank spaces.

4. If we include the code

```
rR_A GREG
rR_B GREG
     GREG @
A    GET  rR_B,rR
     PUT  rR,rR_A
     GO   t,a,0
B    GET  rR_A,rR
     PUT  rR,rR_B
     GO   t,b,0
```

then A can invoke B by "GO a,B" and B can invoke A by "GO b,A".

5. If we include the code

```
a    GREG
b    GREG
     GREG @
A    GET  b,rJ
     PUT  rJ,a
     POP  0
B    GET  a,rJ
     PUT  rJ,b
     POP  0
```

then A can invoke B by "PUSHJ $255,B" and B can invoke A by "PUSHJ $255,A". Notice the similarity between this answer and the previous one. The coroutines should not use the register stack for other purposes except as permitted by the following exercise.

6. Suppose coroutine A has something in the register stack when invoking B. Then B is obliged to return the stack to the same state before returning to A, although B might push and pop any number of items in the meantime.

Coroutines might, of course, be sufficiently complicated that they each do require a register stack of their own. In such cases MMIX's SAVE and UNSAVE operations can be used, with care, to save and restore the context needed by each coroutine.

SECTION 1.4.3′

1. (a) SRU x,y,z; BYTE 0,1,0,#29 .   (b) PBP x,PBTaken+@-0; BYTE 0,3,0,#50 .
(c) MUX x,y,z; BYTE 0,1,rM,#29 .   (d) ADDU x,x,z; BYTE 0,1,0,#30 .

2. The running time of MemFind is $9v + (2\mu + 8v)C + (3\mu + 6v)U + (2\mu + 11v)A$, where C is the number of key comparisons on line 042, $U = [\text{key} \neq \text{curkey}]$, and $A = [\text{new node needed}]$. The running time of GetReg is $\mu + 6v + 6vL$, where $L = [\$k \text{ is local}]$.

If we assume that $C = U = A = L = 0$ on each call, the time for simulation can be broken down as follows:

	(a)	(b)	(c)
fetching (lines 105–115)	$\mu + 17v$	$\mu + 17v$	$\mu + 17v$
unpacking (lines 141–153)	$\mu + 12v$	$\mu + 12v$	$\mu + 12v$
relating (lines 154–164)	$2v$	$2v$	$9v$
installing X (lines 174–182)	$7v$	$\mu + 17v$	$\mu + 17v$
installing Z (lines 183–197)	$\mu + 13v$	$6v$	$6v$
installing Y (lines 198–207)	$\mu + 13v$	$\mu + 13v$	$6v$
destining (lines 208–231)	$8v$	$23v$	$6v$
resuming (lines 232–242)	$14v$	$\mu + 14v$	$16v - \pi$
postprocessing (lines 243–539)	$\mu + 10v$	$11v$	$11v - 4\pi$
updating (lines 540–548)	$5v$	$5v$	$5v$
total	$5\mu + 101v$	$5\mu + 120v$	$3\mu + 105v - 5\pi$

To these times we must add $6v$ for each occurrence of a local register as a source, plus penalties for the times when MemFind doesn't immediately have the correct chunk. In case (b), MemFind *must* miss on line 231, and again on line 111 when fetching the following instruction. (We would be better off with *two* MemFind routines, one for data and one for instructions.) The most optimistic net cost of (b) is therefore obtained by taking $C = A = 2$, for a total running time of $13\mu + 158v$. (On long runs of the simulator simulating itself, the empirical average values per call of MemFind were $C \approx .29$, $U \approx .00001$, $A \approx .16$.)

3. We have $\beta = \gamma$ and $L > 0$ on line 097. Thus $\alpha = \gamma$ *can* arise, but only in extreme circumstances when $L = 256$ (see line 268 and exercise 11). Luckily L will soon become 0 in that case.

4. No problem can occur until a node invades the pool segment, which begins at address #4000 0000 0000 0000; then remnants of the command line might interfere with the program's assumption that a newly allocated node is initially zero. But the data segment is able to accommodate $\lfloor (2^{61} - 2^{12} - 2^4)/(2^{12} + 24) \rfloor = 559{,}670{,}633{,}304{,}293$ nodes, so we will not live long enough to experience any problem from this "bug."

5. Line 218 calls StackRoom calls StackStore calls MemFind; this is as deep as it gets. Line 218 has pushed 3 registers down; StackRoom has pushed only 2 (since rL = 1 on line 097); StackStore has pushed 3. The value of rL on line 032 is 2 (although rL increases to 5 on line 034). Hence the register stack contains $3 + 2 + 3 + 2 = 10$ unpopped items in the worst case.

The program halts shortly after branching to Error; and even if it were to continue, the extra garbage at the bottom of the stack won't hurt anything — we could simply ignore it. However, we could clear the stack by providing second exits as in exercise 1.4.1′–16. A simpler way to flush an entire stack is to pop repeatedly until rO equals its initial value, Stack_Segment.

6.
```
247  Div   DIV   x,y,z     Divide y by z, signed.
248        JMP   1F
249  DivU  PUT   rD,x      Put simulated rD into real rD.
250        DIVU  x,y,z     Divide y by z, unsigned.
251  1H    GET   t,rR
252        STO   t,g,8*rR  g[rR] ← remainder.
253        JMP   XDone     Finish by storing x.  ∎
```

7. (The following instructions should be inserted between line 309 of the text and the Info table, together with the answers to the next several exercises.)

```
Cswap  LDOU   z,g,8*rP
       LDOU   y,res,0
       CMPU   t,y,z
       BNZ    t,1F      Branch if M₈[A] ≠ g[rP].
       STOU   x,res,0   Otherwise set M₈[A] ← $X.
       JMP    2F
1H     STOU   y,g,8*rP  Set g[rP] ← M₈[A].
2H     ZSZ    x,t,1     x ← result of equality test.
       JMP    XDone     Finish by storing x.  ▌
```

8. Here we store the simulated registers that we're keeping in actual registers. (This approach is better than a 32-way branch to see which register is being gotten; it's also better than the alternative of storing the registers every time we change them.)

```
Get   CMPU   t,yz,32
      BNN    t,Error    Make sure that YZ < 32.
      STOU   ii,g,8*rI  Put the correct value into g[rI].
      STOU   cc,g,8*rC  Put the correct value into g[rC].
      STOU   oo,g,8*rO  Put the correct value into g[rO].
      STOU   ss,g,8*rS  Put the correct value into g[rS].
      STOU   uu,g,8*rU  Put the correct value into g[rU].
      STOU   aa,g,8*rA  Put the correct value into g[rA].
      SR     t,ll,3
      STOU   t,g,8*rL   Put the correct value into g[rL].
      SR     t,gg,3
      STOU   t,g,8*rG   Put the correct value into g[rG].
      SLU    t,zz,3
      LDOU   x,g,t      Set x ← g[Z].
      JMP    XDone      Finish by storing x.  ▌
```

9.
```
    Put    BNZ    yy,Error   Make sure that Y = 0.
           CMPU   t,xx,32
           BNN    t,Error    Make sure that X < 32.
           CMPU   t,xx,rC
           BN     t,PutOK    Branch if X < 8.
           CMPU   t,xx,rF
           BN     t,1F       Branch if X < 22.
    PutOK  STOU   z,g,xxx     Set g[X] ← z.
           JMP    Update      Finish the command.
    1H     CMPU   t,xx,rG
           BN     t,Error    Branch if X < 19.
           SUB    t,xx,rL
           PBP    t,PutA     Branch if X = rA.
           BN     t,PutG     Branch if X = rG.
    PutL   SLU    z,z,3      Otherwise X = rL.
           CMPU   t,z,ll
           CSN    ll,t,z     Set rL ← min(z, rL).
           JMP    Update     Finish the command.
    OH GREG #40000
```

```
PutA    CMPU    t,z,0B
        BNN     t,Error      Make sure z ≤ #3fffff.
        SET     aa,z         Set rA ← z.
        JMP     Update       Finish the command.
PutG    SRU     t,z,8
        BNZ     t,Error      Make sure z < 256.
        CMPU    t,z,32
        BN      t,Error      Make sure z ≥ 32.
        SLU     z,z,3
        CMPU    t,z,11
        BN      t,Error      Make sure z ≥ rL.
        JMP     2F
1H      SUBU    gg,gg,8      G ← G − 1.   ($G becomes global.)
        STCO    0,g,gg       g[G] ← 0.   (Compare with line 216.)
2H      CMPU    t,z,gg
        PBN     t,1B         Branch if G < z.
        SET     gg,z         Set rG ← z.
        JMP     Update       Finish the command. ▌
```

In this case the nine commands that branch to either PutOK, PutA, PutG, PutL, or Error are tedious, yet still preferable to a 32-way switching table.

```
10. Pop  SUBU   oo,oo,8
         BZ     xx,1F                Branch if X = 0.
         CMPU   t,ll,xxx
         BN     t,1F                 Branch if X > L.
         ADDU   t,xxx,oo
         AND    t,t,lring_mask
         LDOU   y,l,t                y ← result to return.
1H       CMPU   t,oo,ss
         PBNN   t,1F                 Branch unless α = γ.
         PUSHJ  0,StackLoad
1H       AND    t,oo,lring_mask
         LDOU   z,l,t                z ← number of additional registers to pop.
         AND    z,z,#ff              Make sure z ≤ 255 (in case of weird error).
         SLU    z,z,3
1H       SUBU   t,oo,ss
         CMPU   t,t,z
         PBNN   t,1F                 Branch unless z registers not all in the ring.
         PUSHJ  0,StackLoad          (See note below.)
         JMP    1B                   Repeat until all necessary registers are loaded.
1H       ADDU   ll,ll,8
         CMPU   t,xxx,ll
         CSN    ll,t,xxx             Set L ← min(X, L + 1).
         ADDU   ll,ll,z              Then increase L by z.
         CMPU   t,gg,ll
         CSN    ll,t,gg              Set L ← min(L, G).
         CMPU   t,z,ll
         BNN    t,1F                 Branch if returned result should be discarded.
         AND    t,oo,lring_mask
         STOU   y,l,t                Otherwise set l[(α − 1) mod ρ] ← y.
```

```
1H    LDOU   y,g,8*rJ
      SUBU   oo,oo,z           Decrease α by 1 + z.
      4ADDU  inst_ptr,yz,y     Set inst_ptr ← g[rJ] + 4YZ.
      JMP    Update            Finish the command.  ▌
```

Here it is convenient to decrease oo in two steps, first by 8 and then by 8 times z. The program is complicated in general, but in most cases comparatively little computation actually needs to be done. If $\beta = \gamma$ when the second StackLoad call is given, we implicitly decrease β by 1 (thereby discarding the topmost item of the register stack). That item will not be needed unless it is the value being returned, but the latter value has already been placed in y.

```
11. Save  BNZ    yz,Error          Make sure YZ = 0.
          CMPU   t,xxx,gg
          BN     t,Error           Make sure $X is global.
          ADDU   t,oo,ll
          AND    t,t,lring_mask
          SRU    y,ll,3
          STOU   y,l,t             Set $L ← L, considering $L to be local.
          INCL   ll,8
          PUSHJ  0,StackRoom       Make sure β ≠ γ.
          ADDU   oo,oo,ll
          SET    ll,0              Push down all local registers and set rL ← 0.
    1H    PUSHJ  0,StackStore
          CMPU   t,ss,oo
          PBNZ   t,1B              Store all pushed down registers in memory.
          SUBU   y,gg,8            Set k ← G − 1.    (Here y ≡ 8k.)
    4H    ADDU   y,y,8             Increase k by 1.
    1H    SET    arg,ss
          PUSHJ  res,MemFind
          CMPU   t,y,8*(rZ+1)
          LDOU   z,g,y             Set z ← g[k].
          PBNZ   t,2F
          SLU    z,gg,56-3
          ADDU   z,z,aa            If k = rZ + 1, set z ← 2⁵⁶rG + rA.
    2H    STOU   z,res,0           Store z in M₈[rS].
          INCL   ss,8              Increase rS by 8.
          BNZ    t,1F              Branch if we just stored rG and rA.
          CMPU   t,y,c255
          BZ     t,2F              Branch if we just stored $255.
          CMPU   t,y,8*rR
          PBNZ   t,4B              Branch unless we just stored rR.
          SET    y,8*rP            Set k ← rP.
          JMP    1B
    2H    SET    y,8*rB            Set k ← rB.
          JMP    1B
    1H    SET    oo,ss             rO ← rS.
          SUBU   x,oo,8            x ← rO − 8.
          JMP    XDone             Finish by storing x.  ▌
```

(The special registers saved are those with codes 0–6 and 23–27, plus (rG, rA).)

12.

Unsave	BNZ	xx,Error	Make sure X = 0.
	BNZ	yy,Error	Make sure Y = 0.
	ANDNL	z,#7	Make sure z is a multiple of 8.
	ADDU	ss,z,8	Set rS ← z + 8.
	SET	y,8*(rZ+2)	Set $k \leftarrow rZ + 2$. ($y \equiv 8k$)
1H	SUBU	y,y,8	Decrease k by 1.
4H	SUBU	ss,ss,8	Decrease rS by 8.
	SET	arg,ss	
	PUSHJ	res,MemFind	
	LDOU	x,res,0	Set x ← M_8[rS].
	CMPU	t,y,8*(rZ+1)	
	PBNZ	t,2F	
	SRU	gg,x,56-3	If $k = rZ + 1$, initialize rG and rA.
	SLU	aa,x,64-18	
	SRU	aa,aa,64-18	
	JMP	1B	
2H	STOU	x,g,y	Otherwise set g[k] ← x.
3H	CMPU	t,y,8*rP	
	CSZ	y,t,8*(rR+1)	If $k = rP$, set $k \leftarrow rR + 1$.
	CSZ	y,y,c256	If $k = rB$, set $k \leftarrow 256$.
	CMPU	t,y,gg	
	PBNZ	t,1B	Repeat the loop unless $k = G$.
	PUSHJ	0,StackLoad	
	AND	t,ss,lring_mask	
	LDOU	x,1,t	x ← the number of local registers.
	AND	x,x,#ff	Make sure x ≤ 255 (in case of weird error).
	BZ	x,1F	
	SET	y,x	Now load x local registers into the ring.
2H	PUSHJ	0,StackLoad	
	SUBU	y,y,1	
	PBNZ	y,2B	
	SLU	x,x,3	
1H	SET	ll,x	
	CMPU	t,gg,x	
	CSN	ll,t,gg	Set rL ← min(x, rG).
	SET	oo,ss	Set rO ← rS.
	PBNZ	uu,Update	Branch, if not the first time.
	BZ	resuming,Update	Branch, if first command is UNSAVE.
	JMP	AllDone	Otherwise clear **resuming** and finish. ∎

A straightforward answer
is as good as a kiss of friendship.
— Proverbs 24 : 26

13.

517		SET	xx,0	
518		SLU	t,t,55	Loop to find highest trip bit.
519	2H	INCL	xx,1	
520		SLU	t,t,1	
521		PBNN	t,2B	
522		SET	t,#100	Now xx = index of trip bit.
523		SRU	t,t,xx	t ← corresponding event bit.
524		ANDN	exc,exc,t	Remove t from exc.
525	TakeTrip	STOU	inst_ptr,g,8*rW	g[rW] ← inst_ptr.
526		SLU	inst_ptr,xx,4	inst_ptr ← xx ≪ 4.
527		INCH	inst,#8000	
528		STOU	inst,g,8*rX	g[rX] ← inst + 2^{63}.
529		AND	t,f,Mem_bit	
530		PBZ	t,1F	Branch if op doesn't access memory.
531		ADDU	y,y,z	Otherwise set y ← (y + z) mod 2^{64},
532		SET	z,x	z ← x.
533	1H	STOU	y,g,8*rY	g[rY] ← y.
534		STOU	z,g,8*rZ	g[rZ] ← z.
535		LDOU	t,g,c255	
536		STOU	t,g,8*rB	g[rB] ← g[255].
537		LDOU	t,g,8*rJ	
538		STOU	t,g,c255	g[255] ← g[rJ]. ∎

14.

Resume	SLU	t,inst,40	
	BNZ	t,Error	Make sure XYZ = 0.
	LDOU	inst_ptr,g,8*rW	inst_ptr ← g[rW].
	LDOU	x,g,8*rX	
	BN	x,Update	Finish the command if rX is negative.
	SRU	xx,x,56	Otherwise let xx be the ropcode.
	SUBU	t,xx,2	
	BNN	t,1F	Branch if the ropcode is ≥ 2.
	PBZ	xx,2F	Branch if the ropcode is 0.
	SRU	y,x,28	Otherwise the ropcode is 1:
	AND	y,y,#f	y ← k, the leading nybble of the opcode.
	SET	z,1	
	SLU	z,z,y	z ← 2^k.
	ANDNL	z,#70cf	Zero out the acceptable values of z.
	BNZ	z,Error	Make sure the opcode is "normal."
1H	BP	t,Error	Make sure the ropcode is ≤ 2.
	SRU	t,x,13	
	AND	t,t,c255	
	CMPU	y,t,ll	
	BN	y,2F	Branch if $X is local.
	CMPU	y,t,gg	
	BN	y,Error	Otherwise make sure $X is global.
2H	MOR	t,x,#8	
	CMPU	t,t,#F9	Make sure the opcode isn't RESUME.
	BZ	t,Error	
	NEG	resuming,xx	

```
             CSNN   resuming,resuming,1   Set resuming as specified.
             JMP    Update                Finish the command.    ▌
166  LDOU    y,g,8*rY                     y ← g[rY].
167  LDOU    z,g,8*rZ                     z ← g[rZ].
168  BOD     resuming,Install_Y           Branch if ropcode was 1.
169 OH GREG  #C1<<56+(x-$0)<<48+(z-$0)<<40+1<<16+X_is_dest_bit
170  SET     f,OB                         Otherwise change f to an ORI instruction.
171  LDOU    exc,g,8*rX
172  MOR     exc,exc,#20                  exc ← third-from-left byte of rX.
173  JMP     XDest                        Continue as for ORI.    ▌
```

15. We need to deal with the fact that the string to be output might be split across two or more chunks of the simulated memory. One solution is to output eight bytes at a time with Fwrite until reaching the last octabyte of the string; but that approach is complicated by the fact that the string might start in the middle of an octabyte. Alternatively, we could simply Fwrite only one byte at a time; but that would be almost obscenely slow. The following method is much better:

```
SimFputs   SET    xx,0            (xx will be the number of bytes written)
           SET    z,t             Set z ← virtual address of string.
1H         SET    arg,z
           PUSHJ  res,MemFind
           SET    t,res           Set t ← actual address of string.
           GO     $0,DoInst       (See below.)
           BN     t,TrapDone      If error occurred, pass the error to user.
           BZ     t,1F            Branch if the string was empty.
           ADD    xx,xx,t         Otherwise accumulate the number of bytes.
           ADDU   z,z,t           Find the address following the string output.
           AND    t,z,Mem:mask
           BZ     t,1B            Continue if string ended at chunk boundary.
1H         SET    t,xx            t ← number of bytes successfully put.
           JMP    TrapDone        Finish the operation.    ▌
```

Here DoInst is a little subroutine that inserts inst into the instruction stream. We provide it with additional entrances that will be useful in the next answers:

```
           GREG   @               Base address
:SimInst   LDA    t,IOArgs        DoInst to IOArgs and return.
           JMP    DoInst
SimFinish  LDA    t,IOArgs        DoInst to IOArgs and finish.
SimFclose  GETA   $0,TrapDone     DoInst and finish.
:DoInst    PUT    rW,$0           Put return address into rW.
           PUT    rX,inst         Put inst into rX.
           RESUME 0               And do it.    ▌
```

16. Again we need to worry about chunk boundaries (see the previous answer), but a byte-at-a-time method is tolerable since file names tend to be fairly short.

```
SimFopen   PUSHJ  0,GetArgs       (See below.)
           ADDU   xx,Mem:alloc,Mem:nodesize
           STOU   xx,IOArgs
           SET    x,xx            (We'll copy the file name into this open space.)
1H         SET    arg,z
           PUSHJ  res,MemFind
```

```
              LDBU    t,res,0
              STBU    t,x,0          Copy byte M[z].
              INCL    x,1
              INCL    z,1
              PBNZ    t,1B           Repeat until the string has ended.
              GO      $0,SimInst     Now open the file.
       3H     STCO    0,x,0          Now zero out the copied string.
              CMPU    z,xx,x
              SUB     x,x,8
              PBN     z,3B           Repeat until it is surely obliterated.
              JMP     TrapDone       Pass the result t to the user.   ▌
```

Here GetArgs is a subroutine that will be useful also in the implementation of other I/O commands. It sets up IOArgs and computes several other useful results in global registers.

```
 :GetArgs     GET     $0,rJ          Save the return address.
              SET     y,t            y ← g[255].
              SET     arg,t
              PUSHJ   res,MemFind
              LDOU    z,res,0        z ← virtual address of first argument.
              SET     arg,z
              PUSHJ   res,MemFind
              SET     x,res          x ← internal address of first argument.
              STO     x,IOArgs
              SET     xx,Mem:Chunk
              AND     zz,x,Mem:mask
              SUB     xx,xx,zz       xx ← bytes from x to chunk end.
              ADDU    arg,y,8
              PUSHJ   res,MemFind
              LDOU    zz,res,0       zz ← second argument.
              STOU    zz,IOArgs+8    Convert IOArgs to internal form.
              PUT     rJ,$0          Restore the return address.
              POP     0                      ▌
```

17. This solution, which uses the subroutines above, works also for SimFwrite (!).

```
 SimFread     PUSHJ   0,GetArgs      Massage the input arguments.
              SET     y,zz           y ← number of bytes to read.
       1H     CMP     t,xx,y
              PBNN    t,SimFinish    Branch if we can stay in one chunk.
              STO     xx,IOArgs+8    Oops, we have to work piecewise.
              SUB     y,y,xx
              GO      $0,SimInst
              BN      t,1F           Branch if an error occurs.
              ADD     z,z,xx
              SET     arg,z
              PUSHJ   res,MemFind
              STOU    res,IOArgs     Reduce to the previous problem.
              STO     y,IOArgs+8
              ADD     xx,Mem:mask,1
              JMP     1B
```

```
1H        SUB    t,t,y              Compute the correct number of missing bytes.
          JMP    TrapDone
SimFwrite IS SimFread ;SimFseek IS SimFclose ;SimFtell IS SimFclose ▮
```

(The program assumes that no file-reading error will occur if the first Fread was successful.) Analogous routines for SimFgets, SimFgetws, and SimFputws can be found in the file sim.mms, which is one of many demonstration files included with the author's MMIXware programs.

18. The stated algorithms will work with any MMIX program for which the number of local registers, L, never exceeds $\rho - 1$, where ρ is the lring_size.

19. In all three cases the preceding instruction is INCL 11,8, and a value is stored in location $1 + ((\text{oo} + 11) \wedge \text{lring\_mask})$. So we could shorten the program slightly.

20.
```
560  1H   GETA   t,OctaArgs
561       TRAP   0,Fread,Infile     Input λ into g[255].
562       BN     t,9F               Branch if end of file.
563       LDOU   loc,g,c255         loc ← λ.
564  2H   GETA   t,OctaArgs
565       TRAP   0,Fread,Infile     Input an octabyte x into g[255].
566       LDOU   x,g,c255
567       BN     t,Error            Branch on unexpected end of file.
568       SET    arg,loc
569       BZ     x,1B               Start a new sequence if x = 0.
570       PUSHJ  res,MemFind
571       STOU   x,res,0            Otherwise store x in M₈[loc].
572       INCL   loc,8              Increase loc by 8.
573       JMP    2B                 Repeat until encountering a zero.
574  9H   TRAP   0,Fclose,Infile    Close the input file.
575       SUBU   loc,loc,8          Decrease loc by 8.  ▮
```

Also put "OctaArgs OCTA Global+8*255,8" in some convenient place.

21. Yes it is, up to a point; but the question is interesting and nontrivial.

To analyze it quantitatively, let sim.mms be the simulator in MMIXAL, and let sim.mmo be the corresponding object file produced by the assembler. Let Hello.mmo be the object file corresponding to Program 1.3.2′H. Then the command line 'Hello' presented to MMIX's operating system will output 'Hello, world' and stop after $\mu + 17\upsilon$, not counting the time taken by the operating system to load it and to take care of input/output operations.

Let Hello0.mmb be the binary file that corresponds to the command line 'Hello', in the format of exercise 20. (This file is 176 bytes long.) Then the command line 'sim Hello0.mmb' will output 'Hello, world' and stop after $168\mu + 1699\upsilon$.

Let Hello1.mmb be the binary file that corresponds to the command line 'sim Hello0.mmb'. (This file is 5768 bytes long.) Then the command line 'sim Hello1.mmb' will output 'Hello, world' and stop after $10549\mu + 169505\upsilon$.

Let Hello2.mmb be the binary file that corresponds to the command line 'sim Hello1.mmb'. (This file also turns out to be 5768 bytes long.) Then the command line 'sim Hello2.mmb' will output 'Hello, world' and stop after $789739\mu + 15117686\upsilon$.

Let Hello3.mmb be the binary file that corresponds to the command line 'sim Hello2.mmb'. (Again, 5768 bytes.) Then the command line 'sim Hello3.mmb' will output 'Hello, world' if we wait sufficiently long.

Now let `recurse.mmb` be the binary file that corresponds to the command line 'sim `recurse.mmb`'. Then the command line 'sim `recurse.mmb`' runs the simulator simulating itself simulating itself simulating itself $\cdots$ ad infinitum. The file handle `Infile` is first opened at time $3\mu + 13\upsilon$, when `recurse.mmb` begins to be read by the simulator at level 1. That handle is closed at time $1464\mu + 16438\upsilon$ when loading is complete; but the simulated simulator at level 2 opens it at time $1800\mu + 19689\upsilon$, and begins to load `recurse.mmb` into simulated simulated memory. The handle is closed again at time $99650\mu + 1484347\upsilon$, then reopened by the simulated simulated simulator at time $116999\mu + 1794455\upsilon$. The third level finishes loading at time $6827574\mu + 131658624\upsilon$ and the fourth level starts at time $8216888\mu + 159327275\upsilon$.

But the recursion cannot go on forever; indeed, the simulator running itself is a finite-state system, and a finite-state system cannot produce Fopen–Fclose events at exponentially longer and longer intervals. Eventually the memory will fill up (see exercise 4) and the simulation will go awry. When will this happen? The exact answer is not easy to determine, but we can estimate it as follows: If the kth level simulator needs n_k chunks of memory to load the $(k+1)$st level simulator, the value of n_{k+1} is at most $4 + \lceil (2^{12} + 16 + (2^{12} + 24)n_k)/2^{12} \rceil$, with $n_0 = 0$. We have $n_k = 6k$ for $k < 30$, but this sequence eventually grows exponentially; it first surpasses 2^{61} when $k = 6066$. Thus we can simulate at least 100^{6065} instructions before any problem arises, if we assume that each level of simulation introduces a factor of at least 100 (see exercise 2).

22. The pairs (x_k, y_k) can be stored in memory following the trace program itself, which should appear after all other instructions in the text segment of the program being traced. (The operating system will give the trace routine permission to modify the text segment.) The main idea is to scan ahead from the current location in the traced program to the next branch or GO or PUSH or POP or JMP or RESUME or TRIP instruction, then to replace that instruction temporarily in memory with a TRIP command. The tetrabytes in locations $^\#0$, $^\#10$, $^\#20$, ..., $^\#80$ of the traced program are changed so that they jump to appropriate locations within the trace routine; then all control transfers will be traced, including transfers due to arithmetic interrupts. The original instructions in those locations can be traced via RESUME, as long as they are not themselves RESUME commands.

INDEX AND GLOSSARY

When an index entry refers to a page containing a relevant exercise, see also the *answer* to that exercise for further information. An answer page is not indexed here unless it refers to a topic not included in the statement of the exercise.

WDIF (wyde difference), 11.
Weak binary operators, 38.
Webster, Noah, iii.
Where-interrupted register, 18.
Whitespace character, 67.
Wide strings, 42.
Wilson, George Pickett, 28.
Wirth, Niklaus Emil, 45, 63.
Wordsworth, William, 24.
Wright, Edward Maitland, 105.
Wyde: A 16-bit quantity, 4.
Wyde difference, 11.
Wyde immediate, 14.
WYDE operator, 39.

X field of MMIX instruction, 5.
X_BIT (floating inexact bit), 18, 89.
XOR (bitwise exclusive-or), 10.
XYZ field of MMIX instruction, 6.

Y field of MMIX instruction, 5.

Y operand register, 18.
Yoder, Michael Franz, 95.
Yossarian, John, 3.
Yottabyte, 94.
YZ field of MMIX instruction, 5–6.

Z field of MMIX instruction, 5.
  as immediate constant, 14.
Z operand register, 18.
Z_BIT (floating division by zero bit), 18.
Zero or set instructions of MMIX, 10.
Zettabyte, 94.
ZSEV (zero or set if even), 10.
ZSN (zero or set if negative), 10.
ZSNN (zero or set if nonnegative), 10.
ZSNP (zero or set if nonpositive), 10.
ZSNZ (zero or set if nonzero), 10.
ZSOD (zero or set if odd), 10.
ZSP (zero or set if positive), 10.
ZSZ (zero or set if zero), 10.